THE WORLD'S GREATEST
HOTELS
RESORTS
+SPAS

The rear façade of the
Hotel Aire de Bardenas, in Tudela, Spain.

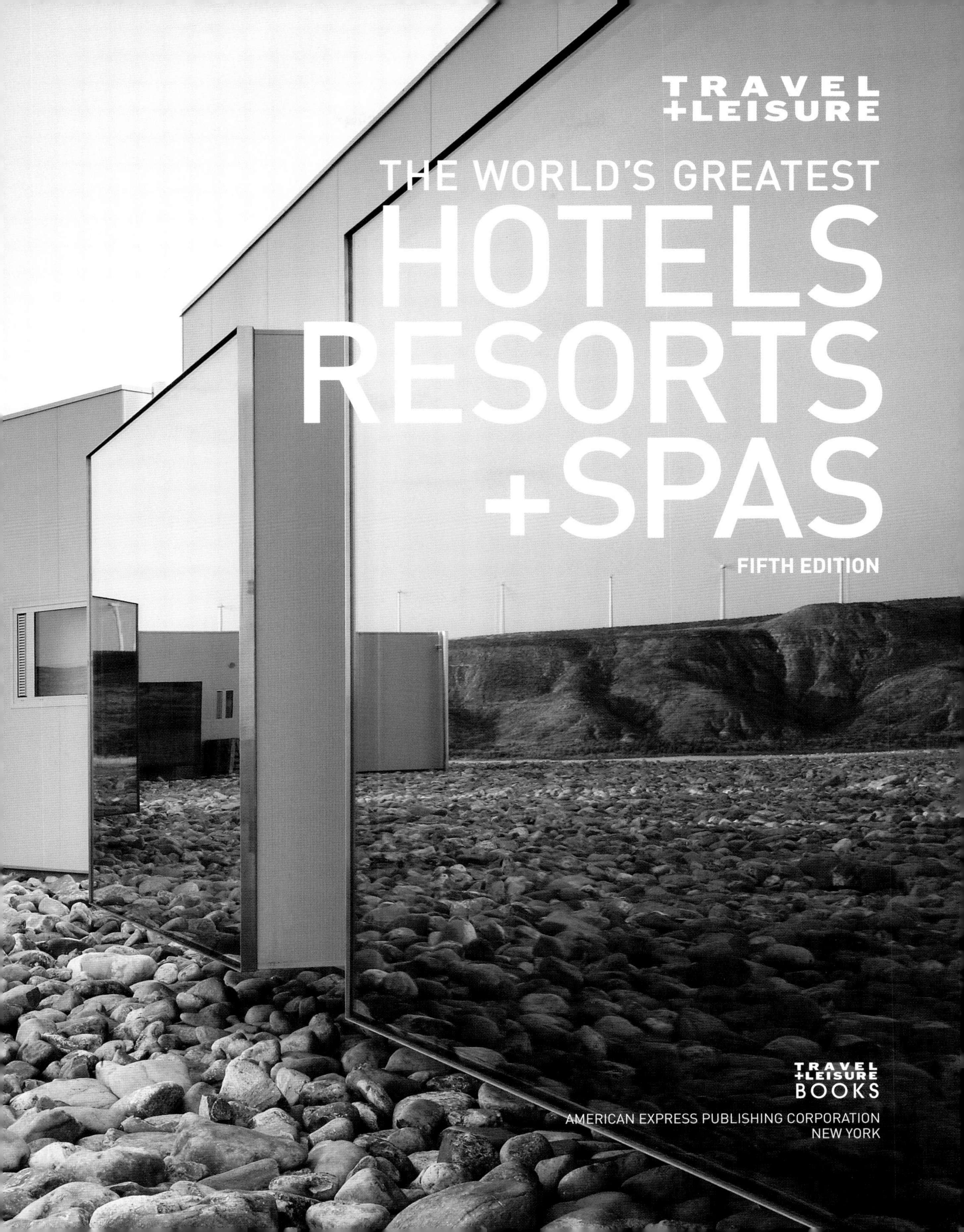

**TRAVEL
+LEISURE**

THE WORLD'S GREATEST
HOTELS
RESORTS
+SPAS

FIFTH EDITION

**TRAVEL
+LEISURE
BOOKS**

AMERICAN EXPRESS PUBLISHING CORPORATION
NEW YORK

TRAVEL+LEISURE
THE WORLD'S GREATEST HOTELS, RESORTS + SPAS
FIFTH EDITION

Editor Irene Edwards
Consulting Editor Laura Begley
Art Director Wendy Scofield
Assistant Book Editor Kathryn O'Shea-Evans
Associate Managing Editor Laura Teusink
Photo Coordinator Beth Garrabrant
Editorial Assistant James Jung
Reporters Christine Ajudua, Lisa Cheng,
Christine Ciarmello, Erin Florio, Jennifer Flowers,
Catesby Holmes, Sarah Kantrowitz, Stirling Kelso,
Sarah Khan, Jane Margolies, Samantha Schoech,
Bree Sposato
Copy Editors David Gunderson, Diego Hadis,
Mike Iveson, Sarah Khan, Elizabeth Sentz
Researchers Oliver Hartman, Yulia Khabinsky,
Shira Nanus
Production Associate David Richey

TRAVEL + LEISURE
Editor-in-Chief Nancy Novogrod
Creative Director Bernard Scharf
Executive Editor Jennifer Barr
Managing Editor Mike Fazioli
Arts/Research Editor Mario R. Mercado
Senior Copy Editor Kathy Roberson
Production Director Rosalie Abatemarco-Samat
Production Manager Ayad Sinawi

AMERICAN EXPRESS PUBLISHING CORPORATION
President, C.E.O. Ed Kelly
S.V.P., Chief Marketing Officer Mark V. Stanich
C.F.O., S.V.P., Corporate Development & Operations
Paul B. Francis
V.P., General Manager Keith Strohmeier, Frank Bland
V.P., Books & Products, Publisher Marshall Corey
Director, Book Programs Bruce Spanier
Senior Marketing Manager, Branded Books
Eric Lucie
Assistant Marketing Manager Lizabeth Clark
Director of Fulfillment & Premium Value Phil Black
Manager of Customer Experience & Product
Development Charles Graver
Director of Finance Tom Noonan
Associate Business Manager Uma Mahabir
Operations Director Anthony White

Front cover: Four Seasons Mauritius at Anahita;
photographed by Markus Gortz.

Copyright © 2010 American Express
Publishing Corporation

ISBN 978-0-7566-6901-0 | ISSN 1559-0372

Published by American Express
Publishing Corporation
1120 Avenue of the Americas
New York, New York 10036

Distributed by DK Publishing, Inc.
375 Hudson Street, New York, New York 10014

Manufactured in China

The shingled exterior of the Red Inn, in Provincetown, Massachusetts.

On a Plantation suite terrace at Barbados's Coral Reef Club.

CONTENTS

KEY TO THE PRICE ICONS $ UNDER $250 $$ $250–$499 $$$ $500–$749 $$$$ $750–$999 $$$$$ $1,000 AND UP

The Breakfast Room at
London's Rough Luxe Hotel.

KEY TO THE PRICE ICONS $ UNDER $250 $$ $250–$499 $$$ $500–$749 $$$$ $750–$999 $$$$$ $1,000 AND UP

The Molelo Presidential Suite at South Africa's Molori Safari Lodge.

A bathroom in a suite at the
Four Seasons Hotel Firenze.

INTRODUCTION

I AM A HOTEL DEPENDENT—NOT AN ADDICT, but a frequent guest whose entire trip experience can rise or fall with a seemingly small detail. I say this with particular feeling, having returned only two days ago from a stay at a much-touted grande dame that had just reopened after an extensive renovation. Sure, it was pretty—very pretty—but did it always work? Not exactly. My biggest complaint was that the light switches were practically impossible to control; even when you arrived at the perfect pressure and removed your finger at the optimum moment, the reward was scant—illumination so low that all you could do was pray for morning light. Thank goodness such disappointments have been relatively few and far between in my years at *Travel + Leisure*. Give or take some scrambling under desks to find outlets for my laptop (or even the hotel's hair dryer), a few absent reading lights, and small service lapses, most hotel experiences have kept me coming back for more.

The 138 properties highlighted in this book—our fifth annual compendium of the top hotels of the year—are an extraordinarily varied lot, from a Rhine Valley castle and a glittering Shanghai skyscraper to a bush camp in the Australian outback. Some are intimate hideaways; others are expansive resorts. (One, the Grand Daddy Hotel in Cape Town, is even an exceptionally chic trailer park.) What unites this diverse collection are the distinctively positive details that embed themselves in your memory, such as the farm-fresh eggs served at the Four Seasons Hotel Firenze, laid by hens raised on fresh goat's milk. The selection of "pillow scents" (from peppermint to rosemary) on offer at the Six Senses Hideaway Zighy Bay, in Oman. Or the bolster, monogrammed with your initials, waiting on your bed at the Montage Beverly Hills.

Of course, a hotel is only as good as the people who work there, and at all truly great properties, it's the attention and expertise of the staff that stands out. Like the concierge at the Mandarin Oriental, in Tokyo, who can lead you to the tiniest and best places for everything from sushi to ceramics; or the one at Charlotte Street Hotel, in London, who helped me buy a wedding gift off the registry at Harrods before I had even arrived; or the night staff at the Bulgari, in Milan, who kept running pages up to my room during a particularly hairy close of an issue of the magazine. Such gracious touches are what separates a merely pleasant stay from an unforgettable one.

In a single year, T+L profiles thousands of hotels and resorts, and our editors and reporters road-test at least twice as many more. Vetting these thousands of contenders and whittling them down to a manageable number is no easy task, and this year's crop was particularly impressive. Our well-traveled readers, as always, were an invaluable resource—and in the second half of the book we present the results of *Travel + Leisure*'s World's Best Awards, our annual survey of your favorite hotels and resorts. Beginning on page 214, you'll find a user-friendly resource section that lets you search for properties by location and by category, from beach resorts to mountain lodges.

Next on my own personal list: the Aman at Summer Palace, in Beijing; and the Parker Palm Springs and Rockhouse, in Jamaica, for destination weddings. There will also be some of the usual suspects—outposts of big-name brands in Italy, France, Bangkok, and Singapore. As always, I'll be on the lookout for details that resonate and embed themselves in memory in the most powerful ways.

NANCY NOVOGROD EDITOR-IN-CHIEF

On a vintage-style cruiser at the Ace Hotel & Swim Club, in Palm Springs.

UNITED STATES
+ CANADA

AINE VERMONT CAPE COD NORTH FORK NEW YORK CIT
RSEY SHORE VIRGINIA ATLANTA CUMBERLAND ISLAN
AMI MICHIGAN SANTA FE CENTRAL NEW MEXICO TUCSO
S VEGAS PALM SPRINGS BEVERLY HILLS BIG SUR NAP
LLEY PORTLAND HONOLULU VANCOUVER MONTREAL MAIN
RMONT CAPE COD NORTH FORK NEW YORK CITY JERSE
ORE VIRGINIA ATLANTA CUMBERLAND ISLAND MIAM
CHIGAN SANTA FE CENTRAL NEW MEXICO TUCSON LA
GAS PALM SPRINGS BEVERLY HILLS BIG SUR NAPA VALLE

HIDDEN POND

Kennebunkport, Maine

OLD MONEY HAS BEEN ENSCONCED in the seaside town of Kennebunkport for ages, as evidenced by the elegant captains' mansions and Federalist houses with luxury sedans parked out front. But in the nearby woods, patrician polish meets carefree simplicity in the manner of an upscale camp. Spread across 60 acres of balsam and birch groves, Hidden Pond's 14 two-bedroom cottages have all the trappings of a breezy summer escape: outdoor showers, screened-in porches, and fully stocked, beadboard-paneled kitchens. Whimsical details—oars used as towel racks, a spa tent decorated with tree trunks—reinforce the rustic nature of the setting. This being Maine, a picturesque lighthouse on a scenic beach is just a lobster-boat ride away.

354 Goose Rocks Rd.; 888/967-9050 or 207/967-9050; hiddenpondmaine. com; cottages from $$$.

The woodsy-chic dining room in Hidden Pond's Daydream cottage.

A vintage chairlift sign in Pitcher Inn's Ski Room. Left: The third-floor stairwell.

PITCHER INN

Warren, Vermont

275 Main St.; 800/735-2478 or 802/496-6350; pitcherinn.com; doubles from $$.

FROM THE ROAD, IT LOOKS LIKE any other house in Vermont's Mad River Valley—a rather austere modern colonial in the heart of a village on the border of 400,000 acres of national forest. Step inside, however, and what you get is a conventional country inn turned on its head. The 11 guest rooms, created by a cast of designers, riff playfully on various pastoral themes. Mountain is a mock fire-lookout cabin with a trompe l'oeil vista; Trout is octagonal, with a river-stone fireplace and tree trunks edging the bed (their "roots" splay out on the wooden floor, echoing the nearby timberland). In the Lodge room, hand-painted stars adorn a twilight-blue ceiling. Visit in late February, when inky streams lie crusted with ice, to see the region at its best: roads lined with old sugar maples bearing tap buckets on their trunks, and woods so still, you can hear the sound of snow crystals as they fall and fill your tracks.

RED INN

Provincetown, Massachusetts

AMONG THE GROOMED INKBERRY HEDGEROWS and white picket fences of the West End sits this rambling Cape Cod–style structure built by a sea captain for his wife in 1805. In 1915, the red-shingled residence—by then covered with climbing roses—became an inn, with decks overlooking the shell-strewn beach where the Pilgrims allegedly first moored the *Mayflower*. With names like Sunset View and Cape Light, the eight rooms and suites are sweetly old-fashioned, featuring wide-plank floors and wrought-iron beds. Modern pilgrims who flock here are more likely to be seeking respite from the parade of characters that turn Commercial Street into a form of open-air theater in high summer. Activities tend toward the quieter side of things—wandering on the sand flats and clamming with the locals, or savoring a platter of Wellfleet oysters and a waterfront view.

15 Commercial St.; 866/473-3466 or 508/487-7334; theredinn.com; doubles from $$.

The lawn and waterfront dining room at the Red Inn.

House-smoked salmon served over a corn blini at the North Fork Table & Inn.

NORTH FORK TABLE & INN

Southold, New York

AN UNASSUMING HAMLET on Long Island Sound, Southold is home to little more than forest, farms, and the North Fork Table & Inn, a small Colonial-style house owned by a pair of Big Apple culinary stars. Chef Gerry Hayden (from the legendary Aureole) and his wife, James Beard Award–winning pastry chef Claudia Fleming (formerly of Gramercy Tavern), turn out seasonally inspired New American dishes that draw on locally sourced biodynamic and organic produce, such as raw *hamachi* and seared Hudson Valley foie gras. The wine list highlights selections from up-and-coming Long Island wineries: a Wölffer Estate Pinot Gris from Sagaponack, a Bedell Cellars Cabernet Franc from Cutchogue. Go for the food, but stay for the night in one of four rooms, which have cherrywood sleigh beds, exposed red-brick chimneys, and artisanal bath products. You'll wake up to the best blueberry and apricot scones you've ever had.
57225 Main Rd.; 631/765-0177; northforktableandinn. com; doubles from $$.

THE STANDARD, NEW YORK

New York, New York

ANDRÉ BALAZS'S FOURTH and largest Standard, a glass-and-concrete behemoth towering 18 stories over Meatpacking District warehouses, serves as both crash pad and playground for the international style set. The Todd Schliemann–designed structure literally straddles the High Line—that 76-year-old elevated freight-train track turned pedestrian greenway—on 60-foot pylons, an attraction in and of itself. Scene-seekers can choose to mingle over Sidecars and single malts in the lobby bar; bratwursts, pretzels, and pilsners in the beer garden, helmed by Wallsé chef Kurt Gutenbrunner; or bacon-topped burgers and duck-fat smashed potatoes in the ground-floor restaurant, the Standard Grill. Accidental exhibitionist alert: the floor-to-ceiling glass windows showcase not only the Hudson River and the Statue of Liberty, but also any in-room shenanigans you care to imagine. *848 Washington St.; 877/550-4646 or 212/645-4646; standardhotels.com; doubles from $.*

The generously sized windows in a guest room at the Standard.

SPOTLIGHT NYC CLASSICS

WHO SAYS ALL THE ACTION HAPPENS DOWNTOWN? Uptown Manhattan's landmark hotels are having their own splashy revival. At the Pierre, new owner Taj Hotels Resorts and Palaces commissioned an ambitious renovation that included bringing in Portuguese artisans to restore the ballroom's hand-painted relief ceilings, and ensconcing the first foreign branch of London's socialite-friendly restaurant Le Caprice. The hotel's original blueprints, now on silver foil, line the corridors. From its decades-long perch on the corner of 77th Street and Madison Avenue, the Mark Hotel recently got a $150 million makeover from French interior designer Jacques Grange. A dizzying Op Art

A Grand Suite's private terrace at the Pierre.

A Jacques Grange–designed bathroom at the Mark Hotel.

THE PIERRE

2 E. 61st St.; 212/838-8000; tajhotels.com; doubles from $$$$.

MARK HOTEL

25 E. 77th St.; 866/744-4300 or 212/744-4300; themarkhotel.com; doubles from $$$$.

marble floor in the eclectically furnished lobby sets the stage for guest rooms in soothing tones of brown and beige. On the southeast (read: prettiest) corner of Central Park, the revamped Plaza Hotel still delivers that cinematic New York experience, with white-gloved butlers, a wood-paneled bar, and stirring park views that spread out before you like an endless summer night. And the Surrey adds a dose of irreverence to the Upper East Side—think cutting-edge video art and an "antique" rug composed of mosaic tile—while still paying the ultimate homage to the ladies who lunch: the walls of the bar's private booths are quilted like a Chanel bag.

The Champagne Bar at the Plaza Hotel.

A guest room with a king-size bed at the Surrey.

PLAZA HOTEL

Fifth Avenue at Central Park South; 888/850-0909 or 212/759-3000; theplaza.com; doubles from $$$$$.

THE SURREY

20 E. 76th St.; 800/978-7739 or 212/288-3700; thesurrey.com; doubles from $$$$.

CONGRESS HALL

Cape May, New Jersey

YOUNG FAMILIES ADORE THIS BUTTERCUP-YELLOW GRANDE DAME—and for good reason. First there is its postcard-perfect setting in one of the best-preserved Victorian districts in America, complete with chiming church bells, gingerbread porches, and old-fashioned trolleys. Then there's the high fun factor: striped cabanas on a private beach, a pool that practically begs for cannonballs, and a sweeping stretch of lawn that's the setting for yoga or a pickup game of lacrosse. It's the summer house where every day is filled with endless play. *251 Beach Ave.; 888/944-1816 or 609/884-8421; congresshall.com; doubles from $$.*

Lacrosse on the Congress Hall lawn.

INN AT LITTLE WASHINGTON

Washington, Virginia

A VERITABLE COCOON of Brunschwig & Fils fabrics and impeccable service, the Inn at Little Washington is as sumptuous as a Henry James period movie. Yet chef-owner Patrick O'Connell's sly sense of humor keeps things from getting too twee. What began as a simple restaurant in a former garage has become a much-lauded destination for haute American fare, where multicourse tasting menus come with a cow-shaped cheese cart announced by the clang of a dairy bell. Along with the inn's guest rooms, awash in Parisian lampshades and Oriental rugs, guests can stay in one of two recently renovated residences: the 1899 Claiborne House, with its two-story veranda and private garden, and the fire-engine red Gamekeeper's Cottage, which has a stone fireplace and an outdoor dining pavilion. Surprisingly, tiny Washington—69 miles from Washington, D.C.—is a hotbed of culture, with two theaters and a clutch of excellent galleries that would impress even the most dedicated urbanite. *Middle and Main Streets; 540/675-3800; theinnatlittle washington.com; doubles from $$$.*

The Inn at Little Washington's courtyard. Above: The master suite at the Claiborne House.

The Mansion Bar at the Mansion on Peachtree.

THE MANSION ON PEACHTREE

Atlanta, Georgia

ARCHITECT ROBERT A.M. STERN'S Neoclassical limestone tower—its full name is the Mansion on Peachtree, a Rosewood Hotel & Residence—provides ready access to the shops and restaurants in the tony enclave of Buckhead, a.k.a. Beverly Hills East. As befits a Rosewood, service is exemplary. The expert choreographers at the door usher guests to reception desks in the lobby, then whisk them up to guest rooms that combine traditional details (marble and velvet) with up-to-the-minute touches (framed landscapes that retract at the touch of a remote, revealing flat-screen TV's). The bathrooms—you'll find TV's here, too—are the biggest of any hotel in town. On the third floor is the 15,000-square-foot spa, overseen by Lydia Mondavi of wine making–family fame. *3376 Peachtree Rd. N.E.; 888/767-3966 or 404/995-7500; rwmansiononpeachtree.com; doubles from $.*

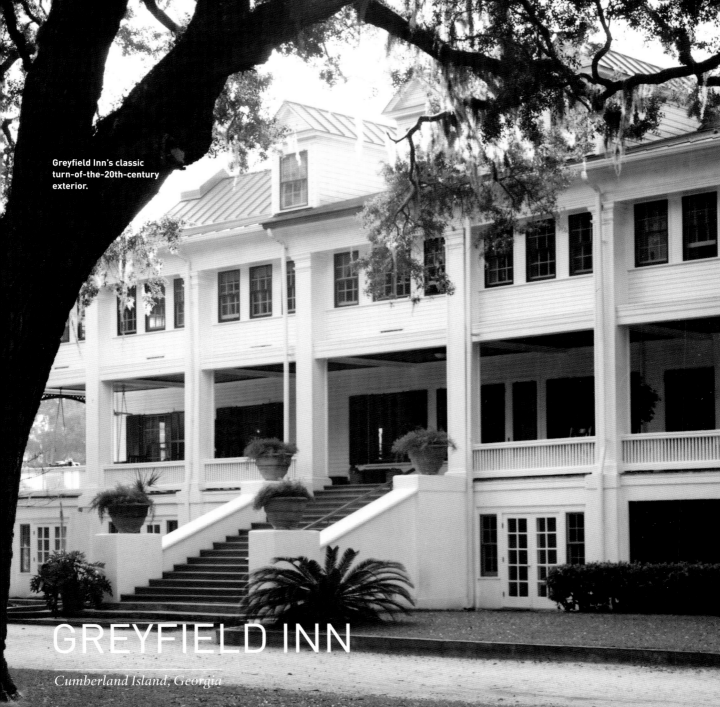

Greyfield Inn's classic turn-of-the-20th-century exterior.

GREYFIELD INN

Cumberland Island, Georgia

WILD HORSES GRAZING ON DUNE GRASSES, live oaks draped with Spanish moss, and creeks scattered with prehistoric sharks' teeth would make this largely undeveloped barrier island feel light-years away from civilization—were it not for the mansion built in 1901 at the behest of industrialist Thomas Carnegie (brother of Andrew) and now run by his descendants as a genteel inn. The 16 rooms are furnished with mahogany beds and Chippendale chairs—but no television, phone, or Internet service. Book the Porch Suite for its morning light, then join a naturalist-led tour of the 18 miles of pristine woodland and marshes.
866/401-8581 or 904/261-6408; greyfieldinn.com, doubles from $$$, including meals and boat transfer from the mainland.

SPOTLIGHT
MIAMI

NEVER A TOWN TO SHY AWAY FROM GLAMOUR, Miami has turned up the heat on its hotel scene. At Canyon Ranch Hotel & Spa in Miami Beach, rooms with residence-style touches—including granite-topped kitchen counters and refrigerators that can be stocked with organic food upon request—join a 70,000-square-foot, David Rockwell–designed spa where three different kinds of "experiential" showers simulate a rainstorm, with sound and lighting effects to match. In downtown Miami, what could have been just another high-rise has become a bold statement, thanks to Hollywood star decorator Kelly Wearstler. The Viceroy Miami is full of charming Wearstlerisms—look for Asian foo dog lamps and fanciful nine-foot-tall cranes painted onto lobby walls. But the showstopper is the two-acre outdoor space and the "floating library" at the all-white spa, as imagined by Philippe Starck. At the Mondrian in South Beach, overlooking the calm waters of Biscayne Bay, Dutch designer Marcel Wanders helped create a Baroque-minimalist palace that's a feast for the imagination. A chandelier turns out to be a showerhead; the bathroom tiles are a trompe l'oeil cloud mosaic. Finally, in mid–Miami Beach, the venerable Fontainebleau—which first welcomed guests in 1954—is swinging once more, thanks to a $1 billion renovation that revived its Rat Pack glamour and design-icon status. The public spaces are truly impressive: an epic lobby, a glowing floor in the Bleau Bar, and a seemingly endless series of palm trees, lounge chairs, and pools that encapsulate what South Florida living is all about.

The outdoor dining area at Canyon Ranch Hotel & Spa in Miami Beach.

The restored "cheese wall" at the Fontainebleau Miami Beach.

The Viceroy Miami's Spa at Icon Brickell.

Overlooking Biscayne Bay at Mondrian in South Beach's Sunset Lounge.

CANYON RANCH HOTEL & SPA IN MIAMI BEACH

6801 Collins Ave.; 800/742-9000; canyonranch miamibeach.com; doubles from $$.

VICEROY MIAMI

485 Brickell Ave.; 866/781-9923 or 305/503-4400; viceroymiami.com; doubles from $$.

MONDRIAN IN SOUTH BEACH

1100 West Ave.; 800/697-1791 or 305/514-1500; mondrian-miami.com; doubles from $$.

FONTAINEBLEAU MIAMI BEACH

4441 Collins Ave.; 800/548-8886 or 305/538-2000; fontainebleau.com; doubles from $$.

INN AT WATERVALE

Arcadia, Michigan

1244 Watervale Rd.; 231/352-9083; watervaleinn.com; doubles from $, including breakfast and dinner; cottages from $$, one-week minimum.

WELCOME TO THE ALL-AMERICAN summer vacation. The Inn at Watervale is something of a time capsule: a 19th-century main house and 17 cottages, set between the sand dunes of Lake Michigan and smaller, warmer Lower Herring Lake. Innkeeper Dori Turner—who makes a mean sour cream coffee cake, often served at breakfast—sourced much of the décor from flea markets and antiques shops, and fosters a love of tradition that draws families generation after generation. Wednesday is barbecue night, with hayrides and ice cream; Thursday brings bingo games in the "casino," a hall once used for town meetings and dances. And while Fourth of July reservations are made months in advance, they're certainly worth the effort—guests gather on the lawn for a cookout, complete with fried chicken and deviled eggs.

On the dock at Lower Herring Lake.

The Inn at Watervale's main building.

ENCANTADO, AN AUBERGE RESORT

Santa Fe, New Mexico

JUST NORTH OF SANTA FE in the enclave of Tesuque is an all-too-rare commodity: a luxe Southwestern desert experience without a hint of dream catcher kitsch. The 65-casita Encantado, the latest from Auberge Resorts, is made for intimate, magical moments. Who wouldn't love late-afternoon sun streaming down over a plush bed while a piñon-scented fire crackles in a nearby kiva-style fireplace? Guests are shuttled to and from the Plaza free of charge in a fleet of Mercedes-Benz sedans, which means they can partake in all the city has to offer, yet leave the tourist hordes behind at day's end. The spa utilizes local ingredients—sage, juniper, and adobe clay—in their treatments, while the restaurant menu echoes the regional emphasis with dishes like grilled tenderloin adobo and a roasted rack of lamb with guajillo-chile *jus*.

198 State Rd. 592; 877/262-4666 or 505/946-5700; encantadoresort.com; doubles from $$$.

A one-bedroom suite at the Encantado.

The sign near the entrance to the Fite Ranch Bed & Breakfast.

FITE RANCH BED & BREAKFAST

San Antonio, New Mexico

164 Fite Ranch Rd.; 575/838-0958; fiteranchbed andbreakfast.com; doubles from $, two-night minimum.

WAY OUT IN CENTRAL NEW MEXICO'S sprawling, craggy desert, this down-home working cattle ranch began life as a coal miners' boarding house. Back then, as rumor has it, parlor girls were hired to keep residents close at hand. Today, the ranch doubles as a quaint bed-and-breakfast made up of four apartment-style suites decorated with Southwestern collectibles— cowgirl-themed art, dude ranch photos, and, in the nearby bunkhouse, 1940's feed stalls from the New Mexico State Fairgrounds. Each room also has a full kitchen and a fridge stocked with ready-to-eat burritos. Kick back on the porch swing and watch the desert sun set over the dusty hamlet, dig for fossils in the canyons, or explore the ruins of nearby ghost towns, vestiges of the area's mining past.

HACIENDA DEL SOL GUEST RANCH RESORT

Tucson, Arizona

YES, IT HAS THE REQUISITE STABLES of any self-respecting ranch. But the adobe-walled Hacienda del Sol is more romantic hideaway than action-packed retreat. Once an exclusive girls' boarding school (the Kelloggs and Vanderbilts reportedly sent their daughters here), the property began welcoming guests in the 1940's, drawing A-list celebrities of the era. Hammered tin lamps, carved-beam ceilings, and saltillo-tile floors add up to an atmosphere of gracious refinement. The restaurant specializes in retro classics, such as Muscovy duck and veal scaloppine, and draws raves for its wine list. Despite such sophisticated flourishes, there's no forgetting you're in the desert; keep an eye out for the odd bobcat or javelina wandering the grounds. *5601 N. Hacienda del Sol Rd · 800/728-6514 or 520/299-1501; haciendadelsol.com; doubles from $*

The bar at Encore's Botero restaurant.

ENCORE

Las Vegas, Nevada

3131 Las Vegas Blvd. S.; 888/320-7125 or 702/770-7171; encorelasvegas.com; doubles from $.

IN A CITY WHERE ONE-UPMANSHIP is the name of the game, the 45-story Encore delivers a degree of intimacy unprecedented on the Strip. The newest resort in mogul Steve Wynn's collection takes a different approach to Vegas glam—one more in keeping with a luxurious desert oasis. Even the sunny casino has glass walls that look out onto gardens and pools. You'll find the obligatory bling in the form of Swarovski-crystal peacock sculptures, a mammoth golden Buddha in the lavish spa, a crystal dragon in Wazuzu restaurant, and massive swiveling flat-screen TV's in each of the 2,034 rooms. Still, the natural touches are just as awe-inspiring, including a botanical backdrop of sculpted flower beds, laurel trees, and potted palms that make the 4.6-million-square-foot expanse feel downright cozy.

A ground-floor guest room with ceramist Stan Bitters's igloo-shaped fireplace at the Ace. Opposite: Towels by the pool.

ACE HOTEL & SWIM CLUB

Palm Springs, California

THE LO-FI, ROCK-AND-ROLL STYLE of Portland, Oregon–based Ace Hotel Group has found a niche among 21st-century bohemians. Its California outpost, a former Westward Ho/Howard Johnson motel, is a carefree, slightly enchanted place where you could easily while away several days without ever leaving the grounds. A pool kiosk forms the base for a stargazing deck with lounge chairs. Three round canvas Mongolian yurts with batik-lined interior walls provide shelter for spa treatments. And just off the lobby, you'll find a well-preserved memento of things past—a cavelike watering hole called the Amigo Room, with upholstered booths, a cork-tiled floor, and Mexican pesos embedded in the transparent tabletops. A playland for adults, the resort seems to encourage regression to a kinder, more nostalgic era, with Ping-Pong on the patio, a mobile bar housed in a vintage camper, hammocks by the pool, turntables in several guest rooms, and cruiser bikes on loan for a spin around town. *701 E. Palm Canyon Dr.; 760/325-9900; acehotel.com; doubles from $.*

MONTAGE BEVERLY HILLS

Beverly Hills, California

THE MAYBACH PARKED OUT FRONT sets an appropriately gilded tone at this testament to unapologetic luxury, which channels vintage Hollywood (wood-beamed ceilings, muraled walls) and nouveau L.A. (a rooftop pool and Pilates studio). Despite the fact that the hotel opened in November 2008, during one of the worst economic moments in recent history, this sister to the super-successful Montage Laguna Beach still pampers with perks like poolside foot massages, complimentary shoe shines, Agraria bath products, and monogrammed bolsters—yes, your initials—on the bed. Oh, and did we mention the Mercedes-Benzes available to guests staying in certain suites, and the hotel's own gold-ink pens? Both are befitting of this glamorous address. *225 N. Canon Dr.; 888/860-0788 or 310/860-7800; montagebeverlyhills.com; doubles from $$.*

An eagle-eye view from the lodge deck at Treebones Resort. Right: Yurts set on the hillside.

TREEBONES RESORT

Big Sur, California

71895 Hwy. 1; 877/424-4787 or 805/927-2390; treebonesresort.com; doubles from $.

THE PHRASE *PERCHED ON THE EDGE* takes on new meaning at this unconventional getaway located high on a bluff along northern California's misty coast. Guests can bunk in a two-person house or in one of 16 spacious and surprisingly comfortable yurts, with polished pine floors, French doors, and quilts that take the chill out of the brisk sea air. The truly adventurous can spend the night in the so-called human nest, a 10-foot-diameter structure crafted out of eucalyptus branches and seemingly suspended over the Pacific. Owners John and Corinne Handy wanted to maximize the oceanfront experience—thus even the outdoor sushi bar, which serves the highest-quality fish around, comes with panoramic views. An organic garden provides most of the produce for the resort's Wild Coast restaurant; all the wines hail from California's Central Coast; and the gray-whale migration, visible during winter months, is another reminder of how breathtaking Big Sur can be.

BARDESSONO

Yountville, California

The rooftop pool at
Bardessono.

THOMAS KELLER'S FRENCH LAUNDRY RESTAURANT put the pint-size Napa Valley town of Yountville on the culinary map—and now the area's accommodations are as memorable as its Michelin-starred establishments. Combining a commitment to the environment with an emphasis on the good life, the year-old Bardessono aims to be the greenest luxury hotel in North America. There's certainly plenty of eco cred to go around. Constructed of salvaged wood and weathered steel and using sustainable building methods, the 62-suite modern inn composts its kitchen scraps and draws much of its electricity from state-of-the-art solar panels. Pampering gets equal attention: rooms have outdoor showers and hidden massage tables, and rooftop cabanas surround a lap pool with views of the valley and vines. *6526 Yount St.; 877/932-5333 or 707/204-6000; bardessono.com; doubles from $$$$.*

The Nines' historic department-store façade.

THE NINES

Portland, Oregon

---

525 SW Morrison St.; 877/229-9995 or 503/222-9996; thenines.com; doubles from $$.

THE POSHEST NEW HOTEL IN TOWN takes up the top nine floors of the iconic 1909 Meier & Frank Building, looking out over downtown Pioneer Courthouse Square and to the Cascade Mountains in the distance. Environmentally sound practices—the Nines gets 100 percent of its electricity from renewable sources like wind turbines—helped it earn LEED Silver certification, one of only 12 hotels in the world to do so. Stylized flourishes are cheeky nods to the structure's department-store glory days: Tiffany-blue corridors lead to the 331 spacious rooms and suites, Ralph Pucci–designed mannequins vamp up public spaces, and a 419-piece modern-art collection showcases the work of local creatives. Oh, and that portrait on the library wall? It's a Gus Van Sant original.

KAHALA HOTEL & RESORT

Honolulu, Hawaii

WORLD'S BEST **IN THE 1960'S, WHEN THIS** tropical compound was a Hilton known as "Kahollywood," the boldfaced names seemed as commonplace as palm trees. Cinematic legends like John Wayne and Julie Andrews shared the pool; Richard Burton and Elizabeth Taylor reportedly hid from the paparazzi and canoodled in a private cabana. These days there's still plenty of name-dropping to be had (President Obama is the latest guest of note), but even the average Joe gets the VIP treatment. Staffers know repeat guests by name, and beach butlers stand at attention with chilled towels and spray bottles to mist sunbathers. Early risers can catch the ultimate extravagance—a Crayola-bright sunrise—by walking to the "kissing point," a sliver of land jutting out from the hotel's beach.

5000 Kahala Ave.; 800/367-2525 or 808/739-8888; kahalaresort.com; doubles from $$$.

The Kahala Hotel & Resort's pool, lined with Italian blue marble.

ROYAL HAWAIIAN

Honolulu, Hawaii

UNLIKE SOME OF THE OTHER HIGH-RISE HOTELS on Waikiki Beach, the Royal Hawaiian puts its heritage front and center—which seems fitting on this particular stretch of Oahu, the former site of Queen Kaahumanu's Summer Palace. The 1927 coral-pink landmark, which just underwent a significant renovation, features Spanish-Moorish design with tasteful Hawaiian-Asian touches: a koa-wood desk here, a Eugene Savage painting there. Every Monday night, locals gather on the beach to perform the Aha Aina luau, dancing the hula, pounding poi, and serving up platters of Island rock-lobster tail and lomilomi salmon. Perhaps the hotel's most buzzed-about new asset is its seafood-centric restaurant, Azure, helmed by Alan Wong–trained chef Jon Matsubara. Each day at 5:30 a.m., a staffer heads to the market to grab the prime catch, resulting in dishes like ginger-steamed opakapaka and seared ahi with a spiced nori crust.
2259 Kalakaua Ave.; 800/325-3589 or 808/923-7311; royal-hawaiian.com; doubles from $$$.

The recently renovated lower lobby. Opposite: A vintage-style phone in the lobby area at the Royal Hawaiian.

A fireplace suite at the Shangri-La Hotel's spa. Right: The lobby.

SHANGRI-LA HOTEL, VANCOUVER

Vancouver, British Columbia

1128 W. Georgia St.; 866/565-5050 or 604/689-1120; shangri-la.com; doubles from $$.

KNOWN FOR ITS VAST HOTELS and opulent, statement-making lobbies, Shangri-La might not be an obvious match for laid-back, mountain-fringed British Columbia. But the Asia-based group's first North American property fits right into downtown Vancouver, thanks to its understated-yet-refined vibe. The 119 spacious rooms are done up in a Zen-like mixture of black-and-white brush paintings and B&B Italia furniture; the discreet L-shaped lobby, with its inviting leather sofas, makes the ideal rainy-day refuge. That's not to say the Shangri-La Hotel did away completely with grandeur. Italian crystal chandeliers hang in public spaces, the Chinese- and Himalayan-inspired spa administers customized treatments in suites with fireplaces, and Jean-Georges Vongerichten's creations, such as Arctic char sashimi and soy-glazed short ribs, have made the third-floor restaurant a culinary hot spot.

VIEUX-MONTREAL HAS ITS SHARE of old-world charm, with its cobblestoned streets and Beaux-Arts buildings. Step beyond the threshold of the Hotel St Paul, however, and the stately columned façade gives way to a lounge-like contemporary space, with low-slung sofas and floor-to-ceiling curtains. The too-cool staffers with their faux-mohawk hairdos would be off-putting if the 120 rooms weren't so comfortable: playful fabrics brighten the dark walnut floors and white walls, and fake-fur throws add texture to beds. On black leather banquettes under dim lighting at the hotel's Vauvert restaurant, diners spoon up market-fresh classics, like a black ink risotto or mini burgers with cheddar and bacon.

355 Rue McGill; 866/380-2202 or 514/380-2222; hotelstpaul.com; doubles from $.

Vauvert restaurant at the Hotel St Paul.

HOTEL ST PAUL

Montreal, Quebec

A villa with private plunge pool at the Viceroy Anguilla.

CARIBBEAN

BAGO BEQUIA BARBADOS DOMINICA ST. BART'S ANGUILL
ERTO RICO DOMINICAN REPUBLIC JAMAICA TOBAGO BEQUI
RBADOS DOMINICA ST. BART'S ANGUILLA PUERTO RIC
MINICAN REPUBLIC JAMAICA TOBAGO BEQUIA BARBADO
MINICA ST. BART'S ANGUILLA PUERTO RICO DOMINICA
PUBLIC JAMAICA TOBAGO BEQUIA BARBADOS DOMINIC
BART'S ANGUILLA PUERTO RICO DOMINICAN REPUBLI
MAICA TOBAGO BEQUIA BARBADOS DOMINICA ST. BART
GUILLA PUERTO RICO DOMINICAN REPUBLIC JAMAICA TOBAG

The stairway to a secluded bay near the hotel. Opposite: A view of the Atlantic from a guest room's private balcony.

BACOLET
BEACH CLUB

Scarborough, Tobago

73 Bacolet St.; 868/639-2357; bacoletbeachclub.com; doubles from $.

HOTELS ON TOBAGO have historically been a rustic lot, but this new 22-room property bucks the trend. Sweeping verandas, espresso-colored rattan chaises, and mahogany four-poster beds swathed in sheer curtains compensate for the rooms' cozy dimensions. The stark white façade and wooden rooftops are a nod to regional design traditions, while the Turkish marble floors and the internationally trained staff reflect owner Gloria Jones-Knapp's background as a globe-trotting fashion model. Alone on a crescent of sugary beach along Bacolet Bay, the resort gives the impression of absolute seclusion; yet the island's capital, Scarborough, with its colorful street markets and seaside bars, lies just five minutes away.

FIREFLY BEQUIA

Spring, Bequia

The pool at the Firefly Bequia. Opposite: One of four guest rooms.

LOOKING FOR THAT FABLED next great Caribbean getaway? Our money's on the Grenadines, part of the Windward Islands just west of Barbados. Bequia, the largest in the archipelago, recently welcomed a slew of new and updated hotels, including the Firefly Bequia, sister property to the Firefly Mustique. The four-room oasis has all the right sophisticated touches: canopied or mosquito-net-draped beds, Italian linens, and waterfall showers that open onto private stone patios. But what really sets it apart is the unparalleled access provided to guests, who can snorkel off the hotel's untamed beach, order a picnic to take to neighboring Isle de Carte, or call for a martini-shaking bartender who arrives at Firefly by speedboat. The ace in the hole is British hotelier Elizabeth Clayton, who has lived in the Grenadines for over a dozen years and has the connections to prove it. *784/458-3414; fireflybequia.com; doubles from $$, including meals.*

A canopied bed in one of Coral Reef Club's Plantation Suites.

SPOTLIGHT
BARBADOS

THE ROMANCE OF THE PAST meets a new wave of spas and hotels as Barbados prepares for a rebirth. It's easy to channel a Somerset Maugham kind of exoticism at the Coral Reef Club, where Bajan green monkeys scamper in the lush gardens; but the buzz is all about its year-old spa, reimagined in part by industry veteran Neil Howard, who worked on the Armani hotels in Dubai and Milan. The 88 guest rooms are crisp and classic, with private balconies or patios (some suites also come with lavish canopy beds). On tranquil Paynes Bay, the House is an intimate retreat with blue-and-white interiors that mimic the surrounding sea and sky. Since its beach is one of the calmest on Barbados, the 34-suite hotel maintains access to a small flotilla—kayaks, banana boats, and the like, all ready for a skim. On the windswept east coast, near the surf village of Bathsheba, a number of idiosyncratic small hotels offer delightful and affordable accommodations. The sweet little Sea-U Guest House, composed of seven simple whitewashed rooms, exudes laid-back charm (fresh coconuts are cut open for visitors). And Barbados's first resort, the Crane, a fixture on the southeast coast since 1887, is in the midst of a multimillion-dollar expansion. One thing that won't change: its signature oceanside pool, which features freestanding columns that seem to buttress the clouds as they float across the horizon.

Looking out on a terrace at the Crane.

The lobby at the House.

A spot to lounge at Sea-U Guest House.

CORAL REEF CLUB

Porters, St. James; 800/223-1108 or 246/422-2372; coralreefbarbados.com; doubles from $$.

THE HOUSE

Paynes Bay, St. James; 888/996-9947 or 246/432-5525; eleganthotels.com; doubles from $$$.

SEA-U GUEST HOUSE

Tent Bay, Bathsheba, St. Joseph; 246/433-9450; seaubarbados.com; doubles from $.

THE CRANE

St. Philip; 246/423-6220; thecrane.com; doubles from $$$.

ON THIS RELATIVELY UNKNOWN ISLAND in the Windward chain, the plantation-style Beau Rive glows like a beacon of civility and elegance amid tropical forest, 240 feet above the Atlantic. The 10 rooms are airy and simple: a cream palette punctuated by dark-wood side tables, jalousie shutters, and colorful paintings of island scenes. Balconies facing the ocean and surrounding jungle—perfect for spotting red-speckled Jacquot parrots—lay hidden behind pairs of double doors. Leave the shutters open at night to let the frangipani-scented breeze and the hum of the tree frogs lull you into a deep, rejuvenating sleep.

Between the villages of Castle Bruce and Sineku; 767/445-8992; beaurive.com; doubles from $.

BEAU RIVE

Dominica

Views of Richmond Bay from a cottage guest room's private veranda at Beau Rive.

The bedroom in Waikiki, one of Salines's five cottages.

SALINES GARDEN COTTAGES

Salines, St. Bart's

590-690/419-429; *salinesgarden.com; doubles from $.*

ALTHOUGH YACHTS AND PRIVATE JETS are a dime a dozen on this exclusive isle, it *is* possible to keep it low-key—and affordable—on St. Bart's. Case in point: Salines Garden Cottages, five *cazes* (traditional Creole houses) framed by bright pink bougainvillea and located just minutes from one of the island's most picturesque beaches, Anse de Salines. The cottages channel the owners' favorite far-flung vacation spots, such as Cap Ferrat and Essaouira. Amenities are simple yet thoughtfully done: the poolside breakfasts, for example, include excellent coffee and freshly baked pain au chocolat from a boulangerie down the road. Given the comparatively modest rates, a $195 post-beach facial in your room from Ligne St Barth, which operates a mobile spa on the island using Caribbean-sourced ingredients, seems like a reasonable indulgence indeed.

VICEROY ANGUILLA

West End, Anguilla

REALITY-TV JUDGE AND HOTEL DESIGNER Kelly Wearstler—whose love of color, layering of texture, and graphic effects appeal to connoisseurs of her retro-Hollywood aesthetic—has found a more subdued vocabulary on an island known for barefoot elegance. At the 166-room Viceroy Anguilla, on 3,200 feet of shorefront where turquoise-hued Meads and Barnes bays meet, Wearstler mixed driftwood lamps, petrified-wood tables, and silvery art objects with cool expanses of travertine marble for a soothing, beach-inspired palette. Full kitchens, private sundecks and plunge pools, outdoor showers with built-in benches and rain-head faucets, and a two-story spa with a meditation garden add to the atmosphere of pampered indolence. *866/270-7798 or 264/497-7000; viceroyanguilla.com; doubles from $$$.*

A villa's luminous exterior at the Viceroy Anguilla.

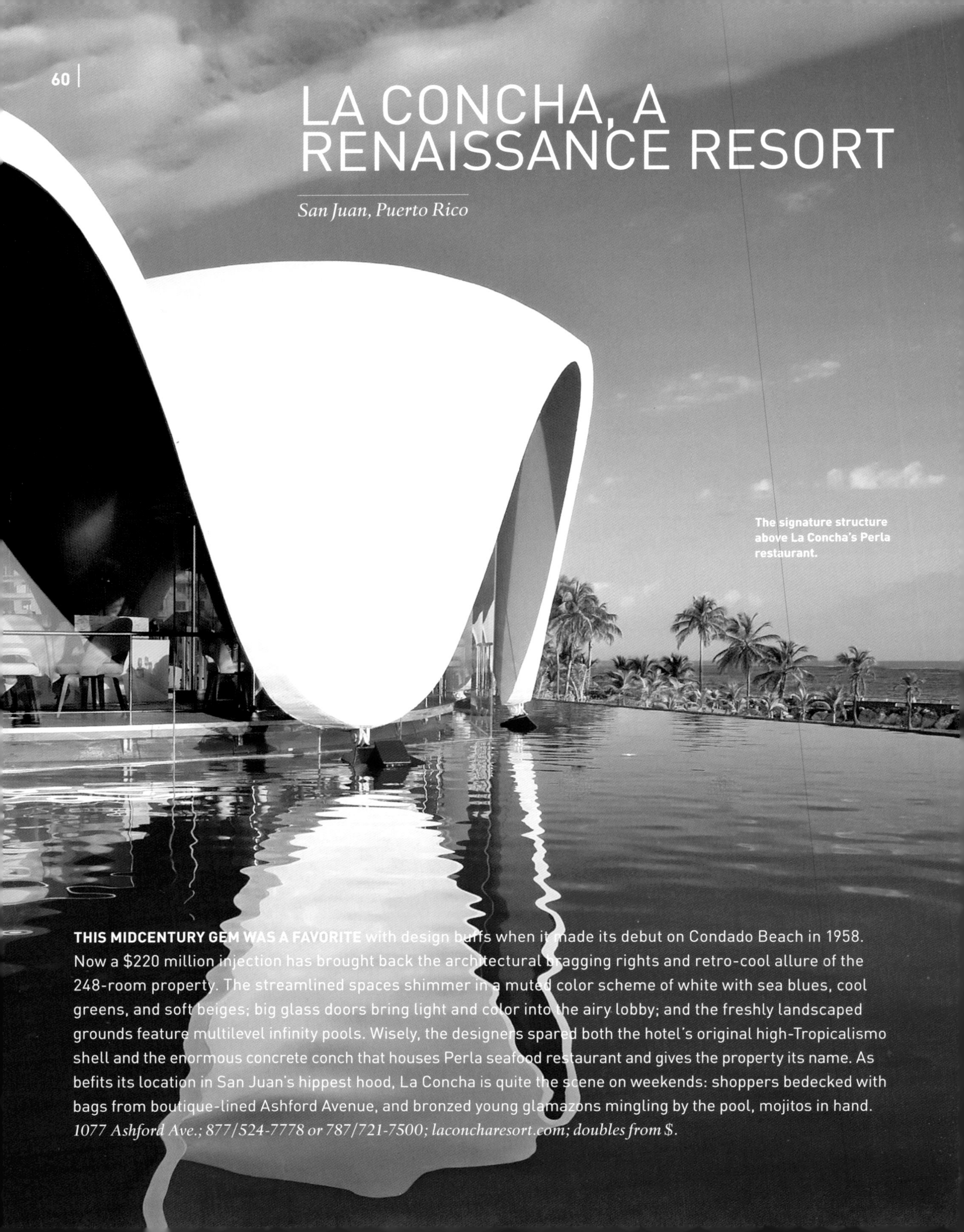

LA CONCHA, A RENAISSANCE RESORT

San Juan, Puerto Rico

The signature structure above La Concha's Perla restaurant.

THIS MIDCENTURY GEM WAS A FAVORITE with design buffs when it made its debut on Condado Beach in 1958. Now a $220 million injection has brought back the architectural bragging rights and retro-cool allure of the 248-room property. The streamlined spaces shimmer in a muted color scheme of white with sea blues, cool greens, and soft beiges; big glass doors bring light and color into the airy lobby; and the freshly landscaped grounds feature multilevel infinity pools. Wisely, the designers spared both the hotel's original high-Tropicalismo shell and the enormous concrete conch that houses Perla seafood restaurant and gives the property its name. As befits its location in San Juan's hippest hood, La Concha is quite the scene on weekends: shoppers bedecked with bags from boutique-lined Ashford Avenue, and bronzed young glamazons mingling by the pool, mojitos in hand. *1077 Ashford Ave.; 877/524-7778 or 787/721-7500; laconcharesort.com; doubles from $.*

A guest room at the
Conrad San Juan Condado Plaza.

CONRAD SAN JUAN CONDADO PLAZA

San Juan, Puerto Rico

THE VISUAL WHIMSY begins in the lobby, with a curved acrylic reception counter that morphs from sultry red to hot pink, backed by an abstract mural of Italian mosaic tiles. And the vibrant hits of color continue throughout, from acid green chairs to boldly patterned rugs. The 570 guest rooms maintain the upbeat mood with bright walls, hibiscus-patterned throws, and blown-up sepia photos of exotic flowers. In keeping with the party atmosphere, celebrity chef Wilo Benet's popular Pikayo restaurant—newly relocated to the property—serves *bistec encebollado* and shrimp with crispy bacon *mofongo* in a space with make-yourself-comfortable sofas and a communal table. *999 Ashford Ave.; 888/722-1274 or 787/721-1000; condadoplaza.com; doubles from $.*

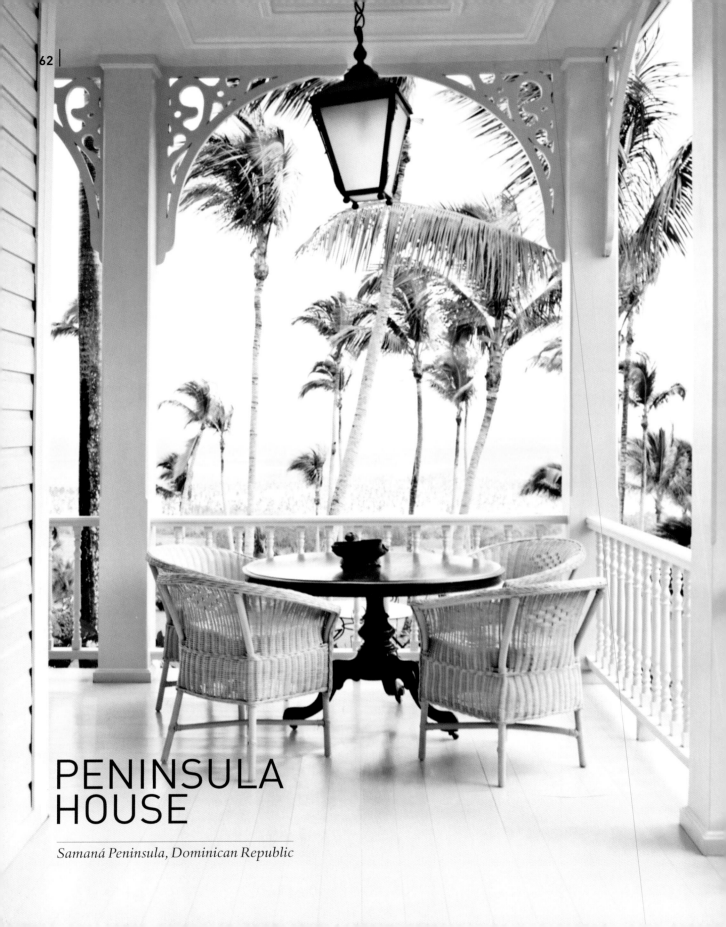

PENINSULA HOUSE

Samaná Peninsula, Dominican Republic

THANKS TO THE EFFORTS of its staff and owners, the Peninsula House feels less like a hotel and more like a residence—albeit an 18,000-square-foot plantation home on a beachside bluff. The six suites, all with terraces, showcase designer Serge Robin's take on global style: Louis XV chairs, handwoven rugs from Turkey, and objets d'art ranging from African masks to Indonesian marionettes. The hotel's refinements belie the tropical mountain setting—your bath linens are Frette, breakfast consists of freshly baked croissants and homemade jam, and even the china has an impressive lineage (a set once owned by the Aga Khan, anyone?). After a day by the pool, guests can follow chef Gonzalo Tizon into the kitchen to watch him whip up a dinner of roast quail and manchego soufflé. *Calle Cosón, Las Terrenas; 809/307-1827; thepeninsula house.com; doubles from $$$.*

A Junior suite at the Peninsula House. Opposite: The front veranda, overlooking Cosón Beach.

GEEJAM

Port Antonio, Jamaica

UNTIL A FEW YEARS AGO, music producer Jon Baker and label owner Steve Beaver rented out their lush eight-acre estate to musicians like Gwen Stefani and India.Arie for use as a recording studio. But now that they have teamed up with Island Outpost, Baker and Beaver's seven-room treetop retreat is open to anyone seeking to channel their inner Lenny Kravitz—easy enough to do, thanks to the hotel's rock-star-cool design (Juergen Teller photographs, Philippe Starck chairs). Due to a staff-to-guest ratio of four to one, anything you ask for seems possible. You can lay down a few tracks in the studio, complete with backup band, or embark on a spontaneous rafting trip on the Rio Grande, followed by a home-cooked lunch of regional specialties served by the river. Relaxation comes easy on the canopied deck, where Tory Burch–clad vacationers bask around the 14-foot-high waterfall. In a world of cookie-cutter boutique hotels, Geejam feels truly bespoke.
San San; 800/688-7678 or 876/993-7000; islandoutpost. com; doubles from $$$.

A canopied daybed at Geejam.

Poolside at UXUA Casa Hotel, in Trancoso, Brazil.

MEXICO
+ CENTRAL
+ SOUTH
AMERICA

ZATLÁN MEXICO CITY RIVIERA MAYA TULUM GRANADA GUANACAST
ZCO COLCHAGUA VALLEY SANTIAGO PATAGONIA BUENOS AIRE
LTA JOSÉ IGNACIO TRANCOSO MAZATLÁN MEXICO CITY RIVIER
YA TULUM GRANADA GUANACASTE CUZCO COLCHAGUA VALLE
NTIAGO PATAGONIA BUENOS AIRES SALTA JOSÉ IGNACIO TRANCOS
ZATLAN MEXICO CITY RIVIERA MAYA TULUM GRANADA GUANACAST
ZCO COLCHAGUA VALLEY SANTIAGO PATAGONIA BUENOS AIRE
LTA JOSÉ IGNACIO TRANCOSO MAZATLÁN MEXICO CITY RIVIER
YA TULUM GRANADA GUANACASTE CUZCO COLCHAGUA VALLE

The view from Casa Lucila
poolside terrace.

The lobby at Casa Lucila.

CASA LUCILA

Mazatlán, Mexico

THE AREA'S FIRST seaside boutique hotel, Casa Lucila heralded Mazatlán's official comeback as an international travel destination. Built on the site of a 19th-century mansion (which later became a 1940's nightclub frequented by John Wayne and Ernest Hemingway), the property harkens back to the town's storied past, when vacationing European and Mexican aristocrats constructed residences with wrought-iron balconies and 16-foot ceilings. Owner Conchita Valadés de Boccard, who oversaw the extensive restoration, named the hotel after her beloved mother, whose portrait hangs above the reception desk. The eight spacious, contemporary rooms bear the names of Conchita and her seven sisters; ask for one on the second floor overlooking long, golden Olas Altas beach and the waterfront Malecón. The family tribute continues in the bar—dubbed Fernando's Jazz Bar for Conchita's jazz-pianist father, whose vinyl releases from the 1950's and 60's are displayed on the walls. *16 Olas Altas; 52-669/982-1100; casalucila.com; doubles from $.*

The dining-room table at the hotel.

DISTRITO
CAPITAL

Mexico City, Mexico

Distrito Capital's main
lobby, with a vintage textile
artwork. Opposite: The
Escape skyscraper, which
houses the hotel.

HOWARD ROARK WOULD CERTAINLY APPROVE of Grupo Habita's latest offering, located in a Santa Fé business-district skyscraper high above the haze that often blankets Mexico City. An elevator takes you up to a cool monochromatic lobby and then to one of 30 gallery-like rooms, which share the same stark sensibility—all linear proportions and geometric angles, with glazed-tile baths, platform beds, studio windows, and lots of gray and white. Minimalism rules, right down to the John Pawson flatware in the restaurant. What saves Distrito Capital from being a mere Modernist box? Clever flourishes by Paris-based designer Joseph Dirand, including Artek light fixtures and Thomas Glassford's silver Asteroid sculptures, plus well-chosen vintage objects and collector-worthy furnishings. A fifth-floor bar and a pool terrace packed nightly with beautiful people—free-flowing tequila, few inhibitions—don't hurt, either. *37 Juan Salvador Agraz; 800/337-4685 or 52-55/5257-1300; hoteldistritocapital.com; doubles from $.*

BANYAN TREE
MAYAKOBA

Riviera Maya, Mexico

Km 298, Crta. Cancún–Playa del Carmen, Playa del Carmen; 800/591-0439
or 52-984/877-3688; banyantree.com; doubles from $$$$$.

The master bedroom in one of Banyan Tree's beachfront-pool villas.

BANYAN TREE'S FIRST FORAY into North America truly ups the ante, beginning with a 50-foot lobby and continuing with its Asian-meets-Mexican villas, all of which have private outdoor pools. Then there's the boat ride in a custom-built gondola that takes you from mangrove forest through an extensive system of lagoons and canals, arriving at a restaurant on a stretch of white sand bordering the Caribbean. You'll catch glimpses of the herons and cormorants that share the waters (the mahogany boats, called *lanchas*, use electric motors to avoid harming wildlife). And as befits an Asian-owned property, the Thai-trained staffers at the spa are well-versed in Eastern healing modalities.

COQUI COQUI

Tulum, Mexico

ALONG AN ULTRA-MELLOW STRETCH of the Riviera Maya, the five-room Coqui Coqui resembles a thatched-roof sand castle. This hotel is not for those seeking lavish attention or fancy amenities (in fact, there's no pool or TV). But if it's a pared-down escape that you're after, you'll find it within the cream-and-cocoa interiors that contrast beautifully with the turquoise sea. Rooms are lit with candles; platform beds are draped with sheer netting; multiple hammocks await. The spa is devoted to natural therapies—try a scrub made from sea salt and coconut. And the location is unimpeachable: Just steps from the Caribbean, it's the essence of barefoot simplicity. *Km 7.5, Carr. Tulum Ruinas Boca Paila; 52-1-984/100-1400; coquicoquispa.com; doubles from $.*

Overlooking the Caribbean from a terrace at Coqui Coqui.

A lobby nook at Hotel La Gran Francia.
Right: The courtyard pool.

HOTEL LA GRAN FRANCIA

Granada, Nicaragua

Southeast corner of Parque Central; 505/2552-6000; lagranfrancia.com; doubles from $.

MOST AMERICANS HAVE YET to update their image of Nicaragua since the tumultuous late 1970's, when the Sandinistas staged an uprising against the ruling Somoza family. It's high time they did: the country is an ecotourism superstar in the making, and Granada, a well-preserved colonial gem, makes a good jumping-off point to several natural wonders, like Lake Nicaragua and Mombacho Volcano. The place to stay is the 16th-century Hotel La Gran Francia, which has 21 rooms on two stories encircling a pool and courtyard open to the sky. Floors of gold-and-terra-cotta tile add a burnished grandeur, and huge carved-hardwood shutters instantly turn sunny rooms into siesta-ready quarters. In a breezy open-air structure next to a garden, the staff serves first-rate breakfasts—decadent French toast, perhaps the largest double espresso ever—at prices that make you realize how much of a secret Nicaragua can still be.

The hotel's Borrancho Beach Club, with views of Islita Beach.

HOTEL PUNTA ISLITA

Guanacaste, Costa Rica

WORLD'S BEST **WITH ITS THATCHED-PALM-FRINGE CASITAS** and hammocks angled to view the sunset, Hotel Punta Islita is a lovely place to kick back—but this ecologically minded resort has also made it a mission to do right. Eighty-five percent of the staff comes from surrounding communities, and 50 acres of the property are a designated protected habitat for native species. The neighboring village of Islita was transformed into a thriving arts center, with an open-air museum and crafts guilds. Keep an eye out for howler monkeys as you whiz through tropical forest on the legendary 50-foot-high zip lines. *866/446-4053 or 506/2656-3036; hotelpuntaislita.com; doubles from $$.*

The courtyard at
Inkaterra La Casona.

INKATERRA LA CASONA

Cuzco, Peru

A MERE 10 YEARS AGO, PERU—despite possessing a world-class attraction like Machu Picchu—had a limited infrastructure for luxury tourism. Then came Inkaterra, the ambitious, eco-minded hotel group responsible for three of the country's finest properties, including this 16th-century mansion once owned by a Spanish conquistador. Secreted behind a massive door on tiny Plaza Las Nazarenas, La Casona has 11 suites with views of the plaza or a charming courtyard. Interiors reflect both Incan and colonial influences, thanks to handwoven blankets and ornate frescoes—though such 21st-century comforts as heated floors and iPod speakers are very much in evidence. Guests are welcomed with hot cups of herbal tea infused with Andean mint and blended with honey.

113 Plaza Las Nazarenas; 800/442-5042 or 51-84/234-010; inkaterra.com; doubles from $$$.

SCATTERED AMONG THE COLONIAL TOWNS and blossom-covered haciendas of Colchagua Valley are more than 30 wineries—making this region, two and a half hours south of Santiago, the very heart of Chilean red wine culture. On a hill overlooking 450 acres of vines, Lapostolle Residence consists of four freestanding casitas, ranging in size from 650 to more than 1,000 square feet and named for the varietals grown at Clos Apalta, one of Lapostolle's two wineries: Cabernet Sauvignon, Petit Verdot, Merlot, and Carmenère. Cambodian silk curtains, vaulted ceilings, and sweeping wraparound decks add up to an atmosphere of such comfort and privacy that it's been known to inspire a nude sunbather or two. In the striking glass-and-wood main building, lunches and dinners are served with robust Lapostolle wines that cement this area's reputation as "the next Napa." *Km 4, Alpata; 56-72/953-360; lapostolle.com; doubles from $$$$, all-inclusive.*

LAPOSTOLLE RESIDENCE

Colchagua Valley, Chile

Lapostolle Residence's infinity pool, which overlooks the vines.

The W Lounge at the W Santiago.

W SANTIAGO

Santiago, Chile

CHILE'S COSMOPOLITAN CAPITAL is abuzz with new energy, but it's nothing compared to what's going on behind the new W Santiago's doors. Classic W features—modern lines, funky prints, a downtempo soundtrack, and a loungey vibe—form the backdrop for witty flourishes from New York designer Tony Chi, like a sheepskin wall guests can play like a drum. Striking allusions to the country's major exports, including a 1,600-bottle wall of wine, were added with help from Chilean designer Sergio Echeverría. Other heavy-hitters on board: Rande and Scott Gerber, the names behind nightspots Whiskey Blue, Red2One, and W Lounge, and fusion master Ciro Watanabe, who serves up Peruvian-Asian fare at Osaka. In the guest rooms, floor-to-ceiling windows allow the cityscape and snowcapped Andes to be the stars.

3000 Isidora Goyenechea; 877/946-8357 or 56-2/770-0000; whotels.com; doubles from $$$.

EXPLORA PATAGONIA, HOTEL SALTO CHICO

Torres del Paine National Park, Chile

Explora Patagonia, Hotel
Salto Chico, atop a bluff
overlooking Lake Pehoé.

WORLD'S BEST **THE EXPLORA GROUP GOES BOLDLY** where others fear to tread, staking its claim in destinations so remote they feel as if they're at the ends of the earth. Overlooking the emerald-colored Salto Chico waterfall, deep in Torres del Paine National Park, this luxury base camp is easily a two-hour drive from the nearest village. Keeping a long, low profile in contrast to the mountains behind it, the hotel is infused with an understated modern sensibility (warm-toned woods, handcrafted furniture). Getting you out in the wilderness is Explora's specialty; seasoned guides will lead you through the scenery on foot, by boat, on horseback, or via four-wheel drive. *866/750-6699; explora.com; doubles from $$$$$, all-inclusive, four-night minimum.*

The downstairs garden patio and terrace at Francis Ford Coppola's Jardin Escondido.

JARDIN ESCONDIDO

Buenos Aires, Argentina

4746 Gorriti; 800/746-3743; coppolajardinescondido. com; doubles from $$$, three-night minimum.

WHEN DIRECTOR FRANCIS FORD COPPOLA was in Buenos Aires shooting his 2009 film, *Tetro,* he bought a villa in the heart of vibrant Palermo Soho—then set about turning it into his own personal paradise. Now a two-suite hotel that still hosts Coppola when he's in town, it feels much more distinctive than your average accommodations. Three levels of intimate gardens, sprawling patios, and trellised outdoor dining areas create a peaceful escape in a buzzy boutique- and café-filled neighborhood. A daily housekeeper, an English-speaking concierge, and Nigel, the on-call sommelier, make it rather tempting to forgo the sights for a day or two spent playing house—or working your way through the impressive wine cellar. Request your own Sunday asado (Argentinean barbecue) by the solar-heated pool.

MORENO HOTEL BUENOS AIRES

Buenos Aires, Argentina

IT'S A WELL-KNOWN FACT: PORTEÑOS—as the residents of B.A. are dubbed—love to have fun, especially after dark. For visitors seeking a taste of the city's late-night joie de vivre, the Moreno Hotel may well be the perfect launching pad. The 39-room loft-style property occupies a restored Deco building in the heart of San Telmo, where Belle Époque bars and tango halls abound. The Moreno even has its own 130-seat theater for concerts and tango performances. Stained-glass windows, leather club chairs, and wrought-iron elevators join modern luxuries, including Egyptian cotton sheets and massive bathtubs. Most important, rooms come with blackout drapes—a boon for revelers arriving home in the predawn hours. *376 Moreno; 54-11/6091-2000; morenobuenosaires.com; doubles from $.*

A king-size bed in the Moreno Buenos Aires's Extra Extra Large Room.

SPOTLIGHT SALTA

AT APPROXIMATELY 7,000 FEET AND A DAY'S DRIVE from Buenos Aires, the northern Argentine province of Salta exudes an almost mythological allure. In this slower-paced land of the Andean altiplano, known for its native artifacts and some of the best wines on the continent, the most memorable hotels are idiosyncratic blends of colonial influences and native ties. Near the main square in the city of Salta, Legado Mítico Salta has 11 rooms named for notable Salteños—poets, sculptors—and decorated with everything from cowhide chaps to a framed set of arrows. Guests linger in the courtyard for hours under swaying poplars while sampling the region's

The patio at Legado Mítico Salta.

LEGADO MÍTICO SALTA

647 Bartolomé Mitre; 54-387/422-8786; legadomitico. com; doubles from $.

ESTANCIA COLOMÉ

Km 20, Ruta Provincial 53, Molinos; 54-3868/494- 200; estanciacolome.com; doubles from $$.

flinty Torrontés wines. Deep in the wilderness, off a bumpy road barely wide enough for a vehicle, the nine-suite Estancia Colomé stands in marked contrast to its desolate surroundings, with heated terra-cotta floors, an enormous pool, and views of the lavender fields and vineyards. And the heart of Salta's viticultural area is Cafayate, set in a bowl surrounded by mountains and home to the 30-room Patios de Cafayate, a Luxury Collection Hotel & Spa. The Spanish-colonial-style structure features a spa specializing in vinotherapy treatments, from an aromatic bath steeped with Cabernet Sauvignon grapes to a decadent evening massage amid the vines.

Estancia Colomé's expansive outdoor pool.

The entrance gate at Patios de Cafayate.

PATIOS DE CAFAYATE

Rutas Nacionales 40 & 68, Cafayate; 800/325-3589 or 54-3868/422-229; luxurycollection.com; doubles from $.

ESTANCIA VIK
JOSÉ IGNACIO

José Ignacio, Uruguay

UNTIL RECENTLY, TINY URUGUAY had largely escaped tourist attention—except for Punta del Este, the definitive South American beach destination. But these days, it's laid-back, glamorous José Ignacio that's luring the boho-chic crowd. The reason? Estancia Vik, the town's first luxury guest lodging and the country's most exclusive new property. Located on 4,000 acres of pasture replete with mounted gauchos and grazing horses, the modern ranch has whitewashed walls, a dining room with arched brick ceilings, and a private 500-bottle wine cellar. All 12 suites display installations by Uruguayan artists; the extravagant public spaces feature works by the country's biggest names (sculptor Pablo Atchugarry, painter Clever Lara), as well as towering fireplaces and walls hung with semiprecious geodes. *Km 8, Cam. Eugenio Saiz Martinez; 598-94/605-212; estanciavik.com; doubles from $$$$.*

A Jacaranda de la India–wood bathtub in an Estancia Vik master suite. Opposite: A shed with a view.

UXUA CASA HOTEL

Trancoso, Brazil

BAHIA'S SEXIEST BEACH VILLAGE takes a giant leap forward with UXUA (pronounced "oo-shoo-ahh") Casa Hotel, a nine-cottage gem masterminded by the creative director of Diesel. The design is rustic-chic—lots of burnished reclaimed timber, billowing muslin curtains, and Midcentury Brazilian furnishings. Six of the nine guest casas are scattered around a garden shaded by a tangle of jackfruit trees and bougainvillea; the three best face the Quadrado, the grassy square at the heart of the village, where hippies and hipsters, high-flying celebrities and assorted artistic types gather in equal measure to the beat of drum circles accompanied by the slapping of Havaianas. Flop into a hammock or stroll five minutes away to UXUA's private beach lounge, where you can take a capoeira lesson on the sand or merely kick back and play the part of a wealthy castaway. *On the Quadrado; 55-73/3668-2166; uxua.com; doubles from $$$.*

Drinks at UXUA Casa Hotel. Opposite: A rustic wooden sofa and pergola at UXUA Praia Bar, its beachfront lounge.

Il Palagio restaurant at the
Four Seasons Hotel Firenze.

EUROPE

THE WEST WING, CROM CASTLE

County Fermanagh, Northern Ireland

Newtownbutler; 44-2867/738-004; cromcastle.com;
weekend rates (three nights) from $$$$$ for up to 12 people.

The West Wing's Victorian Conservatory. Opposite: Crom Castle and its grounds.

FIRST THINGS FIRST: CROM CASTLE (pronounced *crum*) is the historical seat of the Crichtons, a.k.a. the Earls of Erne, a.k.a. the Lords of Fermanagh, one of dozens of English families granted dominion over patches of Ireland back in the day by the British crown. In recent years, the castle's West Wing—all six bedrooms and 1,900 acres of its gardens—has been rented out to groups of up to 12 travelers at a time. (The earl and his wife still reside in the larger south wing.) Admittedly, certain amenities are lacking. You won't find TV's and mini-bars in the bedrooms, or a concierge. And the décor of Crom's innumerable spaces comes not from a designer flown in for the weekend, but from seven generations of Crichtons, who have lived, loved, and laughed in its corridors. In effect, the West Wing is more than a hotel—it's a home.

HOTEL MISSONI EDINBURGH

Edinburgh, Scotland

LEAVE IT TO ITALIAN FASHION HOUSE MISSONI—which revolutionized knitwear with its now-iconic zigzag prints—to add a splash of color to Edinburgh's gray Royal Mile. Its first foray into the boutique hotel scene is a lively, unbridled contrast to the traditional surroundings, layering pattern upon pattern to almost dizzying effect. Rooms run the gamut from black-and-white fabrics in one corner to a fuchsia-colored explosion in another, while shag carpets, graphic pillows, and robes (yes, the robes can be purchased) add to the electric mood.

1 George IV Bridge; 44-131/220-6666; hotelmissoni.com; doubles from $$

The dining room at Holbeck Ghyll. Right: A guest room in the Main House.

HOLBECK GHYLL COUNTRY HOUSE HOTEL

Windermere, England

Holbeck Lane; 800/525-4800 or 44-1539/432-375; holbeckghyll.com; doubles from $$.

LONDONERS WITH AN APPETITE for the outdoors have long flocked to northwest England, famous for its rolling hills and silvery blue lakes. On Windermere, the largest body of water in Lake District National Park, canoeists paddle to and from its tiny islands, while hikers explore the craggy peaks overlooking its shores. Panoramic views abound at nearby Holbeck Ghyll, a 19th-century hunting lodge full of traditional English touches like oak paneling, wing chairs, and a croquet lawn, plus two Labradors. Guests are welcome to bring their own dogs, who often join their masters in the Main House for afternoon aperitifs. Most rooms face the lake, but the two you truly want are the Miss Potter Suite (a nod to local legend Beatrix Potter), with its deep hot tub on a private balcony, and Lowtherwood, a converted barn that can be booked with a chef and butler.

SPOTLIGHT THE COTSWOLDS

THANKS TO AN INFLUX of a modern generation of Londoners—a weekending supermodel, a rocker turned cheese maker—one of England's quaintest areas is also now one of its most glamorous. Amid the rolling hills and limestone villages, the latest breed of boutique hotels fits in surprisingly well. Barnsley House, with its markedly chic interiors, manages to feel laid-back and personal, because of a friendly staff that serves house-baked cookies with afternoon tea. Renowned landscape designer Rosemary Verey owned the property until 2001, resulting in

The reflecting pools at the Barnsley House Spa.

BARNSLEY HOUSE

Barnsley, Cirencester; 44-1285/740-000; barnsleyhouse.com; doubles from $$.

COTSWOLD HOUSE HOTEL & SPA

The Square, Chipping Campden; 44-1386/840-330; cotswoldhouse.com; doubles from $$.

a four-acre plot divided into unbelievably picturesque tableaux. Forty-five minutes away in Chipping Campden, Cotswold House Hotel & Spa melds its Regency façade with abstract light fixtures and carved stone baths. At Cotswolds88hotel, in the medieval town of Painswick, loungy electronic music is piped into common areas where on-trend upholsteries mix with eclectic antiques. But in the dining room, local ingredients are the stars: dishes like a confit of pork belly and slow-braised lamb are yet another mark of the countryside's new sophistication.

A back view of Cotswold House Hotel & Spa and its gardens.

A sitting room at Cotswolds88hotel.

COTSWOLDS88HOTEL

Kemps Lane, Painswick; 44-1452/813-688; cotswolds88hotel.com; doubles from $$.

ROUGH LUXE HOTEL

London, England

THESE AREN'T YOUR AVERAGE ACCOMMODATIONS. For starters, don't expect an elevator, soundproof walls, modern TV's, or en-suite baths in every room at this new hotel in the King's Cross neighborhood. The interiors of the 1820's Georgian town house might even seem a trifle undone (peeling wallpaper, cracked paint, sanded surfaces). But that's entirely the point— this is a visual experiment that mixes opulence and grit. Bespoke textiles, ranging from psychedelic riffs on Fortuny damask to pony skin upholstery, are thrown into the mix, along with faux-crocodile headboards, black lacquered chairs, plaster chandeliers, and a clever collection of contemporary art. Manager Leo Rabelo and his Jack Russell terrier, Spud, will most likely check you in, ushering you past the Jonathan Root portrait of Gilbert & George to a table that can be set for afternoon tea in the jewel of a back garden. Rough Luxe Hotel isn't for everyone—but it's certainly like nothing else.

1 Birkenhead St.; 44-20/7837-5338; roughluxe.co.uk; doubles from $$.

Room No. 1, a suite at the Rough Luxe Hotel.

ME
BARCELONA

Barcelona, Spain

MOST VISITORS MIGHT NEVER VENTURE into Poblenou,
Barcelona's emerging tech district, were it not for
French architect Dominique Perrault's 400-foot-tall
glass-and-steel den of cool. Fifteen minutes from
the center of town, this boutique hotel comes with
its own "aura experience manager," who curates
the artfully hip vibe. The city's stylish set gather on
ebony wingback chairs and chalk-white daybeds
at Angels & Kings, an outpost of musician Pete
Wentz's New York and Chicago bars. Chefs and twin
brothers Sergio and Javier Torres are in the kitchen
at the restaurant Dos Cielos, which has garnered its
own share of hype. Upstairs, the 258 rooms—each
outfitted with a bottle of oxygen in the mini-bar—look
out over vistas of the Sagrada Família, the Agbar
Tower, and the hills of Catalonia.
*272 Carrer Pere IV; 877/954-8363; me-barcelona.com;
doubles from $.*

The Angels & Kings bar at
ME Barcelona.

HOTEL AIRE DE BARDENAS

Tudela, Spain

AT FIRST GLANCE, YOU MIGHT THINK you're gazing at a lunar encampment, given the single-story cubical structures set against a spare, windswept landscape in northeastern Spain. But the Hotel Aire de Bardenas has a recycled kind of simplicity that recalls the traditional buildings of this rural area, a semidesert environment next to a nature preserve. The 22 white-walled rooms are oriented to the outdoors, with large windows that offer views of wheat fields. Deservedly popular with architecture fans, the hotel doesn't disappoint the foodies, either: a meal of Bardenas lamb paired with a chilled Rosado is all the more sybaritic in the midst of such design austerity.
Km 1.5, Ctra. Ejea de los Caballeros; 34/948-116-666; airedebardenas.com; doubles from $.

Room No. 22, with its outdoor bathtub, at the Hotel Aire de Bardenas.

FONTANA PARK HOTEL

Lisbon, Portugal

IN AN ECLECTIC NEIGHBORHOOD at the city's center, the Fontana is housed in a 1908 iron factory whose industrial veneer remains intact. Architect Francisco Aires Mateus reimagined the once-derelict building with sharply angled glass-and-concrete staircases and sheaths of hammered ironwork—homages to the hotel's former life. Designer Nini Andrade Silva stuck with the pared-down theme, adhering to a palette of black, white, and gray in the 139 rooms and achieving a lush-yet-futuristic effect in the lobby with abstract wicker chairs, accents of smooth river rocks, and photographs of verdant forests. *2 Rua Engenheiro Vieira da Silva; 800/337-4685 or 351-210/410-600; fontanap⸱hotel.com; doubles from $*

The lobby at the
Fontana Park Hotel

Memmo Baleeira Hotel's outdoor pool, with views of the Martinhal Islands.

MEMMO BALEEIRA HOTEL

Sagres, Portugal

351-282/624-212; memmobaleeira.com; doubles from $.

ON A WINDSWEPT PENINSULA high above the Atlantic, at the Continent's southwestern edge, this recently renovated 144-room hotel feels just remote enough. White interiors and plush furniture act as a calm counterpoint to the turquoise waters of the harbor. The pool and Turkish bath–equipped spa cater to those seeking nothing more than relaxation, but options abound for the more athletically inclined. Go for a swim off Beliche Beach, where a cove creates the perfect shelter from the wind; take a private lesson from the in-house surf school (Sagres is considered one of the top surf spots in Europe); or dive to explore shipwreck sites and underwater caves, where moray eels and octopuses make their homes in the hollows. Come dusk, the spa staff is available for massages on sun beds overlooking the ocean.

A guest room at Villa l'Arche. Left: The glass-and-aluminum front door.

VILLA L'ARCHE

Bidart, France

Rue Camboénèa; 33-5/59-51-65-95; villalarche.com; doubles from $.

LET THE THRONGS DO BIARRITZ. Just a pebble's throw away, the petite Basque village of Bidart draws surfers, escapists, and travelers in the know with its picturesque streets of half-timbered houses and some of the region's best restaurants. Among the Beaux-Arts estates of summering European families lies Villa l'Arche, a seaside retreat featuring eight rooms and suites done up in pure white with handsome flourishes of crimson, black, and silver. The lobby is soothing and tasteful (gray walls, Kartell lamps, chesterfield sofas), but the sable-hued beach and the swells of the Atlantic act as siren calls to the sea. Vivid blue mosaic tile and white-pebbled accents in the garden smooth the transition between hotel and sand.

MAMA SHELTER

Paris, France

LEAVE IT TO PHILIPPE STARCK to cater to your noirish fantasies in the most imaginative manner possible. Housed in the industrial expanses of a former garage in the less-than-gentrified 20th Arrondissement, the high-style Mama Shelter has a whimsical club-kid quality about it—foosball at the bar, chalk graffiti scrawled on the lobby ceiling, and Batman-mask lamps mounted on the guest rooms' unfinished concrete walls. By nightfall, guests congregate en masse in acclaimed chef Alain Senderens's restaurant, where escargots in herb butter and a tremendous cheese course are served to a sound track mixed by a cast of underground hip-hop and Afro-jazz DJ's. *109 Rue de Bagnolet, 20th Arr.: 33-1/43-48-48-48; mamashelter.com; doubles from $$.*

A secluded back corner in
Mama Shelter's restaurant.

LE COUVENT DES MINIMES

Provence, France

Chemin des Jeux de Maï, Mane; 800/735-2478 or 33-4/92-74-77-77; couventdesminimes-hotelspa.com; doubles from $$.

The indoor and outdoor pools at Le Couvent des Minimes Spa by L'Occitane.

WITH ITS TRANQUIL TOPOGRAPHY of verdant fields and scenic villages, Provence has long been a top destination for Europe's well-heeled set. Now there's one more reason to go, thanks to this Relais & Châteaux hideaway near the eastern edge of the Lubéron. Set in a former nunnery dating to the 17th century, the 46-room Couvent des Minimes features the first spa in France from Provençal skin-care company L'Occitane, with treatments that make use of regional ingredients like verbena, olives, lemon, and almond. In the hotel, restoration mastermind Bruno Legrand chose to showcase the original structure's weathered beauty, subtly accenting the white stone walls with linen drapes and solid oak headboards. One highlight: the Cassine Suite, a romantic nook at the base of the convent's former bell tower.

GRAND HÔTEL DE CALA ROSSA

Porto-Vecchio, Corsica

The spa's swimming pool at Grand Hôtel de Cala Rossa.

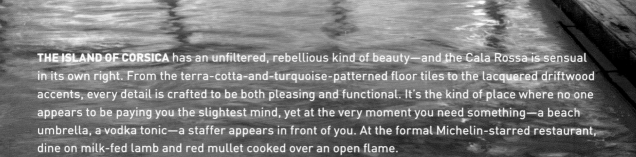

THE ISLAND OF CORSICA has an unfiltered, rebellious kind of beauty—and the Cala Rossa is sensual in its own right. From the terra-cotta-and-turquoise-patterned floor tiles to the lacquered driftwood accents, every detail is crafted to be both pleasing and functional. It's the kind of place where no one appears to be paying you the slightest mind, yet at the very moment you need something—a beach umbrella, a vodka tonic—a staffer appears in front of you. At the formal Michelin-starred restaurant, dine on milk-fed lamb and red mullet cooked over an open flame.
Lecci; 800/735-2478 or 33-4/9571-6151; doubles from $$$$$.

The Moroccan Room at La Villa Hotel.

LA VILLA HOTEL

Mombaruzzo, Italy

7 Via Torino; 39-0141/793-890; lavillahotel.net; doubles from $.

SOME EXCEPTIONAL HOTELS seem to sprout from their surroundings. La Villa, a refurbished 17th-century palazzo set against the languid hills of Piedmont, lies securely in this category. Husband-and-wife duo Chris and Nicola Norton—two Brits who abandoned their corporate careers for the good life in northern Italy—furnished the understated rooms with claw-foot tubs, country-style armoires, and even an antique cobbler's table whose tools remain intact. Vineyards abound not 10 feet from the kitchen door, and excellent bottles populate the 150-strong wine list, including Barolos from La Spinetta and Nebbiolos from Hilberg-Pasquero. The Slow Food–inspired menu pairs perfectly: rabbit and oxtail agnolotti are autumn favorites, while summertime barbecues extend well past sunset.

The private pier in the reception area at the Charming House IQs.

SPOTLIGHT
VENICE

A STROLL THROUGH VENICE is a whirlwind of candy-colored palazzi, ethereal blown glass, and narrow streets where you could get lost for days. Despite the omnipresent weight of its past, the city manages to defy being characterized as a historical amusement park by melding modernity into its heady blend. This deft mix is also evident in its best hotels—including the four-room Charming House IQs, a hidden gem that's popular with privacy-seeking celebs during the Venice Film Festival. Contemporary pieces by Moroso and B&B Italia form an alluring juxtaposition to views of the Rio del Mondo Nuovo canal. In a former school of art behind St. Mark's Square, ivy-covered Hotel Flora is a streamlined take on 16th- and 17th-century maximalism, with a tranquil summer garden for afternoon tea. On the banks of the Grand Canal, the regal suites at Ca' Sagredo Hotel feature both Wi-Fi and frescoes of mythological characters by 18th-century artists Abbondio Stazio and Carpoforo Mazzetti. Nearby, at the lavish Bauer Il Palazzo, a solar-powered boat shuttles guests down one of the most magnificent waterways in Venice. The city's gilded youth flock to the hotel's bar terrace for mixologist Gennaro Fioro's inspired cocktails, served in the shadow of the Chiesa della Salute.

Overlooking the Grand Canal at Bauer Il Palazzo.

Hotel Flora's courtyard garden.

Inside Ca' Sagredo Hotel's Portego Hall.

CHARMING HOUSE IQS

Campiello Querini Stampalia, 4425 Castello; 39-041/241-0062; thecharminghouse.com; doubles from $$.

HOTEL FLORA

2283/A San Marco; 39-041/520-5844; hotelflora.it; doubles from $$.

CA' SAGREDO HOTEL

4198-99 Campo Santa Sofia; 800/525-4800 or 39-041/241-3111; casagredohotel.com; doubles from $$.

BAUER IL PALAZZO

1413/D San Marco; 800/223-6800 or 39-041/520-7022; bauerhotels.com; doubles from $$$$$.

Housekeeping staff at work in Suite 122 at the Four Seasons Hotel Firenze.

The hotel reception area.

Tempio Lawn in the hotel's private garden.

FOUR SEASONS HOTEL FIRENZE

Florence, Italy

HOUSED IN A RENAISSANCE-ERA STRUCTURE with 15th-century frescoes and the largest private garden in town, the Four Seasons puts palazzo-like grandeur at your fingertips. The former papal residence, located on the north side of the Arno and only a short walk from the Duomo, was meticulously revamped by designer Pierre-Yves Rochon, who approached the one-of-a-kind property with an eye for authenticity—swathing the 116 rooms in silks and velvets, and retaining the original 19th-century chandeliers in the Baroque-style ballroom. Add bathrooms laden with soaps and scents by the Florentine perfumer Lorenzo Villoresi; a two-story spa stocked with products from centuries-old apothecary Santa Maria Novella; and chef Vito Mollica's haute Tuscan menu, and you've got a hotel that is as lavish as its history. Even the eggs—sourced from a farmer's estate near Pisa and laid by chickens raised on fresh goat's milk—are works of art. *99 Borgo Pinti; 800/332-3442 or 39-055/26-261; fourseasons.com; doubles from $$.*

DOLDER GRAND

Zurich, Switzerland

65 Kurhausstrasse; 41-44/456-6000; thedolder grand.com; doubles from $$$$.

ARCHITECT NORMAN FOSTER is a genius when it comes to blending the old with the new. At the Dolder, he first restored the 1899 cuckoo clock–style façade, then flanked the main structure with two new stone-and-glass buildings, creating an aesthetic at once stolidly conservative and explosively futuristic. Curving hallways evoke a *2001: A Space Odyssey* mood, and wooden doors open to reveal rooms with off-white leather upholstery and smoked-oak flooring. The spa provides layer-cake views of Lake Zurich, the surrounding farmland, and the Alps.

Part of the Norman Foster–designed addition at the Dolder Grand.

The Schönburg Castle Hotel's entrance. Left: A view of the courtyard.

SCHÖNBURG CASTLE HOTEL

Oberwesel, Germany

ALTHOUGH ONLY AN HOUR'S DRIVE from the soaring skyscrapers of Frankfurt, the Rhine Valley might as well be accessed via time travel. Castles and villages dot the landscape, Riesling vineyards wind along the river's shores, and bicycles are one preferred mode of transportation. A 13th-century former fortress, the hauntingly romantic Schönburg Castle Hotel commands the area with a sphinxlike gravitas. The inner courtyard consists of a multilevel patchwork of Romanesque arches, half-timbered parapets, and tumbledown stonework. In one wood-paneled room—a round chamber at the top of the highest tower that resembles an officer's quarters on a ship—the bed is built into a windowed alcove accessed by climbing a circular stepladder, and a doorway leads to a tiny stone balcony overlooking the valley. You can't help but think of Rapunzel locked away in her belfry.

Auf Schönburg; 49-6744/93930; hotel-schoenburg.com; doubles from $.

An Executive suite at the Ellington Hotel.

ELLINGTON HOTEL

Berlin, Germany

50-55 Nürnberger Str.; 49-30/683-150; ellington-hotel. com; doubles from $.

UNTIL RECENTLY, THE ELLINGTON served as a mammoth office building, but such Teutonic rigidity belies a far more colorful history. In the 1920's and 30's, Berlin's roaring revelers danced beneath the stars as the building's hydraulic roof opened to the night sky. In the 1970's, expat scenesters like David Bowie and Iggy Pop dropped by to get their disco fix in the legendary Dschungel club. These days, the interior evokes Germany's Art Deco heyday, with sleek rooms that envelop guests in a seemingly boundless blanket of space. Restaurant Duke's open kitchen acts as the hotel's main artery; on Sundays in the Mediterranean-style garden, a jazz brunch pays tribute to yet another of the Ellington's previous incarnations—a postwar cabaret drawing the likes of Louis Armstrong and Ella Fitzgerald.

HOTEL COCOON

Munich, Germany

Hotel Cocoon's lobby lounge.

SLICK INTERIORS AND SPACE-AGE ACCENTS, combined with numerous curl-up nooks, make the quirky Hotel Cocoon an inviting crash pad. Located on a residential avenue lined with cafés just outside Sendlinger Tor and the old city, the hotel has small but efficiently organized rooms; bubble chairs, Day-Glo color schemes, recessed lighting, and sage-green sliding partitions make them sexy spaces fit for Barbarella. Window-side reading areas provide cozy spots for sequestering yourself with a good book. Modest travelers, beware— showers have glass walls, so it's best to share a room with someone you know intimately.

35 *Lindwurm* ▪ ▪ ▪ 49-89/5999-3907; *hotel-cocoon.de; doubles f* ▪ ▪ *$*

A Streetview guest room at Hotel Patou.

HOTEL PATOU

Amsterdam, the Netherlands

A NOD TO FRENCH FASHION INNOVATOR Jean Patou, this corner town house on the P.C. Hooftstraat— Amsterdam's version of Rodeo Drive—is refined in a Dutch-Flemish sort of way. A somber-yet-sensuous palette of putty gray, black, and white in the 12 spacious rooms forms the backdrop for Bisazza-tiled step-in showers, beach-blanket-worthy towels, and individually crafted Carpe Diem beds. On the ground floor, Brasserie Patou caters to both hotel guests and boutique-weary shoppers, who pop in for a quick soup and salad or an indulgent midday repast of champagne and oysters. The hotel definitely draws a fashion-centric following, but with both the van Gogh museum and the Concertgebouw concert hall within walking distance, you'll have just as many opportunities to stock up on culture as you will on couture. *63 P.C. Hooftstraat; 31-20/676-0232; hotelpatou.nl; doubles from $.*

The back garden at the Badhotel Bruin.

BADHOTEL BRUIN

Vlieland, the Netherlands

THE SMALL ISLAND OF VLIELAND, which lies 65 miles north of Amsterdam, has long lured Dutch weekenders with its forests and sand dunes, diverse bird life, and network of bike paths. It's especially popular with hip young families, who base themselves at Badhotel Bruin, Vlieland's oldest institution. The recently renovated hotel retains its down-home vibe with plush sofas, shag carpets, and even beds for Fido. Book one of the Hästens rooms, which have linen-covered chesterfields and windows that look out onto red-tiled rooftops and gardens. Sip a morning cappuccino on the terrace before cycling off to one of the island's wide beaches, 10 minutes from the property. In the evening, sample fresh seafood at the restaurant—and don't miss the art-house cinema next door, which features an artisanal–ice cream parlor.

88 Dorpsstraat; 31-562/452-828; badhotelbruin.com; doubles from $.

PÄDASTE MANOR

Muhu Island, Estonia

PICTURE AN ELEGANTLY WILD ISLAND KINGDOM, a forgotten shore revealed by a receding Soviet tide. Along this Baltic riviera lies Pädaste Manor, the setting for a fairy-tale fantasy in which you rule your own ancestral home. The 24 rooms and suites are tucked into historic buildings—from an ironstone cottage next to a juniper forest to a thatched-roof farmhouse in an apple orchard. Fireplaces are lit on brisk fall evenings; mushrooms in the woods are gathered for chanterelle carpaccio; and eiderdown pillows are plumped and laid atop handcrafted beds. *800/525-4800 or 011-372/454-8800; padaste.ee; doubles from $$.*

Jumping into the Baltic Sea from Pädaste Manor's dock

Lánchíd 19's abstract glass exterior.

LÁNCHÍD 19

Budapest, Hungary

19 Lánchíd Utca; 800/337-4685 or 36-1/419-1900; lanchid19hotel.hu; doubles from $.

WITH A LUMINOUS GLASS FAÇADE composed of 150 panels that rotate throughout the day, Lánchíd 19 certainly stands out amid its Romanesque and Gothic neighbors. Yet the 48-room property manages to complement its historic surroundings. The multihued exterior mimics the river's rhythms; its restaurant terrace shares a stone wall with the grounds of a UNESCO World Heritage site, Buda Castle. Even the lobby's transparent floor reveals an excavation of Roman ruins underneath. The hotel is as popular with business travelers as it is with design-minded tourists, who marvel over the airy glass bridges that soar above the lobby and connect some guest rooms. Worthy of the splurge: one of the three Danube-facing Panorama Suites, where a soak in the tub will leave you feeling like you're floating on the river itself.

A Chara Lebessi–decorated guest room at Classical 2, Fashion House Hotel.

CLASSICAL 2, FASHION HOUSE HOTEL

Athens, Greece

2 Pireos St.; 30-210/523-5230; classicalhotels.com; doubles from $.

SOME OF THE COUNTRY'S most stylish names—including Greek *Vogue* fashion director Michalis Pantos—are behind the design of this flamboyant property right in the heart of Athens. The 110 rooms have an almost schizoid charm, with details that run the gamut from faux-tiger-skin rugs and a mural of winged angels to wallpaper reminiscent of Pop art. There's plenty of zany fun to be had on site, what with an in-house fortune-teller, a soccer-themed bar and restaurant, and a café styled like a private jet. But the hotel's best attribute is its prime location. Walking through the labyrinthine streets is like embarking on a tour of the city's vital capillaries: nearby Monastiraki Square teems with flea-market vendors and savvy shoppers, and the Acropolis looms over the scene like a crumbling crown.

KYRIMAI HOTEL

Mani Peninsula, Greece

ALONG THE CRAGGY COASTLINE of Greece's Mani Peninsula, sheer cliffs plunge into clear blue waters where the Ionian meets the Aegean. The architecture is just as dramatic: Byzantine churches abound, and turreted fortresses fleck the landscape. A former mayor's residence now houses the family-owned Kyrimai Hotel, whose stone stairways, arches, and courtyards make it seem like a castle by the sea. Athenians make the 3½-hour drive for the romantic rooms, as well as for the cuisine from award-winning chef Yiannis Baksevanis. *Gerolimenas; 30-27330/54288; kyrimai.gr; doubles from $.*

The Mediterranean, as seen from Kyrimai Hotel's pool terrace.

A Park Spa King room at the Park Hyatt Maçka Palas.

PARK HYATT MAÇKA PALAS

Istanbul, Turkey

4 Bronz Sk.; 800/233-1234 or 90-212/315-1234; park.hyatt.com; doubles from $$.

KNOWN FOR ITS ART NOUVEAU BUILDINGS and high-end boutiques, Istanbul's fashionable Nişantaşi district is also home to the 90-room Park Hyatt Maçka Palas, a favorite with media moguls and creative types. Mirroring the city's distinctive East-meets-West vibe, the 1920's palazzo-style town house fuses traditional motifs (Ottoman-inspired ceramic tiles) with modern conveniences (iPod docks, flat-screen TV's). Chocolate-and-beige guest rooms come with heated floors, color-therapy lighting, freestanding soaking tubs, and products by French *parfumeur* Blaise Mautin; Park Spa King rooms each have a private Turkish hammam. Feast on dry-aged sirloin at the Prime restaurant, but save room for the hotel's custom-made Turkish delight—crafted by a centuries-old confectioner and incorporating rose petals from the city of Isparta.

THE BUTTERFLY

Bodrum, Turkey

CHECK IN TO THE BUTTERFLY and you'll count the country's elite among your neighbors. Near Bodrum's crescent-shaped Bardakçi Bay, the six-room hideaway is surrounded by the summer mansions of a former prime minister and other members of high society. Natural textiles, well-chosen antiques, and details like whisper-light cotton sheets make this seaside villa feel warm and personal—a mood reinforced by owner Patrick Hembrough and staffer Hasan Dogan, who will happily plan boating trips, share insider tips on restaurants, arrange outings to Ephesus, and perhaps even drive you around town to get you acclimated. After dinner, savor a drink on one of the hotel's candlelit garden patios, many of which have CinemaScope-worthy vistas of the Aegean and the Greek island of Kos.
Ünlü Cd., 24 1512 Sk.; 90-252/313-8358; thebutterflybodrum.com; doubles from $$.

Views of the hills around Bodrum from the pool at the Butterfly.

An Executive suite at
La Mamounia, in Marrakesh.

AFRICA
+THE MIDDLE
EAST

RRAKESH NAMIBIA CAPE TOWN CEDAR MOUNTAINS MADIKW
ME RESERVE BOTSWANA KENYA MAURITIUS LUXOR JERUSALE
BAI OMAN MARRAKESH NAMIBIA CAPE TOWN CEDAR MOUNTAIN
DIKWE GAME RESERVE BOTSWANA KENYA MAURITIUS LUXO
RUSALEM DUBAI OMAN MARRAKESH NAMIBIA CAPE TOWN CEDA
UNTAINS MADIKWE GAME RESERVE BOTSWANA KENYA MAURITIU
OR JERUSALEM DUBAI OMAN MARRAKESH NAMIBIA CAPE TOW
DAR MOUNTAINS MADIKWE GAME RESERVE BOTSWANA KENY
URITIUS LUXOR JERUSALEM DUBAI OMAN MARRAKESH NAMIB

LA MAMOUNIA

Marrakesh, Morocco

THE WORD *LEGENDARY* seems coined for this 87-year-old Moorish landmark, which has played host to everyone from Winston Churchill to Kate Winslet. Closed for three years, La Mamounia glows again thanks to Jacques Garcia, known for the opulent interiors of Paris's Hôtel Costes and Monte Carlo's Hotel Métropole. The exuberant designer approached the Marrakesh palace with respect, even reverence, meticulously repairing the intricate mosaics and restoring the marble-floored lobby and mahogany-paneled Churchill Bar. Still, Garcia's trademark touches are very much in evidence, from the new 27,000-square-foot spa (where an indoor soaking pool is lined with hand-cut blue, green, and white tiles) to the smart Moroccan uniforms worn by staff. Tying it all together: little touches of garnet, the Mamounia's signature hue, which gleams on the grand piano in the Majorelle Gallery and on the fleet of Jaguars and Range Rovers parked outside. *Ave. Bab Jdid; 800/223-6800 or 212-52/438-8600; mamounia.com; doubles from $$$$.*

The 1,227-square-foot Majorelle
Suite at La Mamounia. Opposite:
Courtyard views from the Tea Salon.

SPOTLIGHT NAMIBIA

HOME TO VAST DESERTS, volcanic ranges, and towering dunes, otherworldly Namibia can now add a growing number of stylish hideaways to its list of epic attractions. Sprawling game parks provide the secluded settings for these environmentally sensitive lodges. If it's luxury you seek, you'll find it at Little Ongava, three cottages on the southern boundary in Etosha National Park with private infinity pools that seem almost incongruous given the white rhinos nibbling on the nearby foliage. Adjacent to the thousand-foot sand dunes that ripple across the Kulala Wilderness Reserve, each of Little Kulala's 11 villas comes with a deck, a rooftop terrace with "sky

Inside a cottage suite at Little Ongava.

LITTLE ONGAVA

Ongava Game Reserve; 27-11/807-1800; wilderness-safaris.com; doubles from $$$$, all-inclusive.

LITTLE KULALA

Kulala Wilderness Reserve; 27-11/807-1800; wilderness-safaris.com; doubles from $$$$, all-inclusive.

beds" for stargazing, and a minimalist studio with bleached plank floors and leather shag throw rugs. To the northwest, amid the mountains of Kaokoland, Serra Cafema Camp's main lodge overlooks an oasis of green albida trees on the Kunene River, which separates Namibia from Angola. The eight canvas-and-thatch chalets are loftlike yet cozy, with mosquito-netted beds and carved Nguni furniture; bathrooms have copper basins mounted on log pedestals. Take a hike with guide Franco Morao, who will point out goliath herons, foraging tok-tokkie beetles, and fresh sets of long, smooth crocodile tracks.

Little Kulala's main lodge.

A table for two above the Kunene River at Serra Cafema Camp.

SERRA CAFEMA CAMP

Kaokoland, Hartmann Valley; 27-11/807-1800; wilderness-safaris.com; doubles from $$$$$, all-inclusive.

One of the seven redesigned trailers on the rooftop of the Grand Daddy Hotel. Right: Inside the Dorothy Airstream.

GRAND DADDY HOTEL

Cape Town, South Africa

38 Long St.; 27-21/424-7247; granddaddy.co.za; doubles from $.

FROM FOLKSY-CHIC FLEA MARKETS to a flourishing community of collectors and furniture designers, Cape Town is brimming with creative energy and an effortlessly cool vibe. There's no better place to experience it than the Grand Daddy—or, more specifically, at the hotel's cheeky "trailer park" gracing its roof. Curated by one of the talents behind local design collective Whatiftheworld, the seven Airstream trailers come with their own tongue-in-cheek themes, including Afrofunkd (which has a teak-paneled interior inspired by Cape Town street fashion) and Love of Lace (a Marie Antoinette vision of quilted pink satin and chandeliers). Barbecue grills and white mailboxes complete the arch suburban fantasy. Downstairs in the Daddy Cool Bar, an artist enclave, the mood is all playful urban bling: shimmering tile, white leather armchairs, and hits of gold that add up to a space as irrepressible as the city itself.

WORLD'S BEST

THE NUMBER-ONE-RANKED PROPERTY in T+L's 2009 World's Best Awards, Bushmans Kloof lies in a river valley 180 miles north of Cape Town where ancient Bushmen cave paintings were discovered. The archaeological sites can be explored on daily walks with the lodge's guides, who impart the rich history and cultural traditions of the indigenous hunter-gatherers with the skill of born storytellers. Guests can also attend ranger-led discussions at the Heritage Center, where exhibits include hunting kits and musical instruments. The 16 colonial-style rooms are located in the main structure—a thatched farmhouse from the early 1900's—and in newer buildings connected by pebbled paths. Dine under wild fig trees or at a table for two overlooking the valley. *800/735-2478 or 27-21/481-1860; bushmanskloof.co.za; doubles from $$, all-inclusive.*

BUSHMANS KLOOF

Cedar Mountains, South Africa

Dinnertime at Embers, an outdoor restaurant at Bushmans Kloof.

Leadwood trunks leading to an outdoor table at Molori Safari Lodge. Opposite: The master bedroom in the Molelo Suite.

MOLORI SAFARI LODGE

Madikwe Game Reserve, South Africa

27-82/613-5723; molori.com; doubles from $$$$$, all-inclusive.

TUCKED INTO THE HILLS of South Africa's fifth largest game reserve, this five-suite lodge makes a good case for the place of indulgence in a recessionary world. Interiors comprise a knowing mix of local and international designs—a crystal chandelier hangs from a thatched ceiling, and Fendi chaises flank chairs upholstered in African-inspired beadwork. Fancy a wood-fired *braai* (barbecue)? A candlelit table and chef are at the ready. Prefer an intimate feast? An eight-course tasting menu featuring South African wines can be served on a viewing deck built into a mountain. Should you find yourself wondering where the wilderness lies in all of this, you can embark on two game drives daily with a ranger—or simply open the retractable glass walls of your suite, step out onto your deck, and wait till an elephant lumbers into view.

One of nine private roof decks at Xudum Delta Lodge.

A canopied bed in a guest
room. Below: Antelope skulls
on a dresser.

XUDUM DELTA LODGE

Okavango Delta Reserve, Botswana

AMID THE COLONIAL-THROWBACK CAMPS in the richly
varied ecosystem of the Okavango Delta Reserve
comes the iconoclastic new kid in town, courtesy of
safari company &Beyond. The 62,000-acre Xudum
Delta Lodge offers a part-land, part-water experience
on a wildlife reserve that's one of the largest in any
permanent African delta. Scattered among evergreen
figs and ferns, the nine cabins are furnished with
canopied platform beds, freestanding porcelain tubs,
and recycled side tables crafted, astonishingly
enough, from rubber tires and beer cans. (A lookout
with its own king-size daybed and binoculars stands
on top of each pinewood structure.) Guests can
glide along papyrus-lined water channels in sleek
mekoro dugouts, or take jeep rides into the palm-
studded plains, hot on the trail of elephants, giraffes,
and buffalo. The area is also home to a profusion
of wild cats—hence the Lion Research Centre that's
the reserve's only other tenant.
888/882-3742; andbeyond.com; doubles from $$$$$
per person, all-inclusive.

AFTER FASHION DESIGNER ANNA TRZEBINSKI fell in love with a Samburu safari guide named Loyapan Lemarti, the couple built themselves a private retreat on raised wooden platforms at a river bend in the Laikipia Plateau. Now this dreamy, primitive-chic camp is open to guests, providing a rare immersion into a Laikipiak Masai community whose tribesmen still live and dress in traditional ways. Guides carrying spears accompany you on your morning walk in the bush. Camels carry provisions for bedouin-style picnics. Five tents of locally loomed cotton serve as sleeping quarters, decorated with elephant bones, crocodile skulls, and pierced-brass lanterns. *888/436-2040; lemarticamp.com; doubles from $$$$$ per person, all-inclusive, four-day minimum.*

LEMARTI'S CAMP

Laikipia, Kenya

A daybed at Lemarti's Camp.

An aerial view of Four Seasons Resort Mauritius at Anahita.

FOUR SEASONS RESORT MAURITIUS AT ANAHITA

Beau Champ, Mauritius

800/332-3442 or 011-230/402-3100; fourseasons.com; doubles from $$$$.

A RESORT HALFWAY AROUND THE WORLD on an island already known for its luxe hotels had better offer something special—and this one does just that. An old sugarcane plantation with a reef-protected lagoon on Île Maurice's east coast provides the setting. Lush landscaping was added, incorporating the existing flame trees and indigenous palms; an 18-hole golf course was designed with a spectacular finish. The 123 villas, hewn from local hardwoods and volcanic stone, look out onto the lagoon, gardens, or the Bambou Mountains. Oversize bathrooms lead to rustic outdoor showers, and sliding bedroom doors frame plunge pools on private terraces. At the overwater spa, book the signature massage, in which a piece of sugarcane is used as a kneading device—making aches and tensions roll away.

AL MOUDIRA HOTEL

Luxor, Egypt

Luxury Suite No. 3 at Al Moudira Hotel. Opposite: The Mushrabeya seating area in the main courtyard.

ON THE QUIET WEST BANK of the Nile, set in 40 acres of gardens redolent of jasmine, lemon, and mint, this domed palace is the creation of photographer and jewelry designer Zeina Aboukheir. Drawing on a lifetime of influences (Aboukheir was raised in Lebanon, resided in Tuscany, and has traveled extensively in the Middle East), the hotelier lavished the ocher main building with intricate latticework and stained glass. Seven smaller pavilions around a fountain house 54 rooms and suites, each with hand-painted frescoes and mosaic floors, and some with hammam-like baths. As if to tempt the eye toward visual overload, furnishings run to the exotic: marquetry desks, Persian carpets, and Turkish sofas, with embroidered cushions scattered here and there. In keeping with the *Arabian Nights* ambience, camel rides into the desert can be arranged. The ancient Temple of Luxor, on the Nile's east bank, is less than half an hour away.

Hager Al Dabbeya, West Bank Luxor; 20-12/392-8332; moudira.com; doubles from $$.

The American Colony's courtyard and pool.

AMERICAN COLONY HOTEL

Jerusalem, Israel

23 Nablus Rd.; 800/223-6800 or 972-2/627-9777; americancolony.com; doubles from $$.

THOUGH ONCE CAUGHT in the crossfire of Israel's Six-Day War, the American Colony is now a tranquil oasis in a historically divided town. Built around a 19th-century Ottoman pasha's mansion just north of the Damascus Gate, the 86-room hotel gives no hint of turbulent times. The lobby, with its Damascene inlaid tables, turquoise tiles, and Oriental carpets over polished stone floors, exudes affluence and comfort. An interior courtyard with a burbling fountain invites guests to linger and sip Turkish coffee under the shade of an orange tree. Foreign dignitaries, UN officials, and international correspondents make regular appearances on the registry, prompting discreet speculation as to which guests might actually be undercover spies. No wonder the hotel was a favorite with cloak-and-dagger novelists Graham Greene and John le Carré.

IT SEEMS ONLY NATURAL THAT ATLANTIS—already known for its fantasy compound in the Bahamas—would open its second sprawling hotel in Dubai. In a destination that already defines excess, the 114-acre property manages to push the envelope even further. Located on the arch of the Palm Jumeirah artificial island, this incarnation is ersatz-oceanic in style, with a 42-acre water park, almost a mile of man-made beachfront, and a 65,000-creature marine habitat. And then there are the rooms—1,539 in all, with balconies that look out onto resort grounds or the Persian Gulf. But for over-the-top opulence, nothing trumps chef Santi Santamaria's Ossiano, a restaurant submerged in a 3-million-gallon lagoon. It's dramatic enough to wow even the most hardened megalomaniac. *Crescent Road, Palm Jumeirah; 971-4/426-1000; atlantisthepalm.com; doubles from $$$.*

ATLANTIS, THE PALM

Dubai, United Arab Emirates

A view of Atlantis, The Palm, at night.

A Pool villa with views of the Gulf of
Oman at Six Senses Hideaway Zighy Bay.

JUST GETTING HERE—whether by speedboat, by paraglider, or by 4 x 4 on a dirt road cresting a jagged mountain—is an adventure. But once you've arrived at this eco-hideaway, the temptation to hole up for days proves worthy of the effort. The 79 stone villas, all with plunge pools and palm-leaf-shaded terraces, are fashioned after traditional dwellings, while two hammams and a souklike shopping enclave draw further inspiration from Omani culture. As with resorts of this caliber, exquisite details abound. A menu of pillow scents ranges from peppermint to rosemary; larger-than-life excursions include a five-hour cruise aboard a dhow, or fishing boat, in the Arabian Ocean. *Musandam Peninsula; 800/591-7480 or 968/2673-5555; sixsenses.com; doubles from $$$$$.*

SIX SENSES HIDEAWAY ZIGHY BAY

Zighy Bay, Oman

The lobby at the Hyatt Regency Kyoto, in Japan.

ASIA

OTO BEIJING HAINAN ISLAND HONG KONG SHANGHAI KE
WDELHIGOAVARANASIPHUKETBANGKOKGULFOFTHAILAN
NGKAWI BALI LOMBOK KYOTO BEIJING HAINAN ISLAND HON
NGSHANGHAIKEPNEWDELHIGOAVARANASIPHUKETBANGKO
LFOFTHAILANDLANGKAWI BALI LOMBOK KYOTOBEIJINGHAINA
AND HONG KONG SHANGHAI KEP NEW DELHI GOA VARANAS
UKET BANGKOK GULF OF THAILAND LANGKAWI BALI LOMBO
OTO BEIJING HAINAN ISLAND HONG KONG SHANGHAI KEP NEV
LHI GOA VARANASI PHUKET BANGKOK GULF OF THAILAN

A Deluxe King guest room with a silk kimono tapestry at the Hyatt Regency Kyoto.

HYATT REGENCY KYOTO

Kyoto, Japan

644-2 Sanjusangendo-mawari, Higashiyama-ku; 800/233-1234 or 81-75/541-1234; hyatt.com; doubles from $$$.

JAPAN'S ANCIENT CAPITAL—renowned for its temples, shrines, and vibrant geisha culture—has one foot in the 14th century and the other rooted in the 21st. For proof, look to the new Hyatt Regency Kyoto, where interior design firm Super Potato melded contemporary Japanese style with traditional touches. Bamboo trees flank the entrance; an intricately patterned aluminum canopy serves as both ceiling and mood lighting in the lobby; guest rooms of muted white oak have deep-soaking baths or cedar tubs, and headboards composed of colorful panels of silk kimono fabrics. The mesmerizing centerpiece: a Japanese garden with a waterfall and reflection pond. But the biggest draw may be Touzan Bar, where walls are constructed from old hardcover books, and a menu of premium sakes, wines, brandies, and locally brewed beers makes engrossing reading material on its own.

AMAN AT SUMMER PALACE

Beijing, China

Aman at Summer
Palace's bar terrace.

鏡影涵虛

STAYING AT AMANRESORTS' first foray into China is like having your own set of keys to a vanished kingdom. The 51 rooms and suites—housed in what was once a Qing-dynasty imperial complex—are just steps from the Summer Palace, the former residence of the dowager empress Cixi. Go through a private door and you're on the grounds. While many Beijing hotels are razor-edge modern, this resort is a portal in time, referencing its history with Ming-style armoires, Jin clay tiles, and hand-carved wooden screens. In a nod to the glory days of the dowager empress, guests can get their own royal treatment with spa rituals that employ roses and lotuses. *1 Gongmenqian St · 800/477-9180 or 86-10/5987-9999; amanresorts.com; doubles from $$$*

RITZ-CARLTON SANYA

Hainan Island, China

WELCOME TO THE HAWAII of the South China Sea. The 450-room Ritz-Carlton is a standout among the growing number of resorts on Hainan, China's only tropical island. Crowds of sun-seeking Russians and well-heeled mainland Chinese (including lovestruck newlyweds in matching floral shirts) flock here for the lagoon-dotted gardens and private white-sand beach, where hammocks strung on coconut trees afford myriad opportunities to laze and gaze at Yalong Bay. Walkways fringed with greenery connect the 33 villas; eight dining venues offer a range of culinary options, from high-end Cantonese to homey southern Italian. Don't be daunted by the distance to the seawater-themed Espa at the other end of the resort—a personal butler awaits to drive you there.
Yalong Bay National Resort District, Sanya; 800/241-3333 or 86-898/8898-8888; ritzcarlton.com; doubles from $.

An infinity pool with views of Yalong Bay at the Ritz-Carlton Sanya.

A guest room at the
W Hong Kong.

W HONG KONG

Hong Kong, China

THE FIRST OUTPOST IN CHINA from Starwood's boutique-style brand perfectly channels the tastes of its urban clientele. Located in the vibrant West Kowloon district overlooking Victoria Harbor, the hotel features 393 nightclubesque rooms with remote-controlled everything, from blackout curtains to multicolored mood lighting. Joining the fun are the first Bliss Spa in Asia, with its signature decadent bar snacks; a rooftop pool that's one of the highest in the world; and a cocktail lounge with an electric crowd. The W Hotel's Whatever, Whenever motto couldn't feel more appropriate in Asia's frenetic financial capital. Yes, the concierge can have a bespoke suit tailored in just 24 hours; and if money is no object, he can also summon a private jet for a last-minute side trip to Shanghai.

1 Austin Rd. W., Kowloon Station, Kowloon; 877/946-8357 or 85-2/3717-2222; whotels.com; doubles from $$.

PENINSULA SHANGHAI

Shanghai, China

Frette linens on a
guest-room bed at the
Peninsula Shanghai.

A MAESTRO OF LUXE HOSPITALITY, Peninsula Hotels chairman Michael Kadoorie spent his early childhood in Shanghai, where his entrepreneurial forefathers operated four hotels and built the enormous Marble Hall colonial mansion. So the 2009 premiere of Kadoorie's ninth property, the Peninsula Shanghai, is a homecoming of sorts. Located on the historic Bund, the 14-story granite-clad building is a Modernist reflection of its Art Deco–era neighbors the Shanghai Club and Sassoon House. Interiors are boom-time rich—as in carved marble bathroom walls and up-to-the-minute amenities (hands-free telephones, nail dryers in the dressing room). Given Kadoorie's predilection for vintage cars, there's also a 1934 Rolls-Royce Phantom II for guests who want to tour the city in style. *32 Zhongshan Dong Yi Rd.; 866/382-8388 or 86-21/2327-2888; peninsula.com; doubles from $$.*

WITH ITS NECK-CRANING HIGH-RISES and teeming boulevards, Shanghai's Lujiazui district is a neighborhood typically best experienced from afar. That's why this 174-room hotel, nestled between the 79th and 93rd floors of the 101-story Shanghai World Financial Center, is such a luxury. Once up the elevator, you're enveloped in an almost monastic calm: floor-to-ceiling windows give the impression that you're floating in a cocoon, while daily tai chi classes in the Living Room encourage a meditative state of mind. This blissful vibe comes courtesy of interior designer Tony Chi, who used a neutral palette and streamlined furniture to create a sort of visual silence. Amid all the minimalism lurks a stealthy air of indulgence—the restaurant serves a cream-of-artichoke soup garnished with caviar, and the Water's Edge spa features rose-scented foot rubs and healing treatments incorporating traditional Chinese medicine.

100 Century Ave., Pudong; 800/233-1234 or 86-21/6888-1234; park.hyatt.com; doubles from $$$$.

PARK HYATT SHANGHAI

Shanghai, China

The Dining Room restaurant at the Park Hyatt Shanghai.

One of the restored villas at Knai Bang Chatt.

KNAI BANG CHATT

Kep, Cambodia

Phum Thmey, Sangkat Prey Thom, Khan Kep; 855-12/349-742; knaibangchatt.com; doubles from $.

IN ITS 1950'S HEYDAY, before the Khmer Rouge took power, Kep was the weekend destination of choice among French colonials and the Cambodian elite. Decades later, Belgian travelers Jef Moons and Boris Vervoordt stumbled upon a remnant of those bygone times—a series of Modernist villas that were abandoned during the 70's. The two set about transforming the site into a seaside escape that would help revive Cambodia's tourist trade. By all accounts, they've succeeded. Eleven guest rooms, furnished with Khmer fabrics, antiques, and furniture of salvaged driftwood, join a palapa-style dining pavilion, a saltwater infinity pool, and a garden with nooks for yoga or meditation. Lunch at one of the crab shacks on the beach is a must: a simple pleasure in a once sleepy town on the cusp of its next boom.

AMAN NEW DELHI

New Delhi, India

MELDING AMAN'S SIGNATURE hushed vibe with the notorious tumult of New Delhi presented quite the challenge. But architect Kerry Hill rose to the occasion, unleashing the equivalent of design Xanax to set this urban resort apart from the hubbub of its surroundings. Khaki-hued spaces are made of locally quarried Khareda stone; Dholpur marble statues and Lutyens-replica furniture add character to interiors; and manicured lawns enclose the six-acre property like a verdant moat. Most of the 31 rooms and 36 suites come with individual plunge pools on private terraces. A long lap pool beckons guests who have more athletic inclinations, while a bar located beneath its colonnade caters to those feeling parched at the mere thought of physical exertion.
Lodhi Rd.; 800/477-9180 or 91-11/4363-3333; aman resorts.com; doubles from $$$$.

A private plunge pool and daybed on a guest-room terrace at the Aman New Delhi. Opposite: The hotel's lap pool.

SPOTLIGHT GOA

OFTEN THOUGHT OF AS INDIA'S VERSION OF IBIZA, a scene full of dreadlocked ravers and package tourists, Goa gets a bad rap. But stray off the 65-mile-long main beach and you'll discover the destination's tranquil side—a haven of seclusion, gentility, and relaxation, where international glitterati go to kick back. On the Goan island of Corjuem, the four-suite Panchavatti combines the intimate vibe of a jungle hideaway with the atmosphere of an exclusive slumber party. Owner Loulou Van Damme, a spry, sixtysomething interior designer of Belgian descent, encourages social interaction among her guests, who are joined by Van Damme's four dogs, hundreds

Owner Loulou Van Damme at Panchavatti.

Casa Britona's courtyard pool.

PANCHAVATTI

Island of Corjuem, Aldona; 91-082/258-0632; islaingoa.com; doubles from $$.

CASA BRITONA

House No. 14/7, near Charmanos, Badem, Salvador-do-Mundo, Bardez; 91-832/241-6737; casaboutiquehotels.com; doubles from

of crickets, and clusters of enormous striped moths to form one big interspecies family. On the mainland in the fishing village of Britona, Goan architect Dean D'Cruz gutted an old warehouse and turned it into Casa Britona—eight rooms and two riverside studios decorated with brightly painted frescoes, embroidered linens, and colonial antiques. And half an hour away in the quiet coastal hamlet of Siolim, Casa Palacio Siolim House exudes Portuguese-era charm and homey comfort, right down to the superb fresh fish *thali* served in the open-air dining room. No wonder Kate Moss and her entourage once booked all seven suites for their own private retreat.

The Macassar Room at Casa Palacio Siolim House.

CASA PALACIO SIOLIM HOUSE

Wadi, Siolim; 91-832/227-2138; siolimhouse.com;
doubles from $.

QUEEN ELIZABETH II, INDIRA GANDHI, and the Dalai Lama have all been guests at this former maharajah's palace, surrounded by jasmine-scented gardens in the holy city of Varanasi. But after its transformation by Taj Resorts, even less exalted travelers can stay in the columned 18th-century residence. Within the 10 supersize suites, gauzy textiles in luscious lotus-petal pinks and marigold yellows are draped over teakwood four-posters, and etched mirrors hang next to claw-foot tubs. A silk pouch filled with palate-cleansing cardamom pods is left at turndown. The spa draws on ancient Indian wellness and spiritual traditions; in one treatment, Vedic verses are chanted while a blend of milk, honey, yogurt, sugar, and clarified butter is poured over your body, then rinsed off with water from the sacred Ganges River, believed to have miraculous healing powers. *Nadesar Palace Grounds; 866/969-1825 or 91-542/250-300-119; tajhotels.com; doubles from $$.*

The Historical Suite at the Taj Nadesar Palace.

TAJ NADESAR PALACE

Varanasi, India

Daybeds that seem to float over a shallow pool at Anantara Phuket Resort & Spa.

ANANTARA PHUKET RESORT & SPA

Phuket, Thailand

888 Moo 3, Tumbon Mai Khao; 800/223-6800 or 66-76/336-100; anantara.com; doubles from $$$$.

LOCATED ON A PRIVATE STRETCH of Mai Khao Beach, Anantara's first Phuket property is unabashed about its objective: namely, to pamper guests to the point of never wanting to leave. Hidden within a former plantation, on the far side of a man-made lagoon, the 83 bougainvillea-covered villas draw on elements of classic Thai design, with wooden walls and sloping roofs that make guests feel as if they're meandering through a local village. But there's nothing rustic here: each one, clad in teak and raw silk, comes with a swimming pool, an outdoor daybed, and a terrazzo tub. Ritual baths, avocado body wraps, and other lavish treatments are offered at the spa, which features a dedicated Ayurvedic suite and an open-air room for massage and yoga within tropical gardens.

LE MÉRIDIEN
BANGKOK

Bangkok, Thailand

40/5 Surawong Rd., Bangrak;
800/543-4300 or 66-2/232-8888;
lemeridien.com; doubles from $.

Check-in at Le Méridien Bangkok.
Opposite: The lobby, featuring Ralph
Gibson's *Man with Poodle* photograph.

WORLD'S BEST | **THINK OF EACH FLOOR-TO-CEILING WINDOW** as a canvas—one that captures a lively vista of the Thai capital, from the Buddhist Hua Lampong Temple and Phatumwan shopping area to the Chao Phraya River. In fact, a stay at this Silom District hotel functions as an education in the arts and senses. You can choose between a room with a circular bed or a regular square one, then contemplate the geometric shadows on your wall made by sunlight filtered through a perfectly positioned teak panel (its placement is no accident). Your key card, created by artist Michael Lin, not only unlocks your door but also provides access to the Thailand Creative & Design Center, with its wealth of programs and exhibits. If you're curious to know the meaning of the poem inscribed above your bed—written by Sunthon Phu, Thailand's version of Shakespeare—ask for an English translation.

A Deluxe Pool Villa at X2 Kui Buri. Opposite: A Garden Villa bedroom, with walls made of rocks from local quarries.

X2
KUI BURI

Prachuap Khiri Khan, Thailand

52 Moo 13, Ao Noi, Muang; 800/337-4685 or 66/3260-1412; x2resorts.com; doubles from $.

WELCOME TO THE SEASIDE THAILAND of 20 years ago, blessedly free of the banana-boat operators and wandering masseurs who crowd many of the country's beaches. At the end of a dirt road lies X2 Kui Buri, a compound of 23 stone-and-wood bungalows designed by Thai architect Duangrit Bunnag. Boardwalks meander, mazelike, throughout the grounds, pausing at key bursts of colorful landscaping or at views of the Gulf of Thailand. In the villas, glass doors keep the focus on the scenery, while stone walls provide textural contrast. (Such artful visuals might cause you to wonder whether the sea pebbles on the beach were individually placed by Bunnag himself.) There are no Do Not Disturb signs—the assumption being that you never want to be disturbed unless you dial the front desk with a request.

Bon Ton's private dining
room, perched over the
property's lotus lagoon.

BON TON RESTAURANT +RESORT

Langkawi, Malaysia

THE ALLURE OF COLONIAL INDOCHINA lives on at
Bon Ton, a small village of beautifully refurbished
Malay wooden stilt houses that seem to be straight
out of a Marguerite Duras novella. Australian owner
Narelle McMurtrie, who has lived on Langkawi
for the past 23 years, runs her eight-villa resort as
an effort at cultural preservation and finances an
island animal shelter with the profits. Four-poster
beds and plantation shutters create a heady, romantic
ambience. Sultry evenings call for a lychee caipiroska
in the lounge (an old rubber house) before a dinner of
Malay-influenced fare, such as pandan-leaf-wrapped
prawns and eggplant in coconut curry. At sunset
the emerald green rice paddies and golden-tipped
reeds take on a cinematic glow.
*Pantai Cenang; 60-4/955-1688; bontonresort.com.my;
doubles from $.*

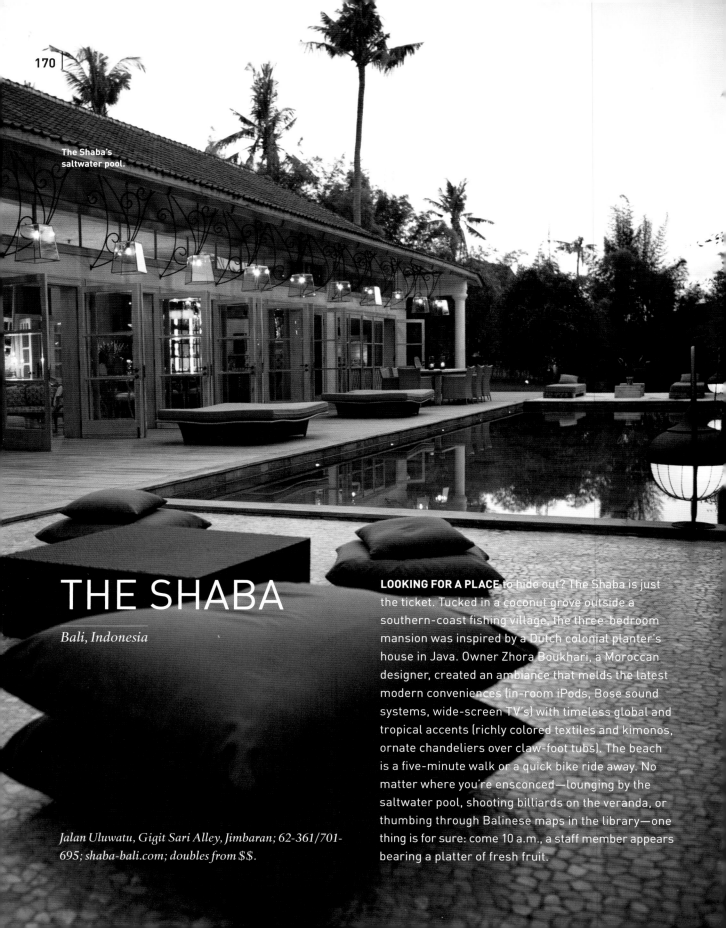

The Shaba's saltwater pool.

THE SHABA

Bali, Indonesia

Jalan Uluwatu, Gigit Sari Alley, Jimbaran; 62-361/701-695; shaba-bali.com; doubles from $$.

LOOKING FOR A PLACE to hide out? The Shaba is just the ticket. Tucked in a coconut grove outside a southern-coast fishing village, the three-bedroom mansion was inspired by a Dutch colonial planter's house in Java. Owner Zhora Boukhari, a Moroccan designer, created an ambiance that melds the latest modern conveniences (in-room iPods, Bose sound systems, wide-screen TV's) with timeless global and tropical accents (richly colored textiles and kimonos, ornate chandeliers over claw-foot tubs). The beach is a five-minute walk or a quick bike ride away. No matter where you're ensconced—lounging by the saltwater pool, shooting billiards on the veranda, or thumbing through Balinese maps in the library—one thing is for sure: come 10 a.m., a staff member appears bearing a platter of fresh fruit.

The open-air dining hall and infinity pool. Above: The Aloon-Aloon suite at Hotel Tugu Lombok.

HOTEL TUGU LOMBOK

Lombok, Indonesia

TRADITIONAL THATCHED HUTS and jade-green fields border the pristine mile-long beach on Lombok's underdeveloped northwest coast. It's a memorable backdrop for this 19-room property, which—true to the island's blend of cultures—deftly combines Dutch, Peranakan, and indigenous design. The reception area is in a century-old wooden building relocated from the former capital of Ampenan. Oil lamps burn dimly in the bar, illuminating giant teak panels and bamboo windows. A freshwater infinity pool is guarded by four giant statues of the god Bhairava. Colonial-style doors and antique window frames, along with Chinese and Indonesian artifacts, add character (the Bhagavad Gita suites also have tubs carved out of boulders and private lotus ponds). The in-room booklet, *101 Dining Options,* reminds you that any corner of the hotel is yours to nosh in, from the spa's temple rooftop to the four-poster daybeds on the beach.
Jalan Pantai Sire; 62-370/620-111; tuguhotels.com; doubles from $.

A deluxe tent at Australia's
Paperbark Camp.

AUSTRALIA
+ NEW ZEALAND
+ THE SOUTH
PACIFIC

SMANIAMOLLYMOOKWOOLLAMIANORTHERN TERRITOR
CKLAND CHRISTCHURCH QUEENSTOWN SOUTHLAN
RA-BORA MARQUESAS ISLANDS TASMANIA MOLLYMOO
OOLLAMIA NORTHERN TERRITORY AUCKLAND CHRIS
URCHQUEENSTOWNSOUTHLANDBORA-BORAMARQUESA
ANDSTASMANIAMOLLYMOOKWOOLLAMIANORTHER
RRITORYAUCKLAND CHRISTCHURCH QUEENSTOW
UTHLANDBORA-BORAMARQUESAS ISLANDSTASMANI
OLLYMOOK WOOLLAMIA NORTHERN TERRITORY AUCKLAN

IN A TASMANIAN VILLAGE near the Central Highlands, a region known for game hunting, this 1848 Tudor Gothic–style lodge offers a roster of traditional country-squire activities. Guests can fill their days with trout fishing (the hotel provides majestically tied flies free of charge); rounds of golf (the nearby course is the oldest in the Southern Hemisphere); visits to a whiskey distillery; and walks through UNESCO World Heritage–designated wilderness. The style meter may be all over the map, but somehow it comes together: antler chandeliers, stained-glass windows from the original priory on the site, lamps made from old pistols, and even the occasional tapestry. *2 Wentworth St., Bothwell; 61-3/6259-4012; thepriorycountrylodge.com.au; doubles from $$, including breakfast, afternoon tea, and dinner.*

RIORY
OUNTRY
ODGE

nia, Australia

The Hunting Room at the Priory Country Lodge. Opposite: One of the lodge's three pavilions, which overlooks a neighboring lake.

THREE HOURS SOUTH OF SYDNEY, on a Pacific Coast headland in a town known mostly for attracting surfers and migrating whales, this revamped motel epitomizes beachy chic. The 33 rooms are done up in white and wicker, with spacious wooden balconies overlooking the ocean (some also have freestanding tubs that look like giant latte cups). Down a flight of stairs lies a saltwater infinity pool, where you can swim and watch the waves through a tangle of casuarina trees. At the much-lauded seafood-centric restaurant—run by British chef Rick Stein—dine on blue swimmer crab or grilled rock lobster, then adjourn to the poolside lounge for cocktails by candlelight.

BANNISTERS POINT LODGE

Mollymook, Australia

191 Mitchell Parade; 61-2/4455-3044;
bannisterspointlodge.com.au; doubles from $$.

Poolside at Bannisters Point Lodge.

One of the 12 tents at Paperbark Camp.

PAPERBARK CAMP

Woollamia, Australia

571 Woollamia Rd.; 800/227-9246 or 61-2/4441-6066; paperbarkcamp.com.au; doubles from $$.

THE PLATINUM-BLOND BEACHES of Jervis Bay are only a five-minute drive—and a world apart—from this posh eco-safari experience, located 2½ hours south of Sydney. Set in a dappled eucalyptus grove on the banks of a babbling creek, the 12 solar-powered tents at Paperbark Camp were imported from Africa and retrofitted with open-air showers, timber decks, and simple, locally made furniture. Come dinnertime, take a flashlight to guide your way down the gravel path to the indoor-outdoor Gunyah, a restaurant high above the eucalyptus trees where the contemporary Australian cuisine incorporates regional ingredients: pepper-berry-spiced kangaroo loin, for example, or lime-cured kingfish. Complimentary bikes and canoes complete the explorer fantasy.

BAMURRU PLAINS

Northern Territory, Australia

KOOKABURRAS AND WHISTLING KITES provide your wake-up call at this remote bush camp just west of Kakadu National Park. The Aussie version of a luxe safari lodge, Bamurru Plains is all about wildlife. Skim in an airboat across the Mary River floodplains in the early morning to see kingfishers and crocodiles amid the rushes and blooming pink lotus lilies. At sunset, ride in an open-air jeep through the savannah woodland, where water buffalo roam. The nine corrugated-iron-roofed bungalows on raised timber platforms have mesh sides for optimal viewing, and comfortable beds made up with organic cotton linens. The solar-powered lodge features a collection of modern Aboriginal art and a communal dining table; dishes might include crocodile risotto and kangaroo shepherd's pie, with coveted Australian vintages on offer in the bar. *Swim Creek Station; 61-2/9571-6399; bamurruplains.com; doubles from $$$$, all-inclusive, two-night minimum.*

A raised safari bungalow
at Bamurru Plains.

Hotel DeBrett's Art Deco exterior. Opposite: A Loft suite, with a spiral staircase and the hotel's signature carpet.

HOTEL DEBRETT

Auckland, New Zealand

*2 High St.; 64-9/925-9000; hoteldebrett.com;
doubles from $.*

EVERY NOOK AND CRANNY OF THE DEBRETT brims with personality—thanks to interior designer Michelle Deery and her husband, John Courtney, who transformed the Art Deco building in downtown Auckland over the course of a two-year renovation. The original 1925 hotel once hosted visiting entertainers like the Beatles; now it's a warmly eclectic, 25-room boutique property with the vibe of a stylish friend's home. Deery designed, commissioned, or chose each little detail, from the mirror tiles in the elevator and the chandeliers by Judy Darragh to the colorful custom carpet of New Zealand wool that runs throughout. A soaring, new glass-roofed atrium bridged by interior balconies serves as the hotel's social heart, but the oak-paneled bar, a restored gem, is the place for an evening tête-à-tête.

OTAHUNA LODGE

Christchurch, New Zealand

*224 Rhodes Rd., Tai Tapu; 800/735-2478 or
64-3/329-6333; otahuna.co.nz; doubles from $$$$$,
including breakfast and dinner.*

SET ON 30 ACRES of soft, sheep-speckled hills that call to mind an episode of *Masterpiece Theatre*, th homestead was once the largest private residence in New Zealand, and is still one of the finest exan Queen Anne architecture in Australasia. Interiors celebrate the Arts and Crafts movement, from the embossed William Morris wallpaper in the dining room to the gingerbread woodwork in guest room romantic patchwork of woodland, lawns, ponds, bridges, and arbors was designed by a landscaper w at Kew Gardens in London. And although the amenities (rain showers, a gym) are more modern, the lodge—including the service—conjures up an era of garden parties attended by ladies with 22-inch

The
Otah
exte

in the
Eichardt's

The hotel's glass atrium.

EICHARDT'S PRIVATE HOTEL

Queenstown, New Zealand

IN THE BRISK CLIMATE of New Zealand's adventure capital, the best way to stay warm is by curling up with a possum-fur throw in front of your own private fireplace, a bottle of champagne within easy reach. At Eichardt's, you'll be tempted to do just that after a day packed with the numerous high-adrenaline activities (bungee jumping, skydiving, white-water rafting) on offer nearby. This jewel box of a hotel opened in the 1860's; its glass atrium was a 21st-century addition. All five guest suites have dressing rooms and sitting areas with deep armchairs; next door, the lakefront cottage has four one- and two-bedroom suites with kitchens, to be rented in any combination that suits your fancy. The views across Lake Wakatipu to Walter Peak draw their share of superlatives, but this scenery is truly worthy of its hype. *Marine Parade; 800/525-4800 or 64-3/441-0450; eichardtshotel.co.nz; doubles from $$$$.*

SPOTLIGHT SOUTHLAND

A SPARSELY POPULATED REGION of forests, lakes, waterfalls, and rugged swaths of coastline, Southland remains New Zealand's secret, a veritable no-man's-land near spectacular Milford Sound. But for nature lovers, the area—home to Fiordland National Park and the Catlins, among other less-visited attractions—represents the next big destination in the making. A good place to start is the university town of Dunedin, in the neighboring region of Otago, where the Mandeno House serves tea in a formal garden with 30-plus varieties of white roses. About three hours west in Winton, the ultra-private Lodge at Tikana (available for single-party bookings of up

A guest room at Mandeno House.

MANDENO HOUSE

667 George St., Dunedin, Otago; 64-3/471-9595; mandenohouse.com; doubles from $.

LODGE AT TIKANA

347 Livingstone Rd., Winton; 64-3/236-4117; tikana.co.nz; from $$$$$, including breakfast and dinner.

to four) is a refined country retreat: buffed butter-colored walls, timber beams, and baths for two with views of undulating paddocks and grazing wapiti deer. Meals, which are mostly locally sourced and organic, are discussed with guests each day and designed around their tastes and timing. An hour and a half away, on the shores of Lake Te Anau, Fiordland Lodge shows off Southland's wild scenery to its full advantage. Owner Ron Peacock, a veteran park ranger, and his wife are eager to share their passion for the surrounding landscape, arranging guided trips that range from fly-fishing and bird-watching to hiking and helicopter tours.

The Lodge at Tikana, which sits amid rolling farmland.

The river-stone fireplace at Fiordland Lodge.

FIORDLAND LODGE

472 Te Anau Milford Hwy., Te Anau; 64-3/249-7832; fiordlandlodge.co.nz; doubles from $$$, including breakfast and dinner.

FOUR SEASONS RESORT BORA BORA

Motu Tehotu, Bora-Bora

ON THE PRIVATE ISLET OF MOTU TEHOTU, where the 100 thatched-roof bungalows of the Four Seasons Resort Bora Bora hover above a lagoon, the splendor of the natural world envelops you like a 24-hour Technicolor extravaganza. Glass floor panels in your room give you a sneak peek into the shallows, an underwater realm tended by the resort's on-site marine biologist. (After dark, simply flip a switch to illuminate the coral and swimming fish below.) Next to your soaking tub, shutters slide open for a view of the lagoon and the green peaks of Mount Otemanu. Even your bungalow's interior, with coral lamps and mother-of-pearl plaster, makes use of the native bounty. A long private deck that connects to walkways over the water means you never have to touch terra firma—not even to visit the spa, suspended above a tropical grove with 72-foot-high ceilings and a glass-floored couple's treatment room. *800/332-3442 or 689/603-130; fourseasons.com; doubles from $$$$$.*

Four Seasons Resort Bora Bora's overwater bungalows, with Mount Otemanu as a backdrop.

An outrigger fishing boat near the harbor.

HIVA OA HANAKEE PEARL LODGE

Hiva Oa, Marquesas Islands, French Polynesia

Atuona; 800/657-3275 or 689/927-587; www.spmhotels. com; doubles from $$.

PART OF FRENCH POLYNESIA'S Marquesas archipelago, Hiva Oa has majestic scenery and a somewhat feral past (think tattoo-tongued warriors with a propensity to dine on their conquests). Its primeval beauty attracted artist Paul Gauguin—and continues to lure intrepid travelers in search of far-flung adventure. At the hilltop Pearl Lodge, those who make the journey are greeted with a *tiare*-flower lei and a chilled lemon-scented towel for mopping the brow. Carved tiki poles, woven-palm wall coverings, and traditional bark-paper paintings add character to the 14 bamboo-lattice bungalows, some of which face the lush Tehueto valley and the Bay of Tahauku. Book a tour with Pearl Lodge guide Lecortier Tematai, who leads the way to pristine waterfalls while expertly maneuvering dirt-road switchbacks under a canopy of acacia and mango trees.

The pool at Hiva Oa
Hanakee Pearl Lodge.

THE
WORLD'S
BEST

In *Travel + Leisure*'s annual World's Best Awards Survey, readers are asked to rate their favorite hotels and spas around the globe, based on location, food, service, and value. Each year, the changing list of winners reveals readers' evolving, but always exacting, standards of excellence. You'll find the most recent results on the following pages, organized by region.

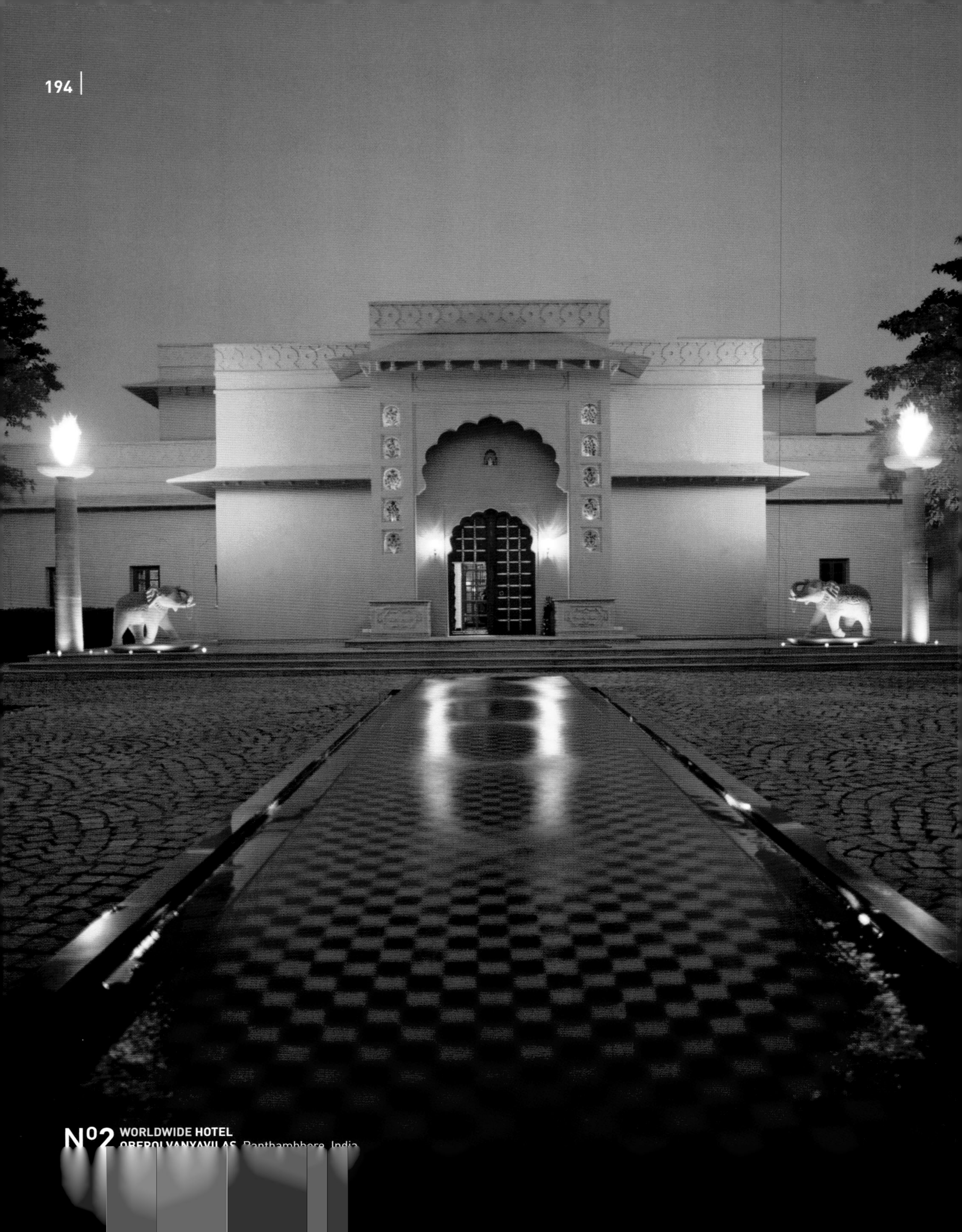

N°2 WORLDWIDE HOTEL
OBEROI VANYAVILAS Ranthambhore, India

TOP 100 HOTELS

1. **BUSHMANS KLOOF** Cedar Mountains, South Africa 98.67
2. **OBEROI VANYAVILAS** Ranthambhore, India 98.00
3. **JADE MOUNTAIN** St. Lucia 97.50
3. **EARTH LODGE AT SABI SABI PRIVATE GAME RESERVE** KrugerNational Park, South Africa 97.50
5. **INN AT MANITOU** McKellar, Ontario 95.59
6. **SINGITA SABI SAND** Kruger National Park, South Africa 95.52
7. **FOUR SEASONS TENTED CAMP GOLDEN TRIANGLE** Chiang Rai, Thailand 95.00
8. **OBEROI UDAIVILAS** Udaipur, India 94.88
9. **GOVERNORS' CAMP** Masai Mara, Kenya 94.82
10. **JACK'S CAMP** Makgadkgadi Pans, Botswana 94.72
11. **PALACIO DUHAU-PARK HYATT** Buenos Aires 94.68
12. **KIRAWIRA LUXURY TENTED CAMP** Serengeti National Park, Tanzania 94.63
13. **EAGLE ISLAND CAMP** Moremi Game Reserve, Botswana 94.17
14. **INN AT PALMETTO BLUFF** Bluffton, South Carolina 94.03
15. **TWELVE APOSTLES HOTEL & SPA** Cape Town 93.91
16. **LODGE AT KAURI CLIFFS** North Island, New Zealand 93.75
16. **SINGITA GRUMETI RESERVES** Serengeti National Park, Tanzania 93.75
18. **ROSEWOOD MAYAKOBÁ** Riviera Maya 93.41
19. **ELIOT HOTEL** Boston 93.40
20. **MANDARIN ORIENTAL** Bangkok 93.34
21. **FARM AT CAPE KIDNAPPERS** North Island, New Zealand 93.33
21. **FOUR SEASONS RESORT** Chiang Mai, Thailand 93.33
23. **ESPERANZA, AN AUBERGE RESORT** Los Cabos, Mexico 93.30
24. **LIONS SAND PRIVATE GAME RESERVE** Kruger National Park, South Africa 93.28
25. **ROYAL MALEWANE** Kruger National Park, South Africa 93.15
26. **WATERMARK HOTEL & SPA** San Antonio, Texas 93.08
27. **SHAMWARI GAME RESERVE** Eastern Cape, South Africa 93.00
28. **OBEROI AMARVILAS** Agra, India 92.91
29. **THE SAXON** Johannesburg 92.86
29. **SINGITA KRUGER NATIONAL PARK** South Africa 92.86
31. **GRAND HOTEL BAGLIONI** Bologna, Italy 92.83
32. **ISLAND SHANGRI-LA** Hong Kong 92.75
33. **GIRAFFE MANOR** Nairobi 92.68
34. **LONDOLOZI PRIVATE GAME RESERVE** Kruger National Park, South Africa 92.68
35. **PENINSULA HONG KONG** 92.23

36. **COUPLES NEGRIL** Jamaica 92.19
37. **ANANTARA DHIGU RESORT & SPA** Maldives 92.14
38. **LONDON WEST HOLLYWOOD** California 92.07
39. **KICHWA TEMBO** Masai Mara, Kenya 91.86
40. **FOUR SEASONS HOTEL CAIRO AT THE FIRST RESIDENCE** Egypt 91.86
41. **HALEKULANI** Oahu 91.81
42. **COUPLES SWEPT AWAY** Negril, Jamaica 91.80
43. **DOMAINE DES HAUTS DE LOIRE** Onzain, France 91.79
44. **KHWAI RIVER LODGE** Moremi Game Reserve, Botswana 91.71
45. **HOTEL NELLIGAN** Montreal 91.47
46. **AMANGANI** Jackson Hole, Wyoming 91.42
47. **IL SAN PIETRO** Positano, Italy 91.39
48. **PUDONG SHANGRI-LA** Shanghai 91.30
49. **TORTILIS CAMP** Amboseli Game Reserve, Kenya 91.28
50. **AMANKORA PARO** Bhutan 91.25
51. **ENCHANTMENT RESORT** Sedona, Arizona 91.22
52. **RABBIT HILL INN** Lower Waterford, Vermont 91.19
53. **ANANTARA GOLDEN TRIANGLE** Chiang Rai, Thailand 91.16
54. **PLACE D'ARMES HOTEL & SUITES** Montreal 91.06
55. **SHANGRI-LA'S TANJUNG ARU RESORT & SPA** Kota Kinabalu, Malaysia 90.98
56. **NGORONGORO CRATER LODGE** Tanzania 90.97
57. **CEYLAN INTERCONTINENTAL** Istanbul 90.90
58. **CAPE GRACE** Cape Town 90.90
59. **WESTIN BUND CENTER** Shanghai 90.82
60. **LE QUARTIER FRANÇAIS** Franschhoek Valley, South Africa 90.79
61. **MARRIOTT HOTEL** Budapest 90.76

Throughout the World's Best Awards, scores are rounded to the nearest hundredth of a point; in the event of a tie, properties share the same ranking.

N°1 WORLDWIDE DESTINATION SPA
MII AMO, A DESTINATION SPA AT ENCHANTMENT, Sedona, Arizona

TOP 10 DESTINATION SPAS

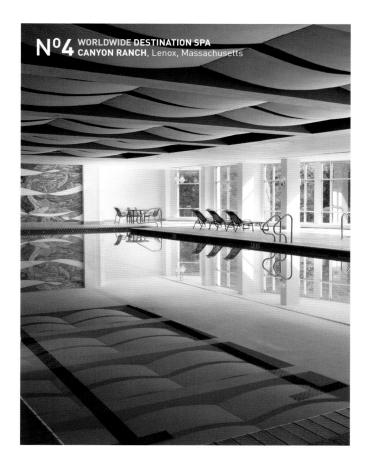

N°**4** WORLDWIDE DESTINATION SPA
CANYON RANCH, Lenox, Massachusetts

N°1 CONTINENTAL U.S. + CANADA RESORT
INN AT PALMETTO BLUFF, Bluffton, South Carolina

CONTINENTAL U.S. + CANADA

TOP HOTELS

➤ RESORTS (40 ROOMS OR MORE)

1. **INN AT PALMETTO BLUFF** Bluffton, South Carolina 94.03
2. **AMANGANI** Jackson Hole, Wyoming 91.42
3. **ENCHANTMENT RESORT** Sedona, Arizona 91.22
4. **SAN YSIDRO RANCH, A ROSEWOOD RESORT** Santa Barbara, California 90.59
4. **POST HOTEL & SPA** Lake Louise, Alberta 90.59
6. **THE CLOISTER** Sea Island, Georgia 89.54
7. **AUBERGE DU SOLEIL** Rutherford, California 89.36
8. **RITZ-CARLTON BACHELOR GULCH** Beaver Creek, Colorado 88.45
9. **LITTLE NELL** Aspen, Colorado 88.27
10. **LODGE AT PEBBLE BEACH** California 88.11
11. **SOLAGE CALISTOGA** California 88.11
12. **LODGE AT SEA ISLAND** Georgia 88.06
13. **FOUR SEASONS RESORT JACKSON HOLE** Wyoming 87.97
14. **MONTAGE LAGUNA BEACH** California 87.81
15. **WHITE ELEPHANT** Nantucket, Massachusetts 87.67
16. **SANCTUARY AT KIAWAH ISLAND GOLF RESORT** South Carolina 87.50
17. **FAIRMONT CHATEAU LAKE LOUISE** Alberta 87.40
18. **CALISTOGA RANCH** California 87.22
19. **RITZ-CARLTON NAPLES** Florida 87.16
20. **CORDEVALLE, A ROSEWOOD RESORT** San Martin, California 87.14
21. **FOUR SEASONS RESORT THE BILTMORE** Santa Barbara, California 86.88
22. **WHITEFACE LODGE RESORT & SPA** Lake Placid, New York 86.45
23. **FOUR SEASONS RESORT** Whistler, British Columbia 86.39
24. **ST. REGIS RESORT** Aspen, Colorado 86.33
25. **RITZ-CARLTON LAGUNA NIGUEL** Dana Point, California 86.23
26. **MIRROR LAKE INN RESORT & SPA** Lake Placid, New York 86.02
27. **HOTEL HEALDSBURG** California 85.94
28. **SONNENALP RESORT** Vail, Colorado 85.89
29. **GRAND DEL MAR** San Diego 85.80
30. **SANCTUARY ON CAMELBACK MOUNTAIN** Paradise Valley, Arizona 85.75
31. **THE BROADMOOR** Colorado Springs, Colorado 85.65
32. **HAWKS CAY RESORT** Duck Key, Florida 85.42
33. **LANGHAM HUNTINGTON** Pasadena, California 85.33
34. **WEQUASSETT RESORT & GOLF CLUB** Chatham, Massachusetts 85.28
35. **TIDES INN** Irvington, Virginia 85.05
36. **INN AT SPANISH BAY** Pebble Beach, California 85.05
37. **STEPHANIE INN** Cannon Beach, Oregon 84.79
38. **VENTANA INN & SPA** Big Sur, California 84.71
39. **PARK HYATT BEAVER CREEK RESORT & SPA** Colorado 84.68
40. **RANCHO VALENCIA RESORT & SPA** Rancho Santa Fe, California 84.67
41. **TOPNOTCH RESORT & SPA** Stowe, Vermont 84.61
42. **WICKANINNISH INN** Vancouver Island, British Columbia 84.60
43. **RIMROCK RESORT HOTEL** Banff, Alberta 84.48
44. **FOUR SEASONS RESORT SCOTTSDALE AT TROON NORTH** Arizona 84.44
45. **PONTE VEDRA INN & CLUB** Ponte Vedra Beach, Florida 84.40
46. **INN ON BILTMORE ESTATE** Asheville, North Carolina 84.23
47. **HYATT REGENCY COCONUT POINT RESORT & SPA** Bonita Springs, Florida 84.17
48. **RITZ-CARLTON AMELIA ISLAND** Florida 83.99
49. **ROYAL PALMS RESORT & SPA** Phoenix 83.91
50. **STEIN ERIKSEN LODGE** Park City, Utah 83.89

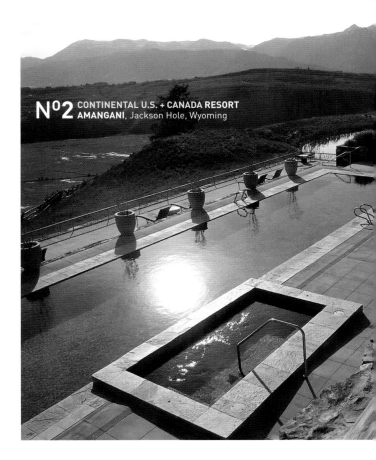

N°2 CONTINENTAL U.S. + CANADA RESORT
AMANGANI, Jackson Hole, Wyoming

CONTINENTAL U.S. + CANADA

➤ LARGE CITY HOTELS (100 ROOMS OR MORE)

1. **LONDON WEST HOLLYWOOD** California 92.07
2. **HOTEL NELLIGAN** Montreal 91.47
3. **PLACE D'ARMES HOTEL & SUITES** Montreal 91.06
4. **OMNI LA MANSIÓN DEL RIO** San Antonio, Texas 90.27
5. **ROSEWOOD MANSION ON TURTLE CREEK** Dallas 89.04
6. **THE CARLYLE, A ROSEWOOD HOTEL** New York City 88.72
7. **PENINSULA CHICAGO** 88.35
8. **RAFFLES L'ERMITAGE BEVERLY HILLS** 88.27
9. **OMNI MANDALAY HOTEL AT LAS COLINAS** Irving, Texas 87.88
10. **PENINSULA BEVERLY HILLS** 87.57
11. **ST. REGIS** San Francisco 87.35
12. **RITZ-CARLTON NEW YORK, CENTRAL PARK** 87.09
13. **WINDSOR COURT HOTEL** New Orleans 87.06
14. **FOUR SEASONS HOTEL** Chicago 87.06
15. **HOTEL OMNI MONT-ROYAL** Montreal 86.93

16. **HOTEL 1000** Seattle 86.81
17. **TRUMP INTERNATIONAL HOTEL & TOWER** New York City 86.44
18. **FOUR SEASONS HOTEL** Las Vegas 86.37
19. **RITZ-CARLTON (A FOUR SEASONS HOTEL)** Chicago 86.35
20. **ROSEWOOD CRESCENT HOTEL** Dallas 86.32
21. **OMNI SAN FRANCISCO HOTEL** 85.68
22. **CHARLESTON PLACE HOTEL** South Carolina 85.67
23. **FOUR SEASONS HOTEL** New York City 85.64
24. **THE HAY-ADAMS** Washington, D.C. 85.37
25. **OMNI CHICAGO HOTEL** 85.33
26. **WYNN LAS VEGAS** 85.31
27. **FAIRMONT VANCOUVER AIRPORT** 85.22
28. **LOEWS HOTEL VOGUE** Montreal 84.95
29. **PENINSULA NEW YORK** 84.88
30. **HÔTEL PLAZA ATHÉNÉE** New York City 84.86
31. **HUNTINGTON HOTEL & NOB HILL SPA** San Francisco 84.85
32. **FAIRMONT OLYMPIC HOTEL** Seattle 84.82
33. **RITZ-CARLTON SAN FRANCISCO** 84.73
34. **MANDARIN ORIENTAL** San Francisco 84.72
35. **SOFITEL PHILADELPHIA** 84.58
36. **FOUR SEASONS RESORT AVIARA** North San Diego 84.43
37. **THE SETAI** Miami Beach 84.38
38. **ST PAUL HOTEL** Minnesota 84.34
39. **HOTEL CASA DEL MAR** Santa Monica, California 84.14
40. **RITZ-CARLTON PHILADELPHIA** 84.13
41. **METROPOLITAN HOTEL** Vancouver 84.11
42. **FOUR SEASONS RESORT** Palm Beach, Florida 83.94
43. **BEVERLY HILLS HOTEL & BUNGALOWS** 83.88
44. **MANDARIN ORIENTAL** New York City 83.88
45. **WILLARD INTERCONTINENTAL** Washington, D.C. 83.86
46. **HOTEL TEATRO** Denver 83.75
47. **CASA MONICA HOTEL** St. Augustine, Florida 83.71
48. **THE PALAZZO** Las Vegas 83.70
49. **BELLAGIO** Las Vegas 83.64
50. **ST. REGIS** New York City 83.62

➤ SMALL CITY HOTELS (FEWER THAN 100 ROOMS)

1. **ELIOT HOTEL** Boston 93.40
2. **WATERMARK HOTEL & SPA** San Antonio, Texas 93.08
3. **AUBERGE SAINT-ANTOINE** Quebec City 87.08
4. **HOTEL BEL-AIR** Los Angeles 86.67
5. **XV BEACON** Boston 86.58
6. **WEDGEWOOD HOTEL & SPA** Vancouver 85.21
7. **BRAZILIAN COURT HOTEL & BEACH CLUB** Palm Beach 85.00
8. **PLANTERS INN** Charleston, South Carolina 84.83
9. **HÔTEL LE ST.-JAMES** Montreal 84.44
10. **MOSAIC HOTEL** Beverly Hills 84.43

➤ INNS (FEWER THAN 40 ROOMS)

1. **INN AT MANITOU** McKellar, Ontario 95.59
2. **RABBIT HILL INN** Lower Waterford, Vermont 91.19
3. **SOOKE HARBOUR HOUSE** Vancouver Island, British Columbia 90.67
4. **RUSTY PARROT LODGE & SPA** Jackson Hole, Wyoming 89.87
5. **POST RANCH INN** Big Sur, California 89.49

Nº1 CONTINENTAL U.S. + CANADA SMALL CITY HOTEL
ELIOT HOTEL, Boston

Nº1 CONTINENTAL U.S. + CANADA **LARGE CITY HOTEL**
LONDON WEST HOLLYWOOD, California

TOP 25 U.S. HOTEL SPAS

1. **HAWKS CAY RESORT** Duck Key, Florida 95.00
2. **SOLAGE CALISTOGA** California 92.55
3. **FAIRMONT SCOTTSDALE** Arizona 91.41
4. **RITZ-CARLTON BACHELOR GULCH** Beaver Creek, Colorado 91.04
5. **THE GREENBRIER** White Sulphur Springs, West Virginia 90.73
6. **AMERICAN CLUB** Kohler, Wisconsin 89.35
7. **RITZ-CARLTON NAPLES** Florida 88.83
8. **MOHONK MOUNTAIN HOUSE** New Paltz, New York 88.66
9. **RITZ-CARLTON LAGUNA NIGUEL** California 87.96
10. **TOPNOTCH RESORT & SPA** Stowe, Vermont 87.89
11. **CALISTOGA RANCH** California 87.87
12. **MONTAGE LAGUNA BEACH** California 87.67
13. **THE PHOENICIAN** Scottsdale, Arizona 87.65
14. **FAIRMONT SONOMA MISSION INN & SPA** California 87.50
15. **CAMELBACK INN, A JW MARRIOTT RESORT & SPA** Scottsdale, Arizona 87.06
16. **AUBERGE DU SOLEIL** Rutherford, California 86.85
17. **GROVE PARK INN RESORT & SPA** Asheville, North Carolina 86.54
18. **THE BREAKERS** Palm Beach, Florida 86.52
19. **WYNN LAS VEGAS** 86.40
20. **ST. REGIS MONARCH BEACH** Dana Point, California 85.80
21. **JW MARRIOTT DESERT RIDGE RESORT & SPA** Phoenix 85.78
22. **RITZ-CARLTON HALF MOON BAY** California 85.52
23. **RITZ-CARLTON AMELIA ISLAND** Florida 84.56
24. **FOUR SEASONS RESORT SCOTTSDALE AT TROON NORTH** Arizona 84.49
25. **HOTEL HERSHEY** Pennsylvania 84.47

N°1 **CONTINENTAL U.S. + CANADA HOTEL SPA**
HAWKS CAY RESORT, Duck Key, Florida

HAWAII
TOP 25 HOTELS

1. **HALEKULANI** Oahu 91.81
2. **FOUR SEASONS RESORT HUALALAI** Hawaii 90.67
3. **HOTEL HÁNA-MAUI & HONUA SPA** Maui 89.74
4. **FOUR SEASONS RESORT MAUI AT WAILEA** 87.65
5. **FOUR SEASONS RESORT LANAI AT MANELE BAY** 86.67
6. **FAIRMONT KEA LANI** Maui 86.48
7. **FOUR SEASONS RESORT LANAI, THE LODGE AT KOELE** 86.43
8. **RITZ-CARLTON KAPALUA** Maui 85.06
9. **KAHALA HOTEL & RESORT** Oahu 84.82
10. **HAPUNA BEACH PRINCE HOTEL** Hawaii 84.71
11. **GRAND HYATT KAUAI RESORT & SPA** 83.46
12. **MAUNA LANI BAY HOTEL & BUNGALOWS** Hawaii 83.40
13. **HYATT REGENCY MAUI RESORT & SPA** 83.10
14. **GRAND WAILEA, THE WALDORF ASTORIA COLLECTION** Maui 82.60
15. **WAILEA BEACH MARRIOTT RESORT & SPA** Maui 82.43
16. **FAIRMONT ORCHID** Hawaii 82.40
17. **JW MARRIOTT IHILANI RESORT & SPA** Oahu 81.84
18. **ST. REGIS PRINCEVILLE RESORT** Kauai 81.13
19. **MAUNA KEA BEACH HOTEL** Hawaii 80.42
20. **KAUAI MARRIOTT RESORT & BEACH CLUB** 79.31
21. **OUTRIGGER WAIKIKI ON THE BEACH** Oahu 79.20
22. **TURTLE BAY RESORT** Oahu 78.70
23. **WESTIN MAUI RESORT & SPA** 78.17
24. **KONA VILLAGE RESORT** Hawaii 78.14
25. **MOANA SURFRIDER, A WESTIN RESORT & SPA** Oahu 78.03

TOP 5 HOTEL SPAS

1. **FOUR SEASONS RESORT HUALALAI** Hawaii 90.43
2. **GRAND WAILEA, THE WALDORF ASTORIA COLLECTION** Maui 87.92
3. **FOUR SEASONS RESORT MAUI AT WAILEA** 85.94
4. **GRAND HYATT KAUAI RESORT & SPA** 83.26
5. **WESTIN MAUI RESORT & SPA** 83.20

Nº3 HAWAII HOTEL SPA + Nº4 HAWAII HOTEL
FOUR SEASONS RESORT MAUI AT WAILEA

N°1 CARIBBEAN HOTEL
JADE MOUNTAIN, St. Lucia

THE CARIBBEAN + BERMUDA + THE BAHAMAS

TOP 25 HOTELS

1. **JADE MOUNTAIN** St. Lucia 97.50
2. **COUPLES NEGRIL** Jamaica 92.19
3. **COUPLES SWEPT AWAY** Negril, Jamaica 91.80
4. **ANSE CHASTANET** St. Lucia 90.14
5. **EDEN ROCK** St. Bart's 89.76
6. **ROYAL PLANTATION OCHO RIOS** Jamaica 88.50
7. **COUPLES SANS SOUCI** Ocho Rios, Jamaica 88.27
8. **COUPLES TOWER ISLE** Ocho Rios, Jamaica 86.98
9. **CAP JULUCA** Anguilla 86.70
10. **FOUR SEASONS RESORT** Nevis 86.55
11. **JAMAICA INN** 86.36
12. **GRACE BAY CLUB** Turks and Caicos 85.77
13. **PETER ISLAND RESORT & SPA** British Virgin Islands 85.14
14. **JUMBY BAY, A ROSEWOOD RESORT** Antigua 84.85
15. **ONE&ONLY OCEAN CLUB** Paradise Island, Bahamas 84.39
16. **LADERA** St. Lucia 84.32
17. **RITZ-CARLTON GRAND CAYMAN** 84.17
18. **THE REEFS** Bermuda 83.33
19. **ROSEWOOD LITTLE DIX BAY** Virgin Gorda, British Virgin Islands 82.96
20. **ROCKHOUSE HOTEL** Negril, Jamaica 82.90
21. **SANDALS WHITEHOUSE EUROPEAN VILLAGE & SPA** Whitehouse, Jamaica 82.29
22. **CANEEL BAY, A ROSEWOOD RESORT** St. John, U.S. Virgin Islands 82.20
23. **HYATT REGENCY ARUBA RESORT & CASINO** 80.64
24. **ROUND HILL HOTEL & VILLAS** Montego Bay, Jamaica 80.56
25. **HALF MOON** Rose Hill, Jamaica 80.22

TOP 10 HOTEL SPAS

1. **COUPLES SANS SOUCI** Ocho Rios, Jamaica 94.54
2. **COUPLES NEGRIL** Jamaica 93.15
3. **COUPLES SWEPT AWAY** Negril, Jamaica 92.23
4. **JADE MOUNTAIN** St. Lucia 91.32
5. **PETER ISLAND RESORT & SPA** British Virgin Islands 90.18
6. **ROSEWOOD LITTLE DIX BAY** Virgin Gorda, British Virgin Islands 90.03
7. **ANSE CHASTANET** St. Lucia 89.67
8. **REGENT PALMS** Turks and Caicos 88.28
9. **HALF MOON** Rose Hill, Jamaica 87.50
10. **ROYAL PLANTATION OCHO RIOS** Jamaica 86.61

Nº1 **CARIBBEAN HOTEL SPA**
COUPLES SANS SOUCI, Ocho Rios, Jamaica

MEXICO+ CENTRAL +SOUTH AMERICA

TOP 10 HOTEL SPAS

1. **ESPERANZA, AN AUBERGE RESORT** Los Cabos, Mexico 95.80
2. **PUEBLO BONITO SUNSET BEACH RESORT & SPA** Los Cabos, Mexico 88.09
3. **RITZ-CARLTON CANCUN** Mexico 85.69
4. **JW MARRIOTT CANCÚN RESORT & SPA** Mexico 85.47
5. **FOUR SEASONS RESORT COSTA RICA AT PENINSULA PAPAGAYO** 85.34
6. **TABACÓN GRAND SPA THERMAL RESORT** Costa Rica 84.04
7. **ONE&ONLY PALMILLA** Los Cabos, Mexico 83.98
8. **LAS VENTANAS AL PARAÍSO, A ROSEWOOD RESORT** Los Cabos, Mexico 83.78
9. **ALVEAR PALACE HOTEL** Buenos Aires 82.59
10. **DREAMS CANCUN RESORT & SPA** Mexico 82.43

TOP MEXICO HOTELS

➤ RESORTS
1. **ROSEWOOD MAYAKOBÁ** Riviera Maya 93.41
2. **ESPERANZA, AN AUBERGE RESORT** Los Cabos 93.30
3. **HOTEL VILLA ROLANDI THALASSO SPA GOURMET & BEACH CLUB** Isla Mujeres 88.33
4. **LA CASA QUE CANTA** Zihuatanejo 88.06
5. **LAS MAÑANITAS** Cuernavaca 87.08
6. **RITZ-CARLTON CANCUN** 86.72
7. **LAS VENTANAS AL PARAÍSO, A ROSEWOOD RESORT** Los Cabos 85.42
8. **ONE&ONLY PALMILLA** Los Cabos 84.95
9. **THE TIDES** Zihuatanejo 84.51
10. **PUEBLO BONITO SUNSET BEACH RESORT & SPA** Los Cabos 84.42
11. **MAROMA RESORT & SPA** Riviera Maya 84.33
12. **FOUR SEASONS RESORT** Punta Mita 83.30
13. **JW MARRIOTT CANCÚN RESORT & SPA** 82.30
14. **LAS BRISAS** Acapulco 82.22
15. **ROYAL HIDEAWAY PLAYACAR** Riviera Maya 82.06

➤ CITY HOTELS
1. **FOUR SEASONS HOTEL** Mexico City 87.71
2. **CASA DE SIERRA NEVADA** San Miguel de Allende 84.18
3. **QUINTA REAL** Guadalajara 82.58
4. **CAMINO REAL POLANCO MÉXICO** Mexico City 80.60
5. **PRESIDENTE MEXICO CITY** 78.83

Nº1 MEXICO RESORT
ROSEWOOD MAYAKOBÁ, Riviera Maya

TOP CENTRAL + SOUTH AMERICA HOTELS

➤ RESORTS

1. **BLANCANEAUX LODGE** San Ignacio, Belize 88.75
2. **FOUR SEASONS RESORT** Carmelo, Uruguay 87.90
3. **EXPLORA PATAGONIA, HOTEL SALTO CHICO** Chile 87.75
4. **INKATERRA MACHU PICCHU PUEBLO HOTEL** Peru 87.30
5. **TURTLE INN** Placencia, Belize 85.99
6. **VICTORIA HOUSE** Ambergris Cay, Belize 85.65
7. **HOTEL PUNTA ISLITA** Guanacaste, Costa Rica 85.58
8. **FOUR SEASONS RESORT COSTA RICA AT PENINSULA PAPAGAYO** 85.20
9. **LLAO LLAO HOTEL & RESORT GOLF-SPA** Bariloche, Argentina 83.55
10. **XANDARI RESORT & SPA** Central Valley, Costa Rica 83.16

➤ CITY HOTELS

1. **PALACIO DUHAU-PARK HYATT** Buenos Aires 94.68
2. **ALVEAR PALACE HOTEL** Buenos Aires 89.22
3. **HOTEL CASA SANTO DOMINGO** Antigua, Guatemala 88.59
4. **HOTEL MONASTERIO** Cuzco, Peru 87.87
5. **FOUR SEASONS HOTEL** Buenos Aires 86.40
6. **RITZ-CARLTON SANTIAGO** Chile 86.08
7. **HOTEL ORO VERDE** Guayaquil, Ecuador 84.54
8. **JW MARRIOTT HOTEL** Rio de Janeiro 84.39
9. **PARK TOWER, A LUXURY COLLECTION HOTEL** Buenos Aires 84.30
10. **BRISTOL** Panama City 84.00

Nº5 CENTRAL + SOUTH AMERICA RESORT
TURTLE INN, Placencia, Belize

EUROPE

TOP HOTELS

➤ LARGE CITY HOTELS
1. **GRAND HOTEL BAGLIONI** Bologna, Italy 92.83
2. **CEYLAN INTERCONTINENTAL** Istanbul 90.90
3. **MARRIOTT HOTEL** Budapest 90.76
4. **WESTIN PALACE** Milan 90.16
5. **FOUR SEASONS HOTEL** Prague 89.69
6. **HÔTEL PLAZA ATHÉNÉE** Paris 89.35
7. **HÔTEL LE ROYAL** Luxembourg 89.08
8. **HOTEL VIER JAHRESZEITEN KEMPINSKI** Munich 89.04
9. **ART'OTEL** Budapest 88.73
10. **FOUR SEASONS HOTEL GEORGE V** Paris 88.26
11. **RITZ PARIS** 88.11
12. **G HOTEL** Galway, Ireland 87.00
13. **HOTEL SACHER WIEN** Vienna 86.59
14. **THE CONNAUGHT** London 86.00
15. **HÔTEL LE MEURICE** Paris 85.62

➤ SMALL CITY HOTELS
1. **SOFITEL BERLIN GENDARMENMARKT** 89.04
2. **THE GORING** London 88.51
3. **HOTEL POD RÓZA** Kraków, Poland 88.04
4. **GRAND HOTEL VILLA CORA** Florence 86.22
5. **41** London 85.88
6. **HOTEL D'INGHILTERRA** Rome 85.61
7. **HOTEL J. K. PLACE** Florence 85.45
8. **HOTEL GOLDENER HIRSCH, A LUXURY COLLECTION HOTEL** Salzburg, Austria 85.21
9. **GRAND HOTEL PALACE** Rome 84.85
10. **MILESTONE HOTEL** London 84.41

➤ RESORTS
1. **IL SAN PIETRO** Positano, Italy 91.39
2. **CONVENTO DO ESPINHEIRO, A LUXURY COLLECTION HOTEL & SPA** Evora, Portugal 87.50
3. **HOTEL VILLA SANT'ANDREA** Taormina, Italy 86.94
4. **MOUNT JULIET ESTATE** County Kilkenny, Ireland 86.28
5. **GRAND HOTEL TIMEO** Taormina, Italy 86.27
6. **HOTEL EXCELSIOR** Venice 86.19
7. **HOTEL CARUSO BELVEDERE** Ravello, Italy 86.14
8. **SEILER HOTEL MONTE ROSA** Zermatt, Switzerland 86.10
9. **GRAND HOTEL PARK** Gstaad, Switzerland 86.06
10. **SUVRETTA HOUSE** St. Moritz, Switzerland 85.42

➤ INNS AND SMALL COUNTRY HOTELS
1. **DOMAINE DES HAUTS DE LOIRE** Onzain, France 91.79
2. **CHÂTEAU EZA** Èze Village, France 89.85
3. **LA ROSA DEI VENTI** Positano, Italy 88.75
4. **HOTEL LA POSTA VECCHIA** Ladispoli, Italy 88.31
5. **CLIVEDEN HOUSE HOTEL** Berkshire, England 88.00
6. **CHÂTEAU DE LA CHÈVRE D'OR** Èze Village, France 87.90
7. **L'OUSTAU DE BAUMANIÈRE** Les Baux-de-Provence, France 86.43
8. **VILLA PISANI** Padua, Italy 85.77
9. **HOTEL LA SCALINATELLA** Capri, Italy 85.44
10. **GRAND HOTEL A VILLA FELTRINELLI** Gargnano, Italy 83.88

Nº1 **EUROPE RESORT**
IL SAN PIETRO, Positano, Italy

AFRICA
+THE MIDDLE EAST

TOP HOTELS

➤ LODGES AND RESORTS
1. **BUSHMANS KLOOF** Cedar Mountains, South Africa 98.67
2. **EARTH LODGE AT SABI SABI PRIVATE GAME RESERVE** Kruger National Park, South Africa 97.50
3. **SINGITA SABI SAND** Kruger National Park, South Africa 95.52
4. **GOVERNORS' CAMP** Masai Mara, Kenya 94.82
5. **JACK'S CAMP** Makgadkgadi Pans, Botswana 94.72
6. **KIRAWIRA LUXURY TENTED CAMP** Serengeti National Park, Tanzania 94.63
7. **EAGLE ISLAND CAMP** Moremi Game Reserve, Botswana 94.17
8. **SINGITA GRUMETI RESERVES** Serengeti National Park, Tanzania 93.75
9. **LION SANDS PRIVATE GAME RESERVE** Kruger National Park, South Africa 93.28
10. **ROYAL MALEWANE** Kruger National Park, South Africa 93.15
11. **SHAMWARI GAME RESERVE** Eastern Cape, South Africa 93.00
12. **SINGITA KRUGER NATIONAL PARK** South Africa 92.86
13. **GIRAFFE MANOR** Nairobi 92.68
14. **LONDOLOZI PRIVATE GAME RESERVE** Kruger National Park, South Africa 92.68
15. **KICHWA TEMBO** Masai Mara, Kenya 91.86
16. **KHWAI RIVER LODGE** Moremi Game Reserve, Botswana 91.71
17. **TORTILIS CAMP** Amboseli Game Reserve, Kenya 91.28
18. **NGORONGORO CRATER LODGE** Tanzania 90.97
19. **LE QUARTIER FRANÇAIS** Franschhoek Valley, South Africa 90.79
20. **MOMBO AND LITTLE MOMBO CAMPS** Moremi Game Reserve, Botswana 90.42

➤ CITY HOTELS
1. **TWELVE APOSTLES HOTEL & SPA** Cape Town 93.91
2. **THE SAXON** Johannesburg 92.86
3. **FOUR SEASONS HOTEL CAIRO AT THE FIRST RESIDENCE** Egypt 91.86
4. **CAPE GRACE** Cape Town 90.90
5. **FOUR SEASONS HOTEL ALEXANDRIA AT SAN STEFANO** Egypt 89.56

N°2 AFRICA + THE MIDDLE EAST **CITY HOTEL**
THE SAXON, Johannesburg

N°2 ASIA HOTEL SPA + N°4 ASIA RESORT
FOUR SEASONS RESORT, Chiang Mai, Thailand

ASIA

TOP HOTELS

➤ RESORTS

1. **OBEROI VANYAVILAS** Ranthambhore, India 98.00
2. **FOUR SEASONS TENTED CAMP GOLDEN TRIANGLE** Chiang Rai, Thailand 95.00
3. **OBEROI UDAIVILAS** Udaipur, India 94.88
4. **FOUR SEASONS RESORT** Chiang Mai, Thailand 93.33
5. **OBEROI AMARVILAS** Agra, India 92.91
6. **ANANTARA DHIGU RESORT & SPA** Maldives 92.14
7. **AMANKORA PARO** Bhutan 91.25
8. **ANANTARA GOLDEN TRIANGLE** Chiang Rai, Thailand 91.16
9. **SHANGRI-LA'S TANJUNG ARU RESORT & SPA** Kota Kinabalu, Malaysia 90.98
10. **OBEROI RAJVILAS** Jaipur, India 90.40
11. **TAJ LAKE PALACE** Udaipur, India 89.87
12. **LE MÉRIDIEN PHUKET BEACH RESORT** Thailand 89.75
13. **AYANA RESORT & SPA (FORMERLY THE RITZ-CARLTON BALI RESORT & SPA)** Bali 89.69
14. **RAMBAGH PALACE** Jaipur, India 89.61
15. **MANDARIN ORIENTAL DHARA DHEVI** Chiang Mai, Thailand 89.55

➤ CITY HOTELS

1. **MANDARIN ORIENTAL** Bangkok 93.34
2. **ISLAND SHANGRI-LA** Hong Kong 92.75
3. **PENINSULA HONG KONG** 92.23
4. **PUDONG SHANGRI-LA** Shanghai 91.30
5. **WESTIN BUND CENTER** Shanghai 90.82
6. **PENINSULA BANGKOK** 90.55
7. **RITZ-CARLTON BEIJING, FINANCIAL STREET** 90.52
8. **ST. REGIS** Shanghai 90.44
9. **FOUR SEASONS HOTEL** Shanghai 90.35
10. **FOUR SEASONS HOTEL TOKYO AT CHINZAN-SO** 89.69
11. **SHANGRI-LA'S FAR EASTERN PLAZA HOTEL** Taipei 89.55
12. **LE MÉRIDIEN** Bangkok 89.48
13. **FOUR SEASONS HOTEL** Hong Kong 89.25
14. **PARK HYATT** Beijing 89.19
15. **PAN PACIFIC** Singapore 89.02
16. **TAJ MAHAL PALACE & TOWER** Mumbai 88.95
17. **KOWLOON SHANGRI-LA** Hong Kong 88.93
18. **DUSITD2** Chiang Mai, Thailand 88.60
19. **SHANGRI-LA HOTEL** Bangkok 88.58
20. **THE REGENT** Beijing 88.37
21. **PENINSULA BEIJING** 87.94
22. **CHINA WORLD HOTEL** Beijing 87.72
23. **FOUR SEASONS HOTEL** Bangkok 87.69
24. **CONRAD** Hong Kong 87.67
25. **MANDARIN ORIENTAL** Hong Kong 87.50

TOP 10 HOTEL SPAS

1. **ANANTARA KOH SAMUI RESORT & SPA** Thailand 95.07
2. **FOUR SEASONS RESORT** Chiang Mai, Thailand 94.96
3. **PENINSULA HONG KONG** 94.69
4. **MANDARIN ORIENTAL** Bangkok 94.61
5. **ANANTARA HUA HIN RESORT & SPA** Thailand 94.21
6. **MANDARIN ORIENTAL DHARA DHEVI** Chiang Mai, Thailand 92.19
7. **SHANGRI-LA HOTEL** Bangkok 91.80
8. **SHANGRI-LA'S RASA SAYANG RESORT & SPA** Penang, Malaysia 91.52
9. **SHANGRI-LA'S TANJUNG ARU RESORT & SPA** Kota Kinabalu, Malaysia 91.15
10. **PENINSULA BANGKOK** 90.63

N°3 ASIA RESORT
OBEROI UDAIVILAS, Udaipur, India

Nº1 AUSTRALIA + NEW ZEALAND + THE SOUTH PACIFIC **LODGE OR RESORT**
LODGE AT KAURI CLIFFS, North Island, New Zealand

AUSTRALIA +
NEW ZEALAND +
SOUTH PACIFIC

TOP HOTELS

➤ LODGES AND RESORTS

1. **LODGE AT KAURI CLIFFS** North Island, New Zealand 93.75
2. **FARM AT CAPE KIDNAPPERS** North Island, New Zealand 93.33
3. **LILIANFELS BLUE MOUNTAINS RESORT & SPA** New South Wales, Australia 88.54
4. **HAYMAN** Great Barrier Reef, Australia 86.80
5. **INTERCONTINENTAL BORA BORA RESORT & THALASSO SPA** French Polynesia 86.56
6. **VOYAGES LONGITUDE 131°** Yulara, Australia 84.56
7. **LIZARD ISLAND RESORT** Great Barrier Reef, Australia 83.75
8. **HUKA LODGE** Taupo, New Zealand 83.53
9. **KEWARRA BEACH RESORT** Cairns, Australia 78.97
10. **TREETOPS LODGE & WILDERNESS EXPERIENCE** Rotorua, New Zealand 77.86

➤ CITY HOTELS

1. **THE LANGHAM** Melbourne 87.69
2. **CROWN TOWERS** Melbourne 85.95
3. **SHANGRI-LA HOTEL** Sydney 85.80
4. **WESTIN AUCKLAND LIGHTER QUAY** New Zealand 85.31
5. **OBSERVATORY HOTEL** Sydney 84.16
6. **PARK HYATT** Sydney 83.87
7. **FOUR SEASONS HOTEL** Sydney 83.27
8. **INTERCONTINENTAL** Sydney 83.27
9. **SYDNEY HARBOUR MARRIOTT HOTEL AT CIRCULAR QUAY** 82.86
10. **THE GEORGE** Christchurch, New Zealand 82.43
11. **SOFITEL MELBOURNE ON COLLINS** 81.66
12. **SOFITEL QUEENSTOWN HOTEL & SPA** New Zealand 80.23
13. **WESTIN SYDNEY** 78.00
14. **PARK HYATT** Melbourne 77.52
15. **HILTON** Auckland, New Zealand 77.19

N°2 AUSTRALIA + NEW ZEALAND + THE SOUTH PACIFIC **LODGE OR RESORT**
FARM AT CAPE KIDNAPPERS, North Island, New Zealand

At the Ace Hotel & Swim Club,
in Palm Springs, California.

HOTELS DIRECTORY

This geographically organized guide includes all the properties profiled in the book and in the World's Best Awards, as well as the 2010 edition of the T+L 500—a list of the 500 highest-rated places to stay in the world as determined by *Travel + Leisure* readers.

HAWAII

Kauai
Oahu
Lanai — Maui
Big Island

VANCOUVER
ISLAND

Whistler
Vancouver
Whidbey Island
Seattle

Banff
Lake Louise

Cannon Beach
Portland

Gold Beach

Jackson Hole

NAPA/SONOMA
San Francisco
Half Moon Bay
San Martin
Pebble Beach
Carmel
Big Sur

Park City

Beaver Creek
Vail
Aspen
Denver

Colorado Springs

Las Vegas

Santa Barbara
Ojai
LOS ANGELES AREA
ORANGE COUNTY
SAN DIEGO AREA

Pasadena

Palm Springs
Escondido

Sedona

Santa Fe

PHOENIX/SCOTTSDALE AREA
San Antonio

Tucson

San Antonio

UNITED STATES
+ CANADA

Quebec City

McKellar

Montreal
Stowe • Lower Waterford
Warren
ADIRONDACKS
Freeport
Kennebunkport

Minneapolis/St. Paul
Arcadia

Lenox
Boston
CAPE COD — Provincetown
Newport • Nantucket

Kohler

New Paltz
Southold
Hawley
New York City

Chicago

Hershey
Philadelphia

Cape May
Washington, D.C.
Washington

Irvington

White Sulphur Springs

Raleigh/Durham

Nashville

Asheville

Atlanta

Charleston
Kiawah Island
Bluffton

DALLAS AREA

Sea Island
Cumberland Island
Amelia Island
Ponte Vedra

Austin

St. Augustine

Houston
Santa Rosa Beach
Orlando

New Orleans

Palm Beach

Bonita Springs
Naples — MIAMI AREA

FLORIDA KEYS

The Grill restaurant at Hacienda del Sol Guest Ranch Resort, in Tucson, Arizona.

ARIZONA

PHOENIX/SCOTTSDALE AREA

Camelback Inn, A JW Marriott Resort & Spa Recently renovated casitas with views of Camelback Mountain, and a spa renowned for its hot-stone massages. 5402 E. Lincoln Dr., Scottsdale; 800/242-2635 or 480/948-1700; camelback inn.com; doubles from $$.

Fairmont Scottsdale Moorish-inspired compound on 450 acres, featuring the 44,000-square-foot Willow Stream Spa. 7575 E. Princess Dr., Scottsdale; 866/540-4495 or 480/585-4848; fairmont. com; doubles from $$.

Four Seasons Resort at Troon North A 210-room Pueblo-inspired complex close to high desert trails. 10600 E. Crescent Moon Dr., Scottsdale; 800/332-3442 or 480/515-5700; fourseasons.com; doubles from $$$.

JW Marriott Desert Ridge Resort & Spa The largest resort in Arizona; the spa uses indigenous ingredients. 5350 E. Marriott Dr., Phoenix; 800/835-6206 or 480/293-5000; jwdesertridgeresort.com; doubles from $$.

The Phoenician Classic resort on 250 acres for the golf-and-tennis set. 6000 E. Camelback Rd., Scottsdale; 800/888-8234 or 480/941-8200; thephoenician.com; doubles from $$.

Royal Palms Resort & Spa Formerly a private residence, a 1929 Spanish-colonial hotel with flower-filled courtyards and an open-air spa. 5200 E. Camelback Rd., Phoenix; 800/672-6011 or 602/840-3610; royalpalmsresortandspa. com; doubles from $$.

Sanctuary on Camelback Mountain Cluster of 105 casitas with contemporary interiors and a new bar on Camelback Mountain's northern slope. 5700 E. McDonald Dr., Paradise Valley; 800/245-2051 or 480/948-2100; sanctuaryaz.com; doubles from $$$.

SEDONA

Enchantment Resort Adobe-style resort in a red-rock canyon, offering Native American–inspired activities (pottery lessons, hikes to sacred ruins) and access to the award-winning Mii amo spa. 800/826-4180 or 928/282-2900; enchantment resort.com; doubles from $$.

Mii amo, A Destination Spa at Enchantment World-class treatments at a 14-casita, two-suite hideaway within a resort. 888/749-2137 or 928/203-8500; miiamo. com; doubles from $$$$, all-inclusive, three-night minimum.

TUCSON

Canyon Ranch in Tucson Innovative classes and an integrated approach to wellness at a veteran destination spa in the Sonoran Desert. 800/742-9000 or 520/749-9000; canyonranch.com; doubles from $$$$$, all-inclusive, four-night minimum.

Hacienda del Sol Guest Ranch Resort Carved-beam ceilings, Saltillo-tile floors, and an acclaimed restaurant add up to a romantic and historic desert hideaway. 5601 N. Hacienda del Sol Rd.; 800/728-6514 or 520/299-1501; haciendadelsol.com; doubles from $.

Miraval Arizona Set at the base of the Santa Catalina Mountains, with a forthcoming wellness center to be overseen by Dr. Andrew Weil. 800/232-3969 or 520/825-4000; miravalresort.com; doubles from $$$$, all-inclusive.

CALIFORNIA

BIG SUR

Post Ranch Inn Along a ridge above the ocean, 41 rooms in wood houses with glass and slate details. 800/527-2200 or 831/667-2200; postranchinn.com; doubles from $$$.

Treebones Resort Sixteen yurts and a guesthouse overlooking one of the most dramatic stretches of the Pacific Coast. 877/424-4787 or 805/927-2390; treebonesresort. com; doubles from $.

Ventana Inn & Spa Rugged-luxe lodges and a renovated organic restaurant surrounded by forest. 800/628-6500 or 831/667-2331; ventanainn.com; doubles from $$$.

KEY TO THE PRICE ICONS   **$** UNDER $250   **$$** $250–$499   **$$$** $500–$749   **$$$$** $750–$999   **$$$$$** $1,000 AND UP

CARMEL

L'Auberge Carmel Twenty-room hotel four blocks from Carmel Beach; the restaurant has a 4,500-bottle wine cellar. 831/624-8578; laubergecarmel.com; doubles from $$.

Tickle Pink Inn The 34 oversize rooms have private balconies with views of the Pacific. 800/635-4774 or 831/624-1244; ticklepinkinn.com; doubles from $$.

ESCONDIDO

Golden Door Modeled after an ancient Japanese inn, a legendary destination spa on 377 acres of landscaped grounds with koi ponds. 800/424-0777 or 760/744-5777; goldendoor.com; doubles from $$$$, all-inclusive, seven-night minimum.

HALF MOON BAY

Ritz-Carlton A 16,000-square-foot spa, two golf courses, and 261 rooms on a bluff that drops away to the ocean. 800/241-3333 or 650/712-7000; ritzcarlton.com; doubles from $$.

LOS ANGELES AREA

Beverly Hills Hotel & Bungalows Two new bungalows will open this year at the "Pink Palace," a gathering spot for the Hollywood elite since 1912. 9641 Sunset Blvd., Beverly Hills; 800/650-1842 or 310/276-2251; beverlyhillshotel.com; doubles from $$.

Chateau Marmont Owned by hotel impresario André Balazs, a 1927 hilltop castle where boldfaced names hide away. 8221 Sunset Blvd., Hollywood; 800/242-8328 or 323/656-1010; chateaumarmont.com; doubles from $$.

Four Seasons Hotel Los Angeles at Beverly Hills Classic Beverly Hills tower known for impeccable service and its prime location near Rodeo Drive and Robertson Boulevard. 300 S. Doheny Dr., Los Angeles; 800/332-3442 or 310/786-2227; fourseasons.com; doubles from $$.

Hotel Bel-Air Cloistered retreat on Stone Canyon, now part of the luxury hotel company Dorchester Collection. 701 Stone Canyon Rd., Los Angeles; 800/650-1842 or 310/472-1211; hotelbelair.com; doubles from $$. Closed for renovations until mid 2011.

Hotel Casa del Mar Oceanfront Spanish colonial–style hotel with hydrotherapy tubs in all 129 rooms and a new 2,580-square-foot spa. 1910 Ocean Way, Santa Monica; 800/898-6999 or 310/581-5533; hotelcasadelmar.com; doubles from $$$.

London West Hollywood All-suite property in the Hollywood Hills with a Gordon Ramsay restaurant and a concierge team that promises access to L.A.'s hip haunts. 1020 N. San Vicente Blvd., West Hollywood; 866/282-4560 or 310/854-1111; thelondonwesthollywood.com; doubles from $.

Montage Beverly Hills Glamorous and gilded, a mix of Old Hollywood and nouveau L.A. 225 N. Canon Dr., Beverly Hills; 888/860-0788 or 310/860-7800; montagebeverlyhills.com; doubles from $$.

Mosaic Hotel Unassuming 49-room boutique hotel, beloved for its service and proximity to Rodeo Drive. 125 S. Spalding Dr., Beverly Hills; 800/463-4466 or 310/278-0303; mosaichotel.com; doubles from $$.

Peninsula Beverly Hills Luxe 196-room property with a rooftop pool and a handsome bar. 9882 S. Santa Monica Blvd., Beverly Hills; 866/382-8388 or 310/551-2888; peninsula.com; doubles from $$$.

Raffles L'Ermitage Beverly Hills Eight-story building with 119 rooms and a bar decorated with famed movie scripts. 9291 Burton Way, Beverly Hills; 800/768-9009 or 310/278-3344; raffles.com; doubles from $$$.

NAPA/SONOMA

Auberge du Soleil Compound of Mediterranean–style cottages with 52 light-filled rooms (each has a soaking tub and private terrace), a French restaurant, and a 17,000-bottle wine cellar. Rutherford; 800/348-5406 or 707/963-1211; aubergedusoleil.com; doubles from $$$$.

The Bathhouse spa at Calistoga Ranch, in California.

The 60-foot garden pool at California's Hotel Healdsburg.

Bardessono Sustainability meets style at this 62-room hotel, which is proud of its commitment to the environment. Yountville; 877/932-5333 or 707/204-6000; bardessono.com; doubles from $$$$.

Calistoga Ranch Wood-and-stone lodges overlooking a lake in a private, oak-tree–filled canyon. Calistoga; 800/942-4220 or 707/254-2800; calistogaranch.com; doubles from $$$$.

Fairmont Sonoma Mission Inn & Spa Sprawling resort with a vast array of amenities, including a spa with ayurvedic and mineral-water treatments. Sonoma; 866/540-4499 or 707/938-9000; fairmont.com; doubles from $$.

Hotel Healdsburg Co-owned by chef Charlie Palmer, this minimalist 55-room hotel is all about the details—teak beds with Frette linens, glass walk-in showers, and spacious balconies. Healdsburg; 800/889-7188 or 707/431-2800; hotelhealdsburg.com; doubles from $$.

Solage Calistoga Eco-focused wine-country resort with mud massages and complimentary cruiser bikes. Calistoga; 866/942-7442 or 707/226-0800; solagecalistoga.com; doubles from $$.

OJAI
The Oaks at Ojai Classic weight-loss regimen, plus pampering treatments, at this destination spa near Santa Barbara. 800/753-6257 or 805/646-5573; oaksspa.com; doubles from $, all-inclusive, two-night minimum on weekends.

ORANGE COUNTY
Montage Laguna Beach Craftsman-style resort with early California artwork on display; a meandering path leads to the beach below. Laguna Beach; 866/271-6953 or 949/715-6000; montagelagunabeach.com; doubles from $$$.

Ritz-Carlton Laguna Niguel Above a legendary wave break, this 396-room resort caters to both surfers and sybarites. Dana Point; 800/241-3333 or 949/240-2000; ritzcarlton.com; doubles from $$.

St. Regis Monarch Beach Tuscan-inspired resort with extensive spa offerings and the largest standard rooms in Orange County. Dana Point; 877/787-3447 or 949/234-3200; stregismonarchbeach.com; doubles from $$$.

PASADENA
Langham Huntington 1907 grande dame with multiple wings and 19th-century English-style common areas (large porcelain vases, gold vaulted ceilings). 800/591-7481 or 626/568-3900; langhamhotels.com; doubles from $.

PALM SPRINGS
Ace Hotel & Swim Club The gold standard of hip budget hotels, with a laid-back, retro-bohemian vibe. 760/325-9900; acehotel.com; doubles from $.

PEBBLE BEACH
Inn at Spanish Bay Amid Monterey pines and next to the famed golf course, with Spanish influences in rooms and restaurant interiors. 800/654-9300 or 831/647-7500; pebblebeach.com; doubles from $$$, two-night minimum required to play Pebble Beach Golf Links.

Lodge at Pebble Beach A 161-room resort best known for the caliber of its on-site golf course (ocean-view rooms look onto the 18th green). 800/654-9300 or 831/624-3811; pebblebeach.com; doubles from $$$, two-night minimum required to play Pebble Beach Golf Links.

SAN DIEGO AREA
Four Seasons Resort Aviara This seaside Spanish colonial has terraced rooms and an Arnold Palmer–designed golf course. Carlsbad; 800/332-3442 or 760/603-6800; fourseasons.com; doubles from $$.

Grand Del Mar Two-year-old property swathed in Italian marble—plus hiking trails, golf, and a kid-friendly pool. Carmel Valley; 888/314-2030 or 858/314-2000; thegranddelmar.com; doubles from $$.

La Valencia Hotel Boutique hideaway filled with murals and mosaics, in a tiny suburb. La Jolla; 800/451-0772 or 858/454-0771; lavalencia.com; doubles from $$.

Rancho Valencia Resort & Spa All-suite property with an award-winning Spanish-Mediterranean restaurant, a 10,000-square-foot spa, and 18 tennis courts. Rancho Santa Fe; 800/548-3664 or 858/756-1123; ranchovalencia.com; doubles from $$$.

SAN FRANCISCO

Four Seasons Hotel A head-to-toe renovation in 2009 perked up the plush high-rise; rooms have floor-to-ceiling windows, granite credenzas, and Eames chairs. 757 Market St.; 800/332-3442 or 415/633-3000; fourseasons.com; doubles from $$.

Huntington Hotel & Nob Hill Spa Reigning over the neighborhood since 1924, this classic property has 136 spacious rooms and complimentary tea at check-in. 1075 California St.; 800/227-4683 or 415/474-5400; huntingtonhotel. com; doubles from $$.

Mandarin Oriental Hotel with Asian influences on the top 11 floors of an ultramodern Financial District tower. 222 Sansome St.; 800/526-6566 or 415/276-9888; mandarin oriental.com; doubles from $$$.

Omni San Francisco Hotel In genteel Nob Hill, Florentine Renaissance-style architecture; guided history walks are available free of charge. 500 California St.; 888/444-6664 or 415/677-9494; omnihotels.com; doubles from $.

Ritz-Carlton Impressive columned hotel with 336 rooms, all with 400-thread-count sheets and rain showers. 600 Stockton St.; 800/241-3333 or 415/296-7465; ritzcarlton. com; doubles from $$.

St. Regis Art-filled spaces draw a dapper crowd to this Yerba Buena hot spot. 125 Third St.; 877/787-3447 or 415/284-4000; stregis.com; doubles from $$$.

SAN MARTIN

CordeValle, A Rosewood Resort Sprawling property that encompasses a 260-acre golf course and an on-site winery. 888/767-3966 or 408/695-4500; rosewoodhotels. com; doubles from $$.

SANTA BARBARA

Four Seasons Resort The Biltmore Ivy-covered property on Butterfly Beach with 1920's-style tiles and gardens. 800/332-3442 or 805/969-2261; fourseasons.com; doubles from $$$.

San Ysidro Ranch, A Rosewood Resort Clusters of cottages around a quaint clapboard main house in posh Montecito. 888/767-3966 or 805/565-1700; rosewoodhotels. com; doubles from $$$.

COLORADO
ASPEN

Hotel Jerome, A RockResort Meticulously preserved 1889 hotel with 94 rooms and four restaurants serving food with locally sourced ingredients. 888/367-7625 or 970/920-1000; rockresorts.com; doubles from $$$.

Little Nell Slopeside landmark now with a more contemporary look, thanks to an $18 million redo last year. 888/843-6355 or 970/920-4600; thelittlenell.com; doubles from $$$$.

St. Regis Resort Brick compound offering impeccable service two blocks from Aspen Mountain's gondola. 877/787-3447 or 970/920-3300; stregis.com; doubles from $$$$$.

BEAVER CREEK

Park Hyatt Beaver Creek Resort & Spa Just yards from two lifts, this contemporary stone-and-timber ski lodge also has a 30,000-square-foot spa. 800/233-1234 or 970/949-1234; park.hyatt.com; doubles from $$.

Ritz-Carlton Bachelor Gulch A 180-room timbered lodge that has its own ski shop and chairlift. 800/241-3333 or 970/748-6200; ritzcarlton. com; doubles from $$$$.

COLORADO SPRINGS

The Broadmoor Lakeside resort on 3,000 acres catering to active families with horseback riding, rock climbing, and fly-fishing. 866/837-9520 or 719/634-7711; broadmoor.com; doubles from $$.

DENVER

Brown Palace Hotel & Spa Downtown landmark known for hosting American presidents; the property's 1,320-square-foot state-of-the-art fitness center was recently refreshed. 321 17th St.; 800/321-2599 or 303/297-3111; brownpalace.com; doubles from $.

Hotel Teatro Renaissance Revival building filled with fascinating theater memorabilia. 1100 14th St.; 888/727-1200 or 303/228-1100; hotelteatro.com; doubles from $$.

VAIL

Sonnenalp Resort Bavarian-style hotel with an air of old-world authenticity, right down to its dirndl-clad staff. 800/654-8312 or 970/476-5656; sonnenalp.com; doubles from $$$.

DISTRICT OF COLUMBIA

Four Seasons Hotel Newly renovated rooms in a red-brick mansion on the eastern edge of Georgetown. 2800 Pennsylvania Ave. NW; 800/332-3442 or 202/342-0444; fourseasons.com; doubles from $$$.

The Hay-Adams 1928 grande dame—named for two former residents, a secretary of state and a well-known author—directly across from the White House. 16th and H Sts. NW; 800/424-5054 or 202/638-6600; hayadams.com; doubles from $$.

Willard InterContinental Beginning in 2007, this 1901 Beaux-Arts icon became completely powered by wind energy; it's also been a D.C. favorite since the Roosevelt era. 1401 Pennsylvania Ave. NW; 800/327-0200 or 202/628-9100; intercontinental.com; doubles from $$.

FLORIDA
AMELIA ISLAND

Ritz-Carlton A 444-room resort on a barrier island; at the pool,

---

KEY TO THE PRICE ICONS   **$** UNDER $250   **$$** $250–$499   **$$$** $500–$749   **$$$$** $750–$999   **$$$$$** $1,000 AND UP

staffers circulate with chilled towels and ice water. 800/241-3333 or 904/277-1100; ritzcarlton.com; doubles from $.

BONITA SPRINGS
Hyatt Regency Coconut Point Resort & Spa Located halfway between Naples and Fort Myers; the resort's child-friendly perks include a 140-foot slide and a climbing wall. 800/233-1234 or 239/444-1234; hyatt.com; doubles from $$.

FLORIDA KEYS
Hawks Cay Resort Family-oriented water world with a dolphin center and a marina, plus a 7,000-square-foot spa. Duck Key; 800/432-2242 or 305/743-7000; hawkscay.com; doubles from $$.

Marquesa Hotel A 27-room clapboard compound flanked by tropical gardens, a block from Duval Street. Key West; 800/869-4631 or 305/292-1919; marquesa.com; doubles from $$.

Sunset Key Guest Cottages, a Westin Resort Series of charming tin-roofed cottages on Sunset Key, 500 yards west of Key West and accessible by ferry. 800/228-3000 or 305/292-5300; westin.com; doubles from $$$.

MIAMI AREA
Canyon Ranch Hotel & Spa in Miami Beach Residential touches in guest rooms, and the ne plus ultra of hotel spas. 6801 Collins Ave.; 800/742-9000; canyonranch.com; doubles from $$.

Fontainebleau Miami Beach Midcentury design icon that just underwent an elaborate renovation, including the construction of a 37-story tower. 4441 Collins Ave.; 800/548-8886 or 305/538-2000; fontainebleau.com; doubles from $$.

Mondrian in South Beach Imaginative flourishes from noted Dutch designer Marcel Wanders, including trompe l'oeil bathroom tiles. 1100 West Ave.; 800/697-1791 or 305/514-1500; morganshotelgroup.com; doubles from $$.

The Setai Art Deco landmark with an adjacent tower. Three pools are heated to varying temperatures and lead the way to the ocean. 2001 Collins Ave.; 888/625-7500 or 305/520-6000; setai.com; doubles from $$$$$.

Viceroy Miami Part of a downtown complex; eclectic Kelly Wearstler interiors meet a white-on-white Philippe Starck–designed spa. 485 Brickell Ave.; 866/781-9923 or 305/503-4400; viceroymiami.com; doubles from $$.

NAPLES
Ritz-Carlton Mediterranean-inspired beachfront resort with a 51,000-square-foot spa, access to premier golf, and a kid-friendly entertainment center. 800/241-3300 or 239/598-3300; ritzcarlton.com; doubles from $$.

ORLANDO
Ritz-Carlton Orlando, Grande Lakes Fourteen-story tower modeled after an Italian palazzo,

with a Greg Norman–designed golf course. 800/241-3333 or 407/206-2400; ritzcarlton.com; doubles from $$.

PALM BEACH
Brazilian Court Hotel & Beach Club Eighty British-colonial rooms, a restaurant by star chef Daniel Boulud, and a new oceanfront beach club. 800/552-0335 or 561/655-7740; braziliancourt.com; doubles from $$$.

The Breakers Italianate legend on the ocean, with a foodie focus (nine restaurants), a serious pedigree, and a surprisingly unstuffy atmosphere. 888/273-2537 or 561/655-6611; thebreakers.com; doubles from $$.

Four Seasons Resort Low-rise beachside property with an old-world feel (sandstone flooring, a marble staircase), 15 minutes from downtown. 800/332-3442 or 561/582-2800; fourseasons.com; doubles from $$.

PONTE VEDRA
Ponte Vedra Inn & Club 1928 golf-and-tennis resort on a 300-acre oceanfront site 20 miles southeast of Jacksonville. 800/234-7842 or 904/285-1111; pvresorts.com; doubles from $$.

ST. AUGUSTINE
Casa Monica Hotel 1888 landmark that's designed to look like a Moorish castle, in the heart of St. Augustine. 800/648-1888 or 904/827-1888; casamonica.com; doubles from $.

SANTA ROSA BEACH
WaterColor Inn & Resort Urbanist enclave with David Rockwell–designed interiors and access to a coastal lake. 866/426-2656 or 850/534-5000; watercolorresort.com; doubles from $$.

GEORGIA
ATLANTA
InterContinental Buckhead All the amenities of a business hotel, plus Jurlique products in the spa and a private chef's table. 3315 Peachtree Rd.; 800/327-0200 or 404/946-9000; intercontinental.com; doubles from $.

Mansion on Peachtree, A Rosewood Hotel & Residence Neoclassical limestone tower with polished interiors and a well-trained staff. 3376 Peachtree Rd. N.E.; 888/767-3966 or 404/995-7500; rwmansiononpeachtree.com; doubles from $.

Ritz-Carlton, Buckhead Renovated high-rise near the city's best shopping. 3434 Peachtree Rd.; 800/241-3333 or 404/237-2700; ritzcarlton.com; doubles from $$.

CUMBERLAND ISLAND
Greyfield Inn Romantic 16-room retreat on a largely undeveloped barrier isle. 866/401-8581 or 904/261-6408; greyfieldinn.com; doubles from $$$, including meals and boat transfer from mainland.

SEA ISLAND
The Cloister Long a favorite of the East Coast Establishment; a mansion set on 1,000 acres of a

Views of Biscayne Bay from the Sunset Lounge at Florida's Mondrian in South Beach.

barrier island. 800/732-4752 or 912/638-3611; seaisland.com; doubles from $$$$.

Lodge at Sea Island Golf Club
English country-manor style meets Southern hospitality, overlooking fairways and the coastline. 800/732-4752 or 912/638-3611; seaisland.com; doubles from $$$.

HAWAII
BIG ISLAND
Fairmont Orchid Kohala Coast resort known for its full roster of activities—from canoeing to seaside yoga. 800/441-1414 or 808/885-2000; fairmont.com; doubles from $$.

Four Seasons Resort Hualalai
Low-slung bungalows with a rock-climbing wall and a newly expanded spa. 800/332-3442 or 808/325-8000; fourseasons.com; doubles from $$$$.

Hapuna Beach Prince Hotel
Business-friendly property set on a white-sand beach. 866/774-6236 or 808/880-1111; princeresorts hawaii.com; doubles from $$.

Mauna Kea Beach Hotel Founded by Laurance S. Rockefeller in 1965; still one of the world's premier golf resorts (designed by Robert Trent Jones Sr. and overlooking the Kohala Coast). 866/977-4589 or 808/882-7222; maunakeabeach hotel.com; doubles from $$.

Mauna Lani Bay Hotel & Bungalows
Eco-friendly hotel with a spa and two championship golf courses.

800/367-2323 or 808/885-6622; maunalani.com; doubles from $$.

Kona Village Resort Kohala Coast property arranged like a thatched-roof Polynesian village. 800/367-5290 or 808/325-5555; konavillage.com; doubles from $$$, including meals and some activities.

KAUAI
Grand Hyatt Kauai Resort & Spa
Sprawling 602-room resort built into oceanside bluffs, with the best spa on the lush island. 800/233-1234 or 808/742-1234; grand.hyatt.com; doubles from $$.

Kauai Marriott Resort & Beach Club Equidistant between the north and south shores of the Garden Isle, with rooms that look out on Kalapaki Beach. 800/220-2925 or 808/245-5050; kauai marriott.com; doubles from $$.

St. Regis Princeville Resort
Freshly revamped, with a first-rate spot on Hanalei Bay. 877/787-3447 or 808/826-9644; stregisprinceville.com; doubles from $$$$.

LANAI
Four Seasons Resort Lanai at Manele Bay This 236-room property has huge marble bathrooms and borders a marine reserve. 800/332-3442 or 808/565-2000; four seasons.com; doubles from $$.

Four Seasons Resort Lanai, The Lodge at Koele Manele Bay's sister hotel feels like a gracious country estate, thanks to its stables and croquet lawn. 800/332-3442 or

808/565-4000; fourseasons.com; doubles from $$.

MAUI
Fairmont Kea Lani Moorish-inspired hideaway (domes, archways, and whitewashed walls) on 22 manicured acres. 800/441-1414 or 808/875-4100; fairmont.com; doubles from $$.

Four Seasons Resort Maui at Wailea Modern 380-room hotel with a new adults-only infinity pool and endless free activities, including snorkeling, scuba diving, and yoga classes. 800/332-3442 or 808/874-8000; fourseasons.com; doubles from $$.

Grand Wailea An intricate network of nine pools and waterslides helps define this mammoth family-friendly complex. 800/888-6100 or 808/875-1234; grandwailea.com; doubles from $$.

Hotel Hana-Maui & Honua Spa
Forty cottages with a low-key vibe—don't expect television or radio in your room. 800/321-4262 or 808/248-8211; hotelhanamaui.com; doubles from $$.

Hyatt Regency Maui Resort & Spa
Upscale resort with Polynesian design details and artful landscaping. 800/233-1234 or 808/661-1234; hyatt.com; doubles from $$.

Ritz-Carlton Kapalua Pineapple plantation turned luxury hotel, with an extensive eco-education program. 800/241-3333 or 808/669-6200; ritzcarlton.com; doubles from $$.

Wailea Beach Marriott Resort & Spa All the classic amenities of a resort, plus koi ponds and old-growth banyan trees. 800/228-9290 or 808/879-2922; marriott.com; doubles from $$$.

Westin Maui Resort & Spa On Kaanapali Beach, a water-focused hotel with an "aquatic playground." 866/716-8112 or 808/667-2525; westinmaui.com; doubles from $$$, three-night minimum.

OAHU
Halekulani Service rules at this recently renovated five-acre Waikiki Beach beauty, which has existed for nearly a century. 2199 Kalia Rd., Honolulu; 800/367-2343 or 808/923-2311; halekulani.com; doubles from $$.

JW Marriott Ihilani Resort & Spa
On a white-sand lagoon, 387 spacious rooms and a popular marine life program. Kapolei; 800/626-4446 or 808/679-0079; ihilani.com; doubles from $$.

Kahala Hotel & Resort Calm and shallow waters on a beach that's perfect for families, plus resident dolphins in a private lagoon. 5000 Kahala Ave., Honolulu; 800/367-2525 or 808/739-8888; kahala resort.com; doubles from $$$.

Moana Surfrider, A Westin Resort & Spa Waikiki's first hotel; some rooms have views of Diamond Head. 2365 Kalakaua Ave., Honolulu; 800/782-9488 or 808/922-3111; moana-surfrider.com; doubles from $$.

Outrigger Waikiki on the Beach Balconied high-rise fronting Waikiki Beach; an activities-rich family favorite. 2335 Kalakaua Ave., Honolulu; 800/688-7444 or 808/923-0711; outrigger.com; doubles from $.

Royal Hawaiian, a Luxury Collection Resort Located on an iconic beach with nearly two miles of white sand. 2259 Kalakaua Ave., Honolulu; 800/325-3589 or 808/923-7311; royal-hawaiian.com; doubles from $$$.

Turtle Bay Resort Luxurious digs on 880 dreamy acres of North Shore, with a famed surfing school founded by Hans Hedemann. 800/203-3650 or 808/293-6000; turtlebayresort.com; doubles from $$.

ILLINOIS
CHICAGO
Four Seasons Hotel On floors 30–46 of a skyscraper; all rooms have Lake Michigan views. 120 E. Delaware Place; 800/332-3442 or 312/280-8800; fourseasons.com; doubles from $$.

Omni Chicago Hotel All-suite mainstay on a prime spot on the Magnificent Mile, near the city's best shops. 676 N. Michigan Ave.; 888/444-6664 or 312/944-6664; omnihotels.com; doubles from $.

Peninsula Chicago Art Deco tower with three restaurants. 108 E. Superior St.; 866/382-8388 or 312/337-2888; peninsula.com; doubles from $$$.

Ritz-Carlton, A Four Seasons Hotel This 21-floor city standby has a fresh contemporary edge, thanks to a recent overhaul. 160

E. Pearson St.; 800/332-3442 or 312/266-1000; fourseasons.com; doubles from $$.

Sofitel Water Tower Prism-shaped glass tower designed by architect Jean-Paul Viguier. 20 E. Chestnut St.; 800/763-4835 or 312/324-4000; sofitel.com; doubles from $$.

LOUISIANA
NEW ORLEANS
Windsor Court Hotel Near the French Quarter, 322 traditional rooms with bay windows and a museum-quality art collection. 300 Gravier St.; 888/596-0955 or 504/523-6000; windsorcourthotel.com; doubles from $$.

MAINE
FREEPORT
Harraseeket Inn In-town white clapboard inn decorated with locally sourced antiques. 800/342-6423 or 207/865-9377; harraseeketinn.com; doubles from $.

KENNEBUNKPORT
Hidden Pond Fourteen two-bedroom cottages in the woods with the atmosphere of a luxe summer camp. 888/967-9050 or 207/967-9050; hiddenpondmaine.com; cottages from $$$.

White Barn Inn & Spa Fronted by perennial gardens, a romantic 26-room property a quarter-mile from the river. 800/735-2478 or 207/967-2321; whitebarninn.com; doubles from $$, including breakfast and afternoon tea.

MASSACHUSETTS
BOSTON
Eliot Hotel Intimate Parisian-inspired retreat with white-and-beige suites in toile and silk, steps from Fenway

Park. 370 Commonwealth Ave.; 800/443-5468 or 617/267-1607; eliothotel.com; doubles from $$.

Four Seasons Hotel Red-brick property known for its attentive service and understated rooms overlooking Boston Common. 200 Boylston St.; 800/332-3442 or 617/338-4400; fourseasons.com; doubles from $$.

The Lenox Historic Back Bay hotel lauded for its environmental

initiatives, which include carbon offsetting and hybrid car service. 61 Exeter St.; 800/225-7676 or 617/536-5300; lenox1900.com; doubles from $.

Taj Boston 1927 urban classic located at the fashionable corner of Arlington and Newbury. 15 Arlington St.; 866/969-1825 or 617/536-5700; tajhotels.com; doubles from $$$.

XV Beacon Beaux-Arts building on Beacon Hill with both traditional elements (dark wood furnishings,

The Fountain Pool at the Four Seasons Resort Maui at Wailea, in Hawaii.

marble busts) and contemporary accents (abstract paintings and gas fireplaces). 15 Beacon St.; 877/982-3226 or 617/ 670-1500; xvbeacon.com; doubles from $$.

CAPE COD

Wequassett Resort & Golf Club Clapboard cottages on Pleasant Bay; recent additions include tennis courts, a lap pool, and a children's center. 800/225-7125 or 508/432-5400; wequassett.com; doubles from $$$.

The Daydream cottage at Hidden Pond, in Kennebunkport, Maine.

LENOX

Canyon Ranch Health-focused 126-room resort spa in the Berkshires; the nutritionist-designed menu wins raves. 800/742-9000 or 413/637-4400; canyonranch.com; doubles from $$$$$ per person, all-inclusive, three-night minimum.

NANTUCKET

The Wauwinet Nantucket's most secluded luxury property, bordering a stretch of rugged coast eight miles from the town center. 800/426-8718 or 508/228-0145; wauwinet.com; doubles from $$$. Open seasonally, May–October.

White Elephant Shingle-style spread overlooking the harbor; rooms are done in organic white linens and handsome walnut woods, and there's a notable restaurant, Brant Point Grill. 800/445-6574 or 508/228-2500; whiteelephanthotel.com; doubles from $$$.

PROVINCETOWN

Red Inn Rambling sea captain's mansion with eight rooms and a seafood-centric restaurant. 866/473-3466 or 508/487-7334; theredinn.com; doubles from $$.

MICHIGAN

ARCADIA

Inn at Watervale Set between two lakes, a multigenerational family favorite and a classic all-American summer escape. 231/352-9083; watervaleinn.com; doubles from $, including breakfast and dinner; cottages from $$, one-week minimum.

MINNESOTA

MINNEAPOLIS

Grand Hotel High-rise with 140 rooms and a huge fitness center, plus access to indoor walkways that connect downtown shops and businesses. 615 Second Ave. S.; 866/843-4726 or 612/288-8888; grandhotelminneapolis.com; doubles from $$.

ST. PAUL

Saint Paul Hotel Top-notch service (a 24-hour concierge and an in-house seamstress) and homey comforts that include a welcoming fireplace and an oak-paneled bar. 350 Market St.; 800/292-9292 or 651/292-9292; saintpaulhotel.com; doubles from $.

NEVADA

LAS VEGAS

Bellagio Mid-Strip extravaganza with outsize amenities: a palatial 55,000-square-foot spa, 14 restaurants, botanical gardens, and dancing fountains. 3600 Las Vegas Blvd. S.; 888/987-6667 or 702/693-7111; bellagio.com; doubles from $.

Encore Luxe desert oasis with a glass-walled casino that looks out onto gardens and pools. 3131 Las Vegas Blvd. S.; 888/320-7125 or 702/770-7171; encorelasvegas. com; doubles from $.

Four Seasons Hotel Understated, slot machine–free hotel on floors 35–39 of the Mandalay Bay tower. 3960 Las Vegas Blvd. S.; 800/332-3442 or 702/632-5000; four seasons.com; doubles from $$.

The Palazzo LEED-certified all-suite property with over-the-top room décor (multiple flat-screen TV's and mini-bars stocked with premium dark chocolate). 3325 Las Vegas Blvd. S.; 877/883-6423 or 702/607-4100; palazzolasvegas. com; doubles from $.

The Venetian Among the largest rooms on the Strip—averaging 650 square feet—in an Italianate fantasyland complete with a faux Grand Canal. 3355 Las Vegas Blvd. S.; 877/883-6423 or 702/414-1000; venetian.com; doubles from $.

Wynn Las Vegas Fifty-story hotel with a much-lauded golf course and a botanical theme, including a 140-foot forested mountain.

A suite patio and private fireplace at Encantado, An Auberge Resort, in Santa Fe, New Mexico.

3131 Las Vegas Blvd. S.; 877/321-9966 or 702/770-7000; wynnlasvegas.com; doubles from $.

NEW JERSEY
CAPE MAY

Congress Hall Federal-style hotel in a picturesque seaside community, with striped cabanas on the beach in summer. 888/944-1816 or 609/884-8421; congresshall.com; doubles from $$.

NEW MEXICO
SAN ANTONIO

Fite Ranch Bed & Breakfast Working cattle ranch in the midst of old mining country; the four rooms are filled with Southwestern memorabilia. 575/838-0958; fiteranchbedandbreakfast.com; doubles from $, two-night minimum.

SANTA FE

Encantado, An Auberge Resort Sixty-five casitas with soothing, tasteful interiors—a 21st-century spin on Southwest style. 198 State Rd. 592; 877/262-4666 or 505/946-5700; encantadoresort.com; doubles from $$$.

Inn on the Alameda It's all about privacy and sense of place: 71 secluded adobe rooms and suites open onto a flower-filled courtyard. 303 E. Alameda; 800/289-2122 or 505/984-2121; innonthealameda.com; doubles from $.

Rosewood Inn of the Anasazi Native American–inspired design at a 58-room hotel steps from the historic Santa Fe plaza. 113 Washington Ave.; 888/767-3966 or

505/988-3030; rosewoodhotels.com; doubles from $$.

NEW YORK
ADIRONDACKS

Mirror Lake Inn Resort & Spa A 131-room lakefront complex favored by families for its endless roster of activities. Lake Placid; 518/523-2544; mirrorlakeinn.com; doubles from $$.

Whiteface Lodge Resort & Spa Rustic lodge featuring white-pine beams, cast-iron fireplaces, and well-equipped rooms abutting the 6 million acre Adirondack Park. Lake Placid; 800/903-4045 or 518/523-0500; thewhitefacelodge.com; doubles from $$.

NEW PALTZ

Mohonk Mountain House Kid-friendly Victorian castle featuring a 16-room spa overlooking a lake. 800/772-6646 or 845/255-1000; mohonk.com; doubles from $$$, including all meals and most activities.

NEW YORK CITY

The Carlyle, A Rosewood Hotel Art Deco bastion of gentility, with a notable bar and new spa. Located near Museum Mile. 35 E. 76th St.; 888/767-3966 or 212/744-1600; rosewoodhotels.com; doubles from $$$$.

Four Seasons Hotel Designed by architect I. M. Pei, the tallest hotel in the city has a limestone lobby and muted interiors. 57 E. 57th St.; 800/332-3442 or 212/758-5700; fourseasons.com; doubles from $$$$.

Hôtel Plaza Athénée Slice of Paris on a quiet Upper East Side block. A recent renovation added bathrooms with deep soaking tubs; four new treatment rooms in the updated fitness center and spa are due to open in late winter. 37 E. 64th St.; 800/447-8800 or 212/734-9100; plaza-athenee.com; doubles from $$$.

Mandarin Oriental Built in 2003 as part of the Time Warner Center, with plush Asian-inspired interiors and views of Central Park. 80 Columbus Circle; 800/526-6566 or 212/805-8800; mandarinoriental.com; doubles from $$$$.

Mark Hotel Recently made over by interior designer Jacques Grange, who added eclectic furnishings and an Op Art marble floor in the lobby. 25 E. 77th St.; 866/744-4300 or 212/744-4300; themarkhotel.com; doubles from $$$$.

Omni Berkshire Place Some of the largest suites in the city, ranging from 400 to 781 square feet; just steps from MOMA and Madison Avenue boutiques. 21 E. 52nd St.; 888/444-6664 or 212/753-5800; omnihotels.com; doubles from $$.

Peninsula New York Landmark Beaux-Arts building with updated rooms (French linens, leather club chairs) and an Asian-inflected spa by Espa. 700 Fifth Ave.; 866/382-8388 or 212/956-2888; peninsula.com; doubles from $$$$.

The Pierre Newly refreshed grande dame on Central Park's southeast corner, with a long-standing reputation for elegance and discretion. 2 E. 61st St.; 212/838-8000; tajhotels.com; doubles from $$$$.

Plaza Hotel White-gloved butlers, the wood-paneled Oak Room & Bar, and cinematic park views. Fifth Ave. at Central Park S.; 888/850-0909 or 212/759-3000; theplaza.com; doubles from $$$$$.

Ritz-Carlton Central Park Elegant 33-story hotel that has Central Park as its front yard. 50 Central Park S.; 800/241-3333 or 212/308-9100; ritzcarlton.com; doubles from $$$.

The Standard, New York Towering above the Meatpacking District, an 18-story glass-and-concrete structure straddling the High Line. 848 Washington St.; 877/550-4646 or 212/645-4646; standardhotels.com; doubles from $.

St. Regis Century-old icon with gracious rooms (silk wall coverings, canopy beds, paisley carpets) and superior service—each floor has its own butler. 2 E. 55th St.; 877/787-3447 or 212/753-4500; stregis.com; doubles from $$$$.

The Surrey Cutting-edge video art and clever design details at an old-guard Upper East Side address. 20 E. 76th St.; 800/978-7739 or 212/288-3700; thesurrey.com; doubles from $$$$.

Trump International Hotel & Tower Occupying 15 floors of a Philip Johnson–designed tower; some rooms have floor-to-ceiling windows overlooking Central Park. 1 Central Park W.; 888/448-7867 or 212/299-1000; trumpintl.com; doubles from $$$$.

SOUTHOLD

North Fork Table & Inn Four rooms in a Colonial-style house, and a restaurant run by two New York culinary stars. 631/765-0177; northforktableandinn.com; doubles from $$.

NORTH CAROLINA
ASHEVILLE

Grove Park Inn Resort & Spa Subterranean spa pools, a recently restored golf course, and a 1913 lodge framed by the Blue Ridge Mountains. 800/438-5800 or 828/252-2711; groveparkinn.com; doubles from $.

Inn on Biltmore Estate A 213-room mansion on a lavish 8,000-acre estate that's also home to George Vanderbilt's Biltmore House. 800/411-3812 or 828/225-1600; biltmore.com; doubles from $$.

Richmond Hill Inn Victorian-style buildings tucked among gardens, seven miles from the Blue Ridge Parkway. 800/545-9238 or 828/

252-7313; richmondhillinn.com; doubles from $$, including breakfast and afternoon tea.

RALEIGH/DURHAM AREA

Umstead Hotel & Spa Art-filled public spaces on 12 wooded acres, minutes from downtown Raleigh. Cary; 866/877-4141 or 919/447-4000; theumstead.com; doubles from $$.

OREGON
CANNON BEACH

Stephanie Inn Shingled hotel overlooking the famous Haystack Rock; the 41 rooms are equipped with fireplaces and private balconies. 800/633-3466 or 503/436-2221; stephanie-inn.com; doubles from $$.

GOLD BEACH

Tu Tu'Tun Lodge Fronting the Rogue River and flanked by old-growth rain forests, with an emphasis on genial service. 800/864-6357 or 541/247-6664; tututun.com; doubles from $.

PORTLAND

Hotel Lucia Buzzy hotel with black-and-white photos on display and a quirky Thai room-service menu for late-night cravings. 400 SW Broadway; 877/225-1717 or 503/225-1717; hotellucia.com; doubles from $.

The Nines Serious eco cred and stylized design flourishes on the top nine floors of a landmark downtown building. 525 SW Morrison St.; 877/229-9995 or 503/222-9996; thenines.com; doubles from $$.

PENNSYLVANIA
HAWLEY

Lodge at Woodloch Destination spa styled after a country retreat, surrounded by bucolic woodland gardens and with a private 15-acre lake. 866/953-8500 or 570/685-8500; doubles from $$$, all-inclusive.

HERSHEY

Hotel Hershey Newly expanded, with a multi-pool swimming complex and a year-round skating rink; the spa incorporates chocolate into its treatments. 800/437-7439 or 717/533-2171; thehotelhershey.com; doubles from $$.

PHILADELPHIA

Omni Hotel at Independence Park Marble-clad hotel near Philly's historic sites, including the Liberty Bell and Independence Hall. 401 Chestnut St.; 888/444-6664 or 215/925-0000; omnihotels.com; doubles from $.

Rittenhouse Hotel Downtown hotel with large rooms starting at 450 square feet. 210 W. Rittenhouse Square; 800/635-1042 or 215/546-9000; rittenhousehotel.com; doubles from $$$.

Ritz-Carlton The entrance to this stately 299-room property is marked by six towering Ionic columns. 10 Ave. of the Arts; 800/241-3333 or 215/523-8000; ritzcarlton.com; doubles from $$.

Sofitel Philadelphia Set in the former stock exchange building, now retrofitted with streamlined

A daybed on the rooftop terrace at the Peninsula New York.

rooms and an intimate brasserie. 120 S. 17th St.; 800/763-4835 or 215/569-8300; sofitel.com; doubles from $.

RHODE ISLAND
NEWPORT

Castle Hill Inn & Resort Restored Victorian mansion and four whitewashed cottages overlooking Narragansett Bay. 888/466-1355 or 401/849-3800; castlehillinn.com; doubles from $$$.

SOUTH CAROLINA
BLUFFTON

Inn at Palmetto Bluff Fifty refined cottage suites (vaulted ceilings, wraparound verandas) in the moss-draped low country along the May River. 866/706-6565 or 843/706-6500; palmettobluffresort. com; doubles from $$$.

CHARLESTON

Charleston Place Hotel Georgian property with grand staircases, Chippendale-style furnishings, and a 1-to-1 staff-to-guest ratio. 205 Meeting St.; 888/635-2350 or 843/722-4900; charlestonplace. com; doubles from $.

Planters Inn A 19th-century building and an adjoining modern addition; a peaceful retreat in the center of town. 112 N. Market St.; 800/845-7082 or 843/722-2345; plantersinn.com; doubles from $$.

KIAWAH ISLAND

Sanctuary at Kiawah Island Golf Resort The golf course and tennis courts are world-class at this family-friendly estate on a barrier island. 800/654-2924 or 843/768-2121; kiawahresort.com; doubles from $$.

TENNESSEE
NASHVILLE

Hermitage Hotel Favored by country music stars, and by far the city's choicest digs, with a stained-glass ceiling and gilded plasterwork. 231 Sixth Ave. N.; 888/888-9414 or 615/ 244-3121; thehermitagehotel.com; doubles from $.

TEXAS
AUSTIN

Four Seasons Hotel Unpretentious oasis on Lady Bird Lake; public spaces are distinctly Southwestern (a hide-covered sofa and the like). 98 San Jacinto Blvd.; 800/332-3442 or 512/685-8100; fourseasons. com; doubles from $$.

Lake Austin Spa Resort Lakefront guest rooms and a spa that blends Hill Country style and New Age sensibility. 800/847-5637 or 512/372-7300; lakeaustin.com; doubles from $$$$$, all-inclusive, three-night minimum.

DALLAS AREA

Omni Mandalay Hotel at Las Colinas A lobby furnished with Burmese-style antiques and larger-than-average rooms, located in the business district of Las Colinas. 221 E. Las Colinas Blvd., Irving; 888/444-6664 or 972/556-0800; omnihotels.com; doubles from $.

Rosewood Crescent Hotel Limestone landmark in Dallas's Uptown neighborhood; an outpost of chef Nobu Matsuhisa's namesake restaurant occupies the first floor. 400 Crescent Court, Dallas; 888/767-3966 or 214/871-3200; rosewood hotels.com; doubles from $$$.

Rosewood Mansion on Turtle Creek The Italian Renaissance interiors are remnants of the hotel's former resident, a 1920's oil baron. 2821 Turtle Creek Blvd., Dallas; 888/ 767-3966 or 214/559-2100; rose woodhotels.com; doubles from $.

HOUSTON

Houstonian Hotel, Club & Spa Stately, lodgelike interiors, surrounded by 18 forested acres in central Houston. 111 N. Post Oak Lane; 800/231-2759 or 713/680-2626; houstonian.com; doubles from $$.

SAN ANTONIO

Omni La Mansión del Rio 1854 Spanish-colonial school that was transformed into a hotel with French doors and courtyard fountains on the city's River Walk. 112 College St.; 888/444-6664 or 210/518-1000; omnihotels.com; doubles from $.

Watermark Hotel & Spa A minute's stroll from the Alamo; historic photographs and paintings by local

The Ski Room at the Pitcher Inn, in Warren, Vermont.

artists are displayed in the guest rooms. 212 W. Crockett St.; 866/605-1212 or 210/396-5800; watermark hotel.com; doubles from $.

UTAH
PARK CITY
Stein Eriksen Lodge Norwegian-style chalet halfway up a peak at Deer Valley ski resort. 800/453-1302 or 435/649-3700; steinlodge.com; doubles from $$$$.

VERMONT
LOWER WATERFORD
Rabbit Hill Inn Romantic getaway occupying a restored house and tavern, both more than 200 years old. 800/762-8669 or 802/748-5168; rabbithillinn.com; doubles from $, including breakfast and afternoon tea.

STOWE
Topnotch Resort & Spa The 68-room hotel is only two miles from Stowe's slopes and has a 35,000-square-foot spa. 800/451-8686 or 802/253-8585; topnotch resort.com; doubles from $$.

WARREN
Pitcher Inn Charming country retreat with 11 individually designed rooms that riff on pastoral themes, and a seasonally inspired restaurant that draws on the region's bounty of ingredients. 802/496-6350; pitcherinn.com; doubles from $$.

VIRGINIA
IRVINGTON
Tides Inn Resort on Chesapeake Bay offering a roster of outdoor activities, from kayaking to croquet. 800/843-3746 or 804/438-5000; tidesinn.com; doubles from $$.

WASHINGTON
Inn at Little Washington Eighteen sumptuous guest rooms and suites and chef Patrick O'Connell's much-lauded restaurant serving haute American fare. 540/675-3800; theinnatlittlewashington.com; doubles from $$$.

WASHINGTON
SEATTLE
Fairmont Olympic Hotel Seattle Italian Renaissance–style landmark, just blocks from the Seattle Art Museum and Pike Place Market. 411 University St.; 800/441-1414 or 206/621-1700; fairmont.com; doubles from $$.

Hotel 1000 Centrally located tower fitted with high-tech details, including scenic vistas displayed in-room on plasma screens and electronic Do Not Disturb signs. 1000 First Ave.; 877/315-1088 or 206/957-1000; hotel1000seattle.com; doubles from $.

WHIDBEY ISLAND
Inn at Langley Intimate retreat on a Puget Sound island; the weekends-only contemporary restaurant is justly famous. 360/221-3033; innatlangley.com; doubles from $$.

WEST VIRGINIA
WHITE SULPHUR SPRINGS
The Greenbrier Classic resort in the Allegheny Mountains, with numerous recreational offerings and a hydrotherapy-focused spa. 800/453-4858 or 304/536-1110; greenbrier.com; doubles from $$.

WISCONSIN
KOHLER
American Club at Destination Kohler 1918 Tudor boardinghouse, now the Midwest's most luxe resort and spa (the golf course is being revamped to host the 2012 U.S. Women's Open). 800/344-2838 or 920/457-8000; destinationkohler.com; doubles from $$.

WYOMING
JACKSON HOLE
Amangani Cliff-top hotel with staggering Teton views, Asian-inspired platform beds, and large soaking tubs. 800/447-9180 or 307/734-7333; amanresorts.com; doubles from $$$.

Four Seasons Resort Ski-in, ski-out lodge with fireplaces in every room and an expert team of adventure concierges at the ready. 800/332-3442 or 307/732-5000; four seasons.com; doubles from $$$.

Jenny Lake Lodge Log cabins at the base of the Teton range. 800/628-9988 or 307/543-2811; gtlc.com; doubles from $$$, including breakfast, dinner, and some activities.

KEY TO THE PRICE ICONS   **$** UNDER $250   **$$** $250–$499   **$$$** $500–$749   **$$$$** $750–$999   **$$$$$** $1,000 AND UP

Rusty Parrot Lodge & Spa Gabled 31-room lodge, only a short stroll from Jackson's town square and its shops and dining spots. 800/458-2004 or 307/733-2000; rustyparrot.com; doubles from $$.

ALBERTA
BANFF

Fairmont Banff Springs Scottish-style castle set amid the snow-capped peaks of Banff National Park. 800/441-1414 or 403/762-2211; fairmont.com; doubles from $$.

Rimrock Resort Hotel Modern lodge carved into Sulphur Mountain. 888/746-7625 or 403/762-3356; rimrockresort.com; doubles from $$.

LAKE LOUISE

Fairmont Chateau Lake Louise 1892 European-style resort flanked by the Rocky Mountains. 800/441-1414 or 403/522-3511; fairmont.com; doubles from $$.

Post Hotel & Spa Family-owned chalet-style lodge with a 32,000-bottle wine cellar, one of the largest in the country. 800/661-1586 or 403/522-3989; posthotel.com; doubles from $$.

BRITISH COLUMBIA
VANCOUVER

Fairmont Vancouver Airport Modern annex situated atop the U.S. departures terminal at Vancouver International Airport. Richmond; 800/441-1414 or 604/207-5200; fairmont.com; doubles from $$.

Fairmont Waterfront A 23-floor glass tower overlooking Coal Harbour and connected via walkway to the convention center. 900 Canada Way; 800/441-1414 or 604/691-1991; fairmont.com; doubles from $$.

Metropolitan Hotel Financial District skyscraper done in muted reds and creams; plus, a novelty—a third-floor putting green. 645 Howe St.; 800/667-2300 or 604/687-1122; metropolitan.com; doubles from $$.

The Opus Yaletown hot spot with design-centric guest rooms (Arne Jacobsen Egg chairs, Philippe Starck bar stools) and a clubby downtempo sound track in its public areas. 322 Davie St.; 866/642-6787 or 604/642-6787; opushotel.com; doubles from $$.

Shangri-La Hotel Occupying the lower 15 floors of the city's tallest building, spacious rooms have a Zen-like mix of furnishings; also an Asian-influenced spa and a restaurant by Jean-Georges Vongerichten. 1128 W. Georgia St.; 604/689-1120; shangri-la.com; doubles from $$.

Wedgewood Hotel & Spa An 83-room boutique property across from Robson Square, featuring European paintings and a piano lounge. 845 Hornby St.; 800/663-0666 or 604/689-7777; wedgewoodhotel.com; doubles from $$.

VANCOUVER ISLAND

Sooke Harbour House Waterfront white clapboard inn renowned for its food, much of which is sourced from the on-site garden. Sooke; 800/889-9688 or 250/642-3421; sookeharbourhouse.com; doubles from $.

Wickaninnish Inn Handmade driftwood furniture is on display at this 75-room hotel on a rocky promontory. Tofino; 800/333-4604 or 250/725-3100; wickinn.com; doubles from $$.

WHISTLER

Fairmont Chateau Ski-in, ski-out resort in the quiet upper village, with a Robert Trent Jones II–designed golf course. 800/606-8244 or 604/938-8000; fairmont.com; doubles from $$.

Four Seasons Resort Stone-and-timber lodge at the base of Blackcomb Mountain. 888/935-2460 or 604/935-3400; fourseasons.com; doubles from $$.

ONTARIO
MCKELLAR

Inn at Manitou A 34-room lakeside resort offering a range of activities, including a championship golf course, 10 tennis courts, and a fleet of sailboats. 800/571-8818 or 705/389-2171; manitou-online.com; doubles from $$$, all-inclusive.

QUEBEC
MONTREAL

Hôtel Le St.-James Old-world ambience in an 1870 Merchant's Bank a few blocks from the Notre Dame Basilica. 355 Rue St.-Jacques; 866/841-3111 or 514/841-3111; hotellestjames.com; doubles from $$.

Hotel Nelligan A 105-room hotel with warm interiors (dark wood furniture and fireplaces) carved out of three 19th-century warehouses in Old Montreal. 106 Rue St.-Paul; 877/788-2040 or 514/788-2040; hotelnelligan.com; doubles from $.

Hotel Omni Mont-Royal Tucked between Old Montreal and buzzing Rue Ste.-Catherine, with a rare-in-these-parts outdoor lap pool. 1050 Rue Sherbrooke Ouest; 800/843-6664 or 514/284-1110; omnihotels.com; doubles from $$.

Hotel St Paul A fashionable staff and equally stylish rooms in historic Vieux-Montréal. 355 Rue McGill; 866/380-2202 or 514/380-2222; hotelstpaul.com; doubles from $.

Loews Hotel Vogue Family-friendly hotel in the heart of downtown near the Notre Dame Basilica, with a popular bar. 1425 Rue de la Montagne; 888/465-6654 or 514/285-5555; loewshotels.com; doubles from $$.

Place d'Armes Hotel & Suites Hotel Nelligan's sister property, also occupying three 19th-century commercial buildings in Old Montreal. 55 Rue St.-Jacques St. Ouest; 888/450-1887 or 514/842-1887; hotelplacedarmes.com; doubles from $.

QUEBEC CITY

Auberge Saint-Antoine Hotel with 95 rooms—some showcasing 300-year-old artifacts found on-site—surrounded by the walls of a 19th-century maritime warehouse on the St. Lawrence River. 8 Rue St.-Antoine; 888/692-2211 or 418/692-2211; saint-antoine.com; doubles from $$.

KEY TO THE PRICE ICONS   **$** UNDER $250   **$$** $250–$499   **$$$** $500-$749   **$$$$** $750–$999   **$$$$$** $1,000 AND UP

BERMUDA

Great Sound

Atlantic Ocean

THE BAHAMAS

Atlantic Ocean

TURKS AND CAICOS

CAYMAN ISLANDS

DOMINICAN REPUBLIC

BRITISH VIRGIN ISLANDS

JAMAICA

PUERTO RICO

ANGUILLA

ST. BART'S

NEVIS

ANTIGUA

U.S. VIRGIN ISLANDS

DOMINICA

Caribbean Sea

ST. LUCIA

BEQUIA

BARBADOS

ARUBA

TOBAGO

THE CARIBBEAN
+BERMUDA
+THE BAHAMAS

Enjoying fresh coconut water at Firefly Bequia.

ANGUILLA

Cap Juluca Collection of Moorish-style villas that underwent a major restoration in 2008. 888/858-5822 or 264/497-6666; capjuluca.com; doubles from $$$$.

Viceroy Anguilla Designer Kelly Wearstler opts for a softer, nature-inspired aesthetic at this beachfront resort. 866/270-7798 or 264/497-7000; viceroyanguilla.com; doubles from $$$.

ANTIGUA

Jumby Bay, A Rosewood Resort Ultra-elite island hideaway off the coast of Antigua with updated rooms, a new 4,000-square-foot spa, and two restaurants. 888/767-3966 or 268/462-6000; jumbybay resort.com; doubles from $$$$$, all-inclusive.

ARUBA

Hyatt Regency Aruba Resort & Casino A 357-room high-rise with a fish-filled, 5,000-square-foot freshwater lagoon. 800/554-9288 or 011-297/586-1234; hyatt.com; doubles from $$$.

THE BAHAMAS

One&Only Ocean Club Beachfront plantation with Versailles-inspired gardens and a Jean-Georges Vongerichten restaurant. Paradise Island; 866/552-0001 or 242/363-2501; oneandonlyresorts.com; doubles from $$$$.

BARBADOS

Coral Reef Club Crisp and classic rooms, but the buzz is all about its new spa, from hotel industry veteran Neil Howard. St. James; 800/223-1108 or 246/422-2372; coralreefbarbados.com; doubles from $$.

The Crane The first resort hotel in the Caribbean; in the midst of a multimillion-dollar expansion. St. Philip; 246/423-6220; thecrane.com; doubles from $$$.

The House On Paynes Bay, a 34-suite hotel that treats each guest to a 30-minute massage. St. James; 888/996-9947 or 246/432-5525; eleganthotels.com; doubles from $$$.

Sea-U Guest House Laid-back and charming, with whitewashed rooms in a main house and cottage on the east coast of the island. St. Joseph; 246/433-9450; seau barbados.com; doubles from $.

BERMUDA

The Reefs A 65-room limestone hotel on a hillside overlooking a pink-sand beach. 800/742-2008 or 441/238-0222; thereefs.com; doubles from $$$.

BEQUIA

Firefly Bequia On a working 30-acre plantation, a four-room oasis with private patios and a beach made for snorkeling. 784/458-3414; fireflybequia.com; doubles from $$, including meals.

BRITISH VIRGIN ISLANDS

Peter Island Resort & Spa On an 1,800-acre private isle, a collection of two-story bungalows and a 10,000-square-foot spa. Peter Island; 800/346-4451 or 284/495-2000; peterisland.com; doubles from $$$, all-inclusive.

Rosewood Little Dix Bay Set on 500 beachy acres, with a slew of water activities (sailing lessons, snorkeling, kayaking) and a hilltop spa. Virgin Gorda; 888/767-3966 or 284/495-5555; rosewoodhotels.com; doubles from $$$.

CAYMAN ISLANDS

Ritz-Carlton Grand Cayman Oceanfront property with world-class diving and a water-themed kids' program designed by Jean-Michel Cousteau. 800/241-3333 or 345/943-9000; ritzcarlton.com; doubles from $$.

DOMINICA

Beau Rive Ringed by tropical forest, with balconies facing the Atlantic and easy access to the island's coves, hills, and jungle trails. 767/445-8992; beaurive.com; doubles from $, two-night minimum.

DOMINICAN REPUBLIC

Peninsula House Refined plantation house whose luxuries belie its remote tropical mountain setting. 809/307-1827; thepeninsulahouse.com; doubles from $$$.

KEY TO THE PRICE ICONS   **$** UNDER $250   **$$** $250–$499   **$$$** $500–$749   **$$$$** $750–$999   **$$$$$** $1,000 AND UP

JAMAICA

Couples Negril A 234-room resort on Bloody Bay Beach. 800/268-7537 or 876/957-5960; couples.com; doubles from $$$, all-inclusive, three-night minimum.

Couples Sans Souci Adults-only resort with an excellent spa. Ocho Rios; 800/268-7537 or 876/994-1206; couples.com; doubles from $$$, all-inclusive, three-night minimum.

Couples Swept Away Wellness-minded travelers love the lap pool and open-air gym. Negril; 800/268-7537 or 876/957-4061; couples.com; doubles from $$$, all-inclusive, three-night minimum.

Couples Tower Isle (formerly Ocho Rios) The first Couples resort, freshly renovated with 20 new rooms, a dive pool, and 10 spa treatment rooms. 800/268-7537 or 876/975-4271; couples.com; doubles from $$$, all-inclusive, three-night minimum.

Geejam Treetop retreat with a music-centric crowd and a ratio of four staff members to every guest. Port Antonio; 800/688-7678; islandoutpost.com; doubles from $$$.

Half Moon On 400 verdant acres, 15 minutes from the airport. Rose Hall; 800/626-0592 or 876/953-2211; halfmoon.com; doubles from $$.

Jamaica Inn Recently updated cove-front manor long favored by Britain's upper crust—Winston Churchill was a frequent guest in the 1950's. Ocho Rios; 800/837-4608 or 876/974-2514; jamaicainn.com; doubles from $$$.

Rockhouse Hotel Hip scene atop the cliffs of Pristine Cove; the 20 villas have terraces, thatched roofs, and outdoor showers. Negril; 876/957-4373; rockhousehotel.com; doubles from $.

Round Hill Hotel & Villas Beloved hideaway of presidents and Hollywood starlets, with a piano bar that was designed by Ralph Lauren. Montego Bay; 800/972-2159 or 876/956-7050; roundhilljamaica.com; doubles from $$$.

Royal Plantation Ocho Rios Steps from the city center, with a Mediterranean feel and a host of classes open to guests, from drawing to cooking. 888/487-6925 or 876/974-5601; royalplantation.com; doubles from $$$$$.

Sandals Whitehouse European Village & Spa An adult Disneyland (including a "Venetian" plaza and "French" café) abutting a 500-acre nature reserve. Whitehouse; 800/726-3257 or 876/640-3000; sandals.com; doubles from $$$$, all-inclusive, two-night minimum.

NEVIS

Four Seasons Resort Plantation-style cottages—some of the island's best—in a palm grove on Pinney's Beach. 800/332-3442 or 869/469-1111; fourseasons.com; doubles from $$$. The hotel is re-opening in April after a renovation.

PUERTO RICO

Conrad San Juan Condado Plaza Revamped hotel with vibrant hits of color in the buzzy Condado neighborhood; now home to chef Wilo Benet's Pikayo restaurant. 999 Ashford Ave.; condadoplaza.com; 888/722-1274 or 787/721-1000; doubles from $.

La Concha, A Renaissance Resort Midcentury gem that sports newly streamlined rooms, multilevel infinity pools, and the iconic Perla seafood restaurant. 1077 Ashford Ave., San Juan; 877/524-7718 or 787/721-7500; laconcharesort.com; doubles from $.

ST. BART'S

Eden Rock Jet-set favorite on a rocky promontory jutting out into the Baie de St. Jean; the resort just unveiled a 16,000-square-foot villa with a private recording studio. 877/563-7105 or 590-590/297-999; edenrockhotel.com; doubles from $$$$$.

Salines Garden Cottages Five cozy *cazes* (traditional Creole houses) located just minutes from picturesque Anse de Salines beach. 590-690/419-429; salinesgarden.com; doubles from $.

ST. LUCIA

Anse Chastanet Brightly decorated hillside cottages above a volcanic-sand beach. 800/223-1108 or 758/459-7000; ansechastanet.com; doubles from $$.

Jade Mountain At the island's most exclusive new resort, 28 expansive open-air suites with either infinity pools or private Jacuzzis. 800/223-1108 or 758/459-7000; jademountain.com; doubles from $$$$$.

Ladera On a forested ridge 1,100 feet above the Piton mountains, 26 open-air suites and six villas. 866/290-0978 or 758/459-6618; ladera.com; doubles from $$$.

TOBAGO

Bacolet Beach Club New beach-side property that lies just five minutes away from the lively island capital of Scarborough. 868/639-2357; bacoletbeachclub.com; doubles from $.

TURKS AND CAICOS

Grace Bay Club Mediterranean-style resort with family villas and an adults-only wing. 800/946-5757 or 649/946-5050; gracebayclub.com; doubles from $$$$.

Regent Palms On celebrated Grace Bay Beach, 72 suites and a spa that uses indigenous ingredients in some of its treatments. 800/545-4000 or 649/946-8666; regenthotels.com; doubles from $$$.

U.S. VIRGIN ISLANDS

Caneel Bay, A Rosewood Resort Sprawling property with a famed wellness retreat; located inside Virgin Islands National Park. St. John; 888/767-3966 or 340/776-6111; caneelbay.com; doubles from $$.

KEY TO THE PRICE ICONS **$** UNDER $250 **$$** $250–$499 **$$$** $500–$749 **$$$$** $750–$999 **$$$$$** $1,000 AND UP

The beach bar and restaurant at Anse Chastenet, on St. Lucia.

Tecate

Los Cabos
Mazatlán
RIVIERA
MAYA
Punta Mita
Guadalajara
Isla Mujeres
Mexico City
Cancún
San Miguel de Allende
Cuernavaca
Tulum
Zihuatanejo
Acapulco
BELIZE

Antigua

Granada

Guanacaste
Central Valley
La Fortuna

Panama City

Quito

Guayaquil

Machu Picchu
Cuzco

Trancoso

Rio de Janeiro

SALTA
PROVINCE

Santiago
Buenos Aires
Carmelo
Colchagua Valley
José Ignacio

Bariloche

PATAGONIA

MEXICO + CENTRAL
+ SOUTH AMERICA

ARGENTINA

BARILOCHE

Llao Llao Hotel & Resort, Golf-Spa 1940 lakeside lodge outfitted with fireplaces and antler chandeliers in the snowcapped Nahuel Huapi mountain range. 800/223-6800 or 54-29/4444-8530; llaollao.com; doubles from $$.

BUENOS AIRES

Alvear Palace Hotel French-inspired 1932 building in Recoleta. 1891 Avda. Alvear; 800/223-6800 or 54-11/4808-2100; alvearpalace.com; doubles from $$.

Caesar Park Buenos Aires On a quiet downtown side street, 175 rooms and a marble-clad lobby. 1232 Posadas; 877/223-7272 or 54-11/4819-1100; caesar-park.com; doubles from $$.

Faena Hotel & Universe Philippe Starck–designed interiors along Puerto Madero and Río de la Plata. 445 Martha Salotti; 800/223-6800 or 54-11/4010-9000; faenahotel anduniverse.com; doubles from $$.

Four Seasons Hotel 1916 mansion and a modern 13-story tower, connected by gardens. 1086 Posadas; 800/332-3442 or 54-11/4321-1200; fourseasons.com; doubles from $$.

Jardin Escondido Director Francis Ford Coppola's villa in Palermo Soho, consisting of two suites on separate floors and a solar-heated swimming pool. 4746 Gorriti; 800/7460-3743; coppola jardinescondido.com; doubles from $$$, three-night minimum.

Moreno Hotel Buenos Aires Loft-style rooms and a 130-seat theater in San Telmo. 376 Moreno; 54-11/6091-2000; morenbuenosaires.com; doubles from $.

Palacio Duhau–Park Hyatt State-of-the-art hotel with a 700-label wine cellar and an on-site cheese cave. 1661 Avda. Alvear; 800/233-1234 or 54-11/5171-1234; park.hyatt.com; doubles from $$.

Park Tower, a Luxury Collection Hotel Every guest gets a butler at this downtown mainstay with stellar service. 1193 Avda. Leandro N. Alem; 800/325-3589 or 54-11/4318-9100; luxurycollection.com; doubles from $$.

Sofitel Buenos Aires Pierre-Yves Rochon–designed rooms in a 1929 Neoclassical high-rise. 841 Arroyo; 800/763-4835 or 54-11/4131-0123; sofitel.com; doubles from $$$.

SALTA PROVINCE

Estancia Colomé Surrounded by lavender fields and vineyards, nine suites with mountain views. Molinos; 54-3868/494-200; estanciacolome.com; doubles from $$.

Legado Mítico Salta Eleven rooms inspired by notable Salteños, in a restored former mansion near the city center. 647 Bartolomé Mitre, Salta; 54-387/422-8786; legado mitico.com; doubles from $.

Patios de Cafayate, a Luxury Collection Hotel & Spa Spanish colonial–style structure with a spa specializing in vinotherapy.

Cafayate; 800/325-3589 or 54-3868/422-229; luxurycollection.com; doubles from $.

BELIZE

AMBERGRIS CAY

Victoria House Located on an island 10 minutes by boat from the world's second-largest barrier reef. 800/247-5159 or 011-501/226-2067; victoria-house.com; doubles from $.

PLACENCIA

Turtle Inn Francis Ford Coppola's Balinese-inspired beachfront cottages on the country's southern coast. 800/746-3743 or 011-501/523-3244; coppola resorts.com; doubles from $$, two-night minimum.

SAN IGNACIO

Blancaneaux Lodge Jungle hideaway also owned by Coppola, near the Mayan ruins of Caracol. 800/746-3743 or 011-501/824-3878; coppolaresorts.com; doubles from $$, two-night minimum.

BRAZIL

RIO DE JANEIRO

Copacabana Palace Hotel Recently redecorated French Riviera–style hotel on Rio's most famous beach. 1702 Avda. Atlântica; 800/237-1236 or 55-21/2548-7070; copacabana palace.com.br; doubles from $$.

JW Marriott Hotel A 249-room pink-marble hotel with a rooftop pool across from Copacabana Beach. 2600 Avda. Atlântica; 800/228-9290 or 55-21/2545-6500; marriott.com; doubles from $$.

TRANCOSO

UXUA Casa Hotel Stylish nine-cottage hideaway in Bahia's sexiest beach village. 55-73/3668-2166; uxua.com; doubles from $$$.

CHILE

COLCHAGUA VALLEY

Lapostolle Residence Four expansive casitas overlooking the vineyards in the heart of Chile's wine country. 56-72/953-360; lapostolle.com; doubles from $$$$, including meals and tour.

PATAGONIA

Explora Patagonia, Hotel Salto Chico Luxe 50-room wilderness lodge with a wealth of guided activities. 866/750-6699; explora.com; doubles from $$$$$, all-inclusive, four-night minimum.

SANTIAGO

Ritz-Carlton In the tony El Golf neighborhood, a 221-room business hotel with a seafood restaurant that offers more than 365 Chilean wines. 15 Calle el Alcalde; 800/241-3333 or 56-24/708-500; ritzcarlton.com; doubles from $$.

W Santiago High-energy public spaces, including three nightspots, a rooftop pool, and a lobby with a 1,600-bottle wall of wine. 3000 Isidora Goyenechea; 877/946-8357 or 56-2/770-0000; whotels.com; doubles from $$$.

COSTA RICA

CENTRAL VALLEY

Xandari Resort & Spa Villas with brightly colored tapestries and sculptures designed by the artist

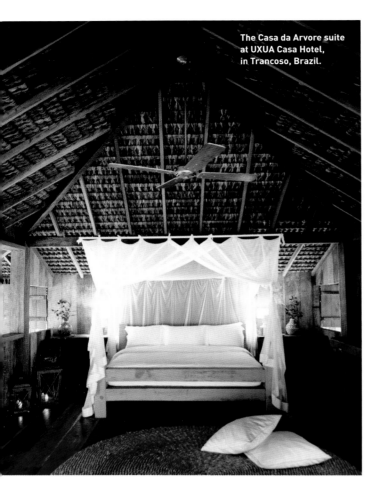

The Casa da Arvore suite at UXUA Casa Hotel, in Trancoso, Brazil.

owners. Alajuela; 866/363-3212 or 506/2443-2020; xandari.com; doubles from $$.

GUANACASTE
Four Seasons Resort at Peninsula Papagayo Hotel with L'Occitane bath products and beachfront access in a tropical dry forest. 800/332-3442 or 506/2696-0000; fourseasons.com; doubles from $$$.

Hotel Punta Islita Eco-resort offering cultural visits to nearby villages. 866/446-4053 or 506/2656-3036; hotelpuntaislita.com; doubles from $$.

LA FORTUNA
Tabacón Grand Spa Thermal Resort Located two miles from Arenal Volcano in Costa Rica's verdant rain forest; the resort is a favorite with families and spa goers. 877/277-8291 or 506/2519-1999; tabacon.com; doubles from $.

ECUADOR
GUAYAQUIL
Hotel Oro Verde Downtown high-rise just eight minutes from the international airport, with good business amenities. 414 Avda. 9 de Octubre; 800/223-6800 or 593-4/232-7999; oroverde guayaquil.com; doubles from $.

QUITO
JW Marriott Hotel Pyramid-shaped hotel with a glass atrium in Quito's financial and entertainment district. 1172 Avda. Orellana; 800/228-9290 or 593-2/297-2000; marriott.com; doubles from $.

GUATEMALA
ANTIGUA
Hotel Casa Santo Domingo Former 16th-century convent and colonial-art museum in a UNESCO World Heritage site. 502/7820-1220; casa santodomingo.com.gt; doubles from $.

MEXICO
ACAPULCO
Las Brisas High above Acapulco Bay, with jeeps to transport guests from casita to private beach club. 800/223-6800 or 52-744/469-6900; brisas hotelonline.com; doubles from $.

CANCÚN
Dreams Cancun Resort & Spa On seven oceanfront acres, with a well-appointed spa. 866/237-3276 or 52-998/848-7000; dreams resorts.com; doubles from $$, all-inclusive.

JW Marriott Cancún Resort & Spa Family-friendly beachfront tower with unprecedented service for a hotel its size. 866/401-8907 or 52-998/848-9600; jwmarriottcancun resort.com; doubles from $$.

Ritz-Carlton Hacienda-style retreat and an on-site culinary center offering weekly tequila tastings. 800/241-3333 or 52-998/881-0808; ritzcarlton.com; doubles from $$.

CUERNAVACA
Las Mañanitas Hotel, Restaurant, Garden & Spa Colonial hotel with three acres of gardens and an art collection that includes works by José Luis Cuevas. 888/413-9199 or 52-777/362-0000; lasmananitas.com.mx; doubles from $, all-inclusive.

GUADALAJARA
Quinta Real In a residential neighborhood set back from the busy streets of Mexico's second-largest city. 2727 Avda. México; 866/621-9288 or 55-33/3669-0600; quintareal.com; doubles from $.

ISLA MUJERES
Hotel Villa Rolandi Thalasso Spa Gourmet & Beach Club Waterfront views and a Swiss-Italian restaurant on a four-mile island off Cancún. 52-998/999-2000; villa rolandi.com; doubles from $$.

LOS CABOS
Esperanza, An Auberge Resort Rooms with oversize tubs and handcrafted furniture (plus an infinity pool overlooking a private cove) on the Sea of Cortés. Punta Ballena; 866/311-2226 or 310/453-6212; esperanzaresort.com; doubles from $$.

Las Ventanas al Paraíso, A Rosewood Resort Mediterranean-style beachfront property known for superb service. San José del Cabo; 888/767-3966 or 52-624/144-2800; lasventanas.com; doubles from $$$$.

One&Only Palmilla All the trappings of a mega-resort, but with

KEY TO THE PRICE ICONS   **$** UNDER $250   **$$** $250–$499   **$$$** $500–$749   **$$$$** $750–$999   **$$$$$** $1,000 AND UP

the sensibility of a boutique hotel. San José del Cabo; 866/552-0001 or 52-624/146-7000; oneandonly resorts.com; doubles from $$$.

Pueblo Bonito Sunset Beach Resort & Spa Family-friendly all-suite resort on Baja's quiet western coast. 800/990-8250 or 52-624/142-9999; pueblobonito. com; doubles from $$.

MAZATLÁN
Casa Lucila Overlooking Olas Altas beach, eight contemporary rooms with locally made wood furniture. 52-669/982-1100; casalucila.com; doubles from $.

MEXICO CITY
Camino Real Polanco México Striking architecture by Ricardo Legorreta with a garden oasis. 700 Mariano Escobedo, Col. Anzures; 52-55/5263-8888; caminoreal.com; doubles from $.

Distrito Capital Minimalist interiors in a business-district skyscraper. 37 Juan Salvador Agraz; 800/337-4685 or 52-55/5257-1300; hotel distritocapital.com; doubles from $.

Four Seasons Hotel Large rooms in an eight-story colonial-style ha-cienda. 500 Paseo de la Reforma; 800/332-3442 or 52-55/5230-1818; fourseasons.com; doubles from $$.

Presidente Mexico City Business-traveler favorite near Chapultepec Park. 218 Campos Eliseos, Col. Polanco; 888/424-6835 or 52-55/5327-7700; ichotelsgroup.com; doubles from $.

PUNTA MITA
Four Seasons Resort Secluded casitas on an isthmus outside Puerto Vallarta. 800/332-3442 or 52-329/291-6000; fourseasons. com; doubles from $$$.

RIVIERA MAYA
Banyan Tree Mayakoba Villas with full-size private pools and a spa staffed with Thai-trained therapists. Playa del Carmen; 800/591-0439; banyantree.com; doubles from $$$$$.

Maroma Resort & Spa Cluster of thatched-roof aeries with their own terraces. Quintana Roo; 866/454-9351 or 52-998/872-8200; maromahotel.com; doubles from $$$$, including airport transfers.

Rosewood Mayakobá The most private new hotel in the area, with a spa built around a natural limestone pool. 888/767-3966 or 52-984/875-8000; rosewoodhotels. com; doubles from $$$$.

Royal Hideaway Playacar Adults-only beach resort with 200 rooms and six restaurants. Playa del Carmen; 800/999-9182 or 52-984/873-4500; royalhideaway.com; doubles from $$$, all-inclusive.

SAN MIGUEL DE ALLENDE
Casa de Sierra Nevada Six Spanish-colonial mansions with 37 rooms. 800/701-1561 or 52-415/152-7040; casa desierranevada.com; doubles from $.

TECATE
Rancho La Puerta The granddaddy of destination spas, on 3,000 acres

with an organic farm and a renowned cooking school. 800/443-7565 or 858/764-5500; rancholapuerta.com; doubles from $$$$, all-inclusive, seven-night minimum.

TULUM
Coqui Coqui Residence & Spa Five-room resort just steps from the sea. 52-1-984/100-1400; coqui coquispa.com; doubles from $.

Maya Tulum Wellness Retreat & Spa Thatched-roof cabanas at a beachfront resort that's a mecca for yoga devotees, with Mayan-influenced spa offerings. 888/515-4580 or 770/483-0238; mayatulum. com; doubles from $.

ZIHUATANEJO
La Casa Que Canta Adobe hide-away built into the rocks above Zihuatanejo Bay. 888/523-5050 or 52-755/555-7030; lacasaquecanta. com; doubles from $$.

The Tides Recently reopened palm-shrouded villas on quiet La Ropa beach. 866/905-9560 or 52-755/5555-500; tideszihuatanejo. com; doubles from $$$.

NICARAGUA
GRANADA
Hotel La Gran Francia 16th-century property just off the plaza. Southeast corner of Parque Central; 505/2552-6000; lagran francia.com; doubles from $.

PANAMA
PANAMA CITY
The Bristol In the business district; the bar serves more than

50 types of rum. Avda. Aquilino de la Guardia; 800/223-6800 or 011-507/264-0000; thebristol.com; doubles from $.

PERU
CUZCO
Hotel Monasterio Converted 16th-century monastery that's by far Cuzco's most luxurious hotel. 136 Calle Palacio, Plazoleta Nazarenas; 800/237-1236 or 51-84/604-000; monasteriohotel.com; doubles from $$$.

Inkaterra La Casona On Plaza Las Nazarenas, a former conquistador's mansion. 113 Plaza Las Nazarenas; 800/442-5042 or 51-84/234-010; inkaterra. com; doubles from $$$.

MACHU PICCHU
Inkaterra Machu Picchu Pueblo Hotel Andean-style casitas steps from the ruins of Machu Picchu. 800/442-5042 or 51-1/610-0400; inkaterra.com; doubles from $$, including breakfast and dinner.

URUGUAY
CARMELO
Four Seasons Resort Set in a forest along the Río de la Plata and known for championship golf course. 800/332-3442 or 011-598/542-9000; fourseasons.com; doubles from $$.

JOSÉ IGNACIO
Estancia Vik José Ignacio Modern ranch with 12 suites and over-the-top public spaces. 598-94/605-212; estanciavik.com; doubles from $$$$.

ISLE OF SKYE

CO. FERMANAGH

Edinburgh

CO. KILDARE

Galway

Dublin

Windermere

CO. LIMERICK

Vlieland

Berlin

CO. KILKENNY

THE COTSWOLDS

Amsterdam

Helsinki

Muhu Island

CO. KERRY

Bath

London

Berkshire

Brussels

Kraków

Oberwesel

Prague

LUXEMBOURG

Reims

Vienna

Paris

Munich

Salzburg

Budapest

LOIRE VALLEY

Zurich

BURGUNDY

Lausanne

St. Moritz

Gstaad

Zermatt

Gargnano

Venice

Milan

Padua

Mombaruzzo

Botogna

Nice

Monte Carlo

Florence

PROVENCE

San Sebastián

Bidart

CÔTE D'AZUR

Tudela

Ladispoli

Rome

Porto-Vecchio

Sorrento

Barcelona

Capri

Ravello

Positano

Madrid

Lisbon

Évora

Taormina

Sagres

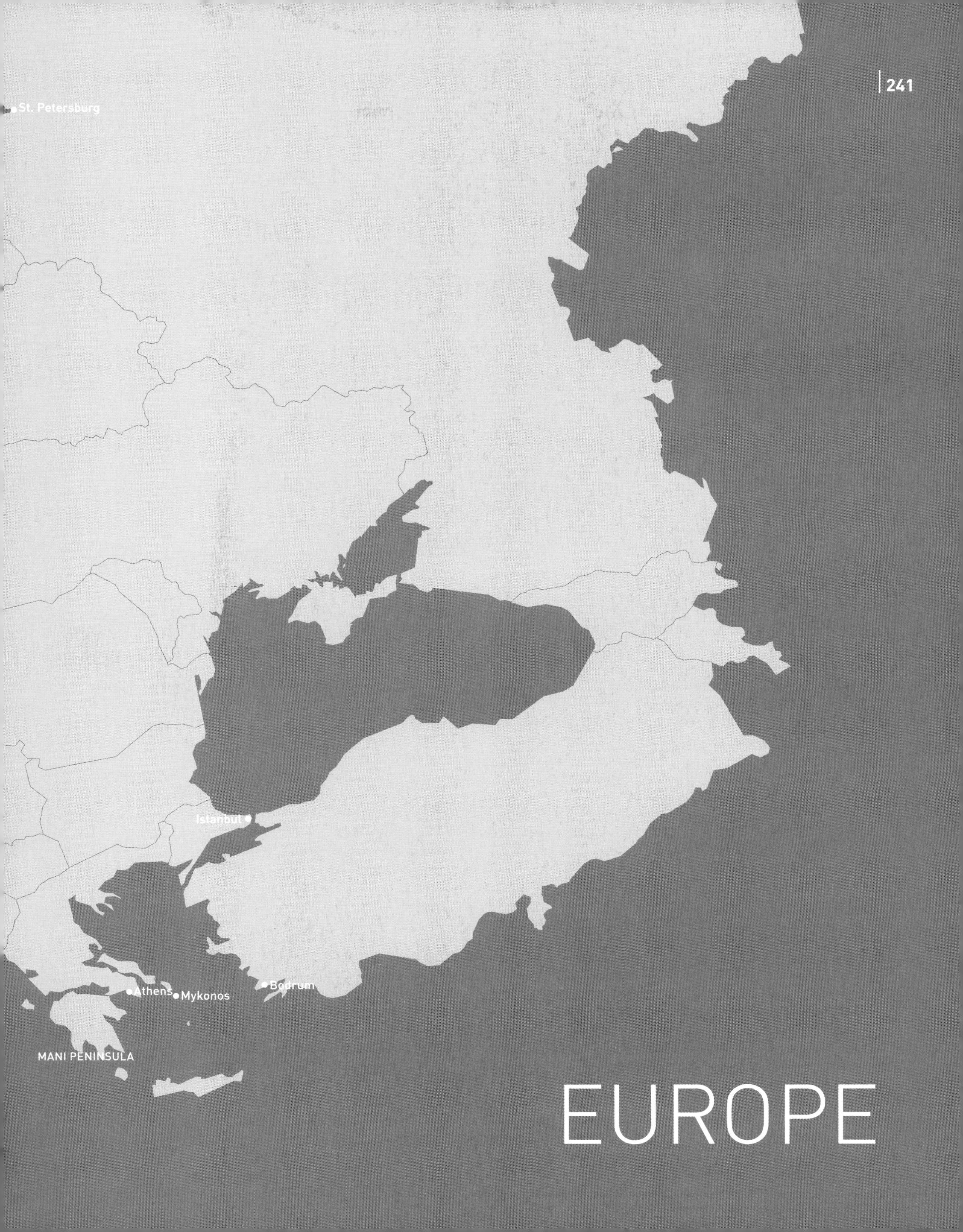

St. Petersburg

Istanbul

Athens Mykonos

Bodrum

MANI PENINSULA

EUROPE

AUSTRIA
SALZBURG
Hotel Goldener Hirsch, a Luxury Collection Hotel Down the block from Mozart's former residence, with Austrian-made furniture in all 69 guest rooms. 37 Getreidegasse; 800/325-3589 or 43-662/86840; goldenerhirschsalzburg.com; doubles from $$.

VIENNA
Grand Hotel Wien Revived 1870 Belle Époque building near the boutique-filled Kohlmarkt street. 9 Kärntner Ring; 800/223-6800 or 43-1/515-800; grandhotelwien.com; doubles from $$.

Hotel Imperial, a Luxury Collection Hotel Palace turned hotel for the 1873 World's Fair that's also known for its superb concierge department (staffers are adept at securing last-minute opera tickets). 16 Kärntner Ring; 800/325-3589 or 43-1/501-100; luxurycollection.com; doubles from $$$.

Hotel Sacher Wien An 1876 property opposite the opera house, with a restaurant redesigned by interiors guru Pierre-Yves Rochon. 4 Philharmonikerstrasse; 800/223-6800 or 43-1/514-560; sacher.com; doubles from $$$.

BELGIUM
BRUSSELS
Hotel Amigo Former 16th-century brick prison, now a light-filled hotel with surrealist art. 1-3 Rue de l'Amigo; 888/667-9477 or 32-2/547-4747; roccofortecollection.com; doubles from $$$$.

CORSICA
PORTO-VECCHIO
Grand Hôtel de Cala Rossa Polished island retreat for the well-heeled, with a formal Michelin-starred restaurant. 33-4/9571-6151; hotel-calarossa.com; doubles from $$$$$.

CZECH REPUBLIC
PRAGUE
Four Seasons Hotel Four buildings from different architectural eras (Neo-Renaissance, Baroque, Neo-classical), on the east bank of the Vltava River. 2A/1098 Veleslavinova; 800/332-3442 or 420-221/427-000; fourseasons.com; doubles from $$$.

ENGLAND
BATH
Royal Crescent Hotel Two 18th-century row houses on an immaculate lawn made for picnics at the center of Bath's Royal Crescent, a series of Georgian-era residences. 16 Royal Crescent; 800/735-2478 or 44-1225/823-333; royalcrescent.co.uk; doubles from $$.

BERKSHIRE
Cliveden House Hotel Encircled by National Trust gardens, an Italianate manor where some rooms have handcrafted beds, and other rooms look onto the Berkshire hills. Taplow, Maidenhead; 44-1628/668-561; clivenhouse.co.uk; doubles from $$.

THE COTSWOLDS
Barnsley House Eighteen-room hotel that feels laid-back and personal, with four acres of lavishly landscaped gardens. Barnsley, Cirencester; 44-1285/740-000; barnsleyhouse.com; doubles from $$.

Cotswold House Hotel & Spa Behind a Regency façade, modern and traditional furnishings and a restaurant serving refined, inventive food. Chipping Campden; 44-1386/840-330; cotswoldhouse.com; doubles from $$.

Cotswolds88hotel Swinging boutique property with eclectic décor and a menu drawing from the region's wealth of ingredients. Painswick; 44-1452/813-688; cotswolds88hotel.com; doubles from $$.

LONDON
The Connaught Red-brick Victorian in Mayfair offering 121 expertly restored rooms and a bar with silver-leaf walls designed by David Collins. Carlos Place; 800/637-2869 or 44-20/7499-7070; the-connaught.co.uk; doubles from $$$$.

The Dorchester Art Deco landmark across from Hyde Park with an Alain Ducasse restaurant and a newly renovated spa. Park Lane; 800/650-1842 or 44-20/7629-8888; thedorchester.com; doubles from $$$$.

41 Black-and-white interiors and the air of a private club. 41 Buckingham Palace Rd.; 44-20/7300-0041; 41hotel.com; doubles from $$.

Four Seasons Hotel Reopening at the end of this year after a Pierre-Yves Rochon–designed redo that includes the launch of a new rooftop spa. Hamilton Place, Park Lane; 800/332-3442 or 44-20/7499-0888; fourseasons.com; doubles from $$$$$.

The Goring Behind Buckingham Palace, a 71-room family-run hotel that balances glitz and English charm. Beeston Place, Grosvenor Gardens; 44-20/7396-9000; the goring.com; doubles from $$.

The Lanesborough On Hyde Park Corner, 95 rooms in a Georgian-style building; the oak-paneled Library Bar stocks hard-to-find Cognacs and whiskeys. Hyde Park Corner; 877/787-3447 or 44-20/7259-5599; stregis.com; doubles from $$$.

Mandarin Oriental Hyde Park An 1889 gentlemen's club converted into a hotel combining British accents (button-back wing chairs) with Asian flair (bamboo terrace furniture). 66 Knightsbridge; 800/526-6566 or 44-20/7235-2000; mandarinoriental.com; doubles from $$$$.

Milestone Hotel Each of the 63 rooms is individually decorated, giving this turreted Victorian opposite Kensington Palace a residential feel. 1 Kensington Court; 800/223-6800 or 44-20/7917-1000; milestonehotel.com; doubles from $$.

The Ritz A 137-room Belle Époque hotel between Green Park and Piccadilly Circus, with gilded Louis

A sitting room at Cotswolds88hotel, in Painswick, England.

Views of Gerolimenas Bay from the Kyrimai Hotel, on Greece's Mani Peninsula.

XVI–style interiors. 150 Piccadilly; 877/748-9536 or 44-20/7493-8181; the ritzlondon.com; doubles from $$$$.

Rough Luxe Hotel 1820's Georgian with unorthodox interiors that mix opulent details and stripped-down surfaces. 1 Birkenhead St.; 44-20/7837-5338; roughluxe.co.uk; doubles from $$.

The Stafford Well-appointed town house behind Green Park, plus a restored 17th-century stable courtyard; a Master Sommelier oversees an in-house wine cellar specializing in Burgundy and Bordeaux. St. James's Place;

44-20/7493-0111; thestaffordhotel. co.uk; doubles from $$$.

WINDERMERE
Holbeck Ghyll Country House Hotel Within Lake District National Park, a 19th-century hunting lodge full of traditional English touches. 800/525-4800 or 44-1539/432-375; holbeckghyll. com; doubles from $$.

ESTONIA
MUHU ISLAND
Pädaste Manor Sixteenth-century manor and stone outbuildings in a landscaped park, on an island in the Baltic Riviera. 800/525-4800

or 011-372/454-8800; padaste.ee; doubles from $$.

FINLAND
HELSINKI
Hotel Kämp, a Luxury Collection Hotel Old-world opulence meets modern-day restraint across from Esplanade Park; the front desk has bicycles and area cycling maps on hand. 29 Pohjoisesplanadi; 800/325-3589 or 358-9/576-111; hotelkamp.com; doubles from $$.

FRANCE
BIDART
Villa l'Arche In a tiny Basque village, eight crisp rooms and suites in a villa overlooking a sandy beach. Rue Camboénèa; 33-5/59-51-65-95; villalarche.com; doubles from $.

BURGUNDY
Hôtel Le Cep Cluster of 14th-, 15th-, and 16th-century buildings housing 64 antiques-filled rooms (each named after a grand cru wine), in the heart of Burgundy wine country. 800/525-4800 or 33-3/80-22-35-48; hotel-cep-beaune. com; doubles from $$.

CÔTE D'AZUR
Château de la Chèvre d'Or Complex of stone buildings and a Michelin two-starred restaurant on a cliff above the Mediterranean. Èze Village; 800/735-2478 or 33-4/92-10-66-66; chevredor.com; doubles from $$.

Château Eza Seventeenth-century hotel with modern bathrooms, stone balconies, and panoramic

views abutting ancient rock walls in the medieval village. Èze Village; 800/525-4800 or 33-4/93-41-12-24; chateaueza.com; doubles from $$$.

LOIRE VALLEY
Domaine des Hauts de Loire Nineteenth-century former hunting lodge with 31 Empire-style rooms on 178 forested acres between Blois and Amboise. Onzain; 800/735-2478 or 33-2/54-20-72-57; domaine-hautsloire.com; doubles from $.

NICE
Le Negresco A 141-room hotel that's a national historic monument on the Promenade des Anglais and is notable for its pink dome overlooking Nice's Baie des Anges. 37 Promenade des Anglais; 800/223-6800 or 33-4/93-16-64-00; hotel-negresco.com; doubles from $$$. The hotel is reopening in July after a major renovation.

PARIS
Four Seasons Hotel George V Sparkling 1928 grande dame with up-to-the-minute technology (Wi-Fi; iPod docking stations) and extraordinary flower arrangements, near the Champs-Élysées. 31 Ave. George V; 800/332-3442 or 33-1/49-52-70-00; fourseasons. com; doubles from $$$$$.

Hôtel de Crillon Louis XV–commissioned palace on the Place de la Concorde; the Obé restaurant was just refurbished. 10 Place de la Concorde; 800/223-6800 or 33-1/44-71-15-00; crillon. com; doubles from $$$$$.

Hôtel Le Meurice Feminine Louis XVI–style interiors and a lobby redesigned by Philippe Starck, across from the Tuileries. 228 Rue de Rivoli; 800/650-1842 or 33-1/44-58-10-10; lemeurice.com; doubles from $$$$.

Hôtel Plaza Athénée A 191-room hotel with a Michelin three-starred restaurant and a 35,000-bottle wine cellar. 25 Ave. Montaigne; 800/650-1842 or 33-1/53-67-66-65; plaza-athenee-paris.com; doubles from $$$$.

Mama Shelter Funky high-concept hotel in a former parking garage that was given a whimsical redo by designer Philippe Starck. 109 Rue de Bagnolet; 33-1/43-48-48-48; mamashelter.com; doubles from $$.

Park Hyatt Paris-Vendôme Palatial hotel with sexy interiors—a daring design departure from its more traditional neighbors—just off the Place Vendôme. 5 Rue de la Paix; 800/233-1234 or 33-1/58-71-12-34; park.hyatt.com; doubles from $$$$$.

Ritz Paris Grand manse built by César Ritz; the on-site L'Espadon restaurant was awarded a second Michelin star. 15 Place Vendôme; 800/223-6800 or 33-1/43-16-30-30; ritzparis.com; doubles from $$$$$.

PROVENCE
Le Couvent des Minimes Evocative 17th-century former nunnery housing the first spa in France

from Provençal skincare company L'Occitane. Mane; 800/735-2478 or 33-4/92-74-77-77; couventdes minimes-hotelspa.com; doubles from $$.

L'Oustau de Baumanière Three former residences in Provençal style, two swimming pools, an organic kitchen garden, and a stellar French restaurant. Les-Baux-de-Provence; 33-4/90-54-33-07; oustaudebaumaniere.com; doubles from $$.

REIMS
Les Crayères Impeccable turn-of-the-20th-century château in the heart of the Champagne region. 800/735-2478 or 33-3/26-82-80-80; lescrayeres.com; doubles from $$.

GERMANY
BERLIN
Ellington Hotel Streamlined interiors in a historic former office building on Nürnberger Strasse, the main artery of former West Berlin. 50-55 Nürnberger Str.; 49-30/683-150; ellington-hotel.com; doubles from $.

Kempinski Hotel Bristol Semi-circular property with 301 rooms and a leafy inner courtyard. 27 Kurfürstendamm; 800/426-3135 or 49-30/884-340; kempinski-berlin.com; doubles from $$$.

Sofitel Berlin Gendarmenmarkt Contemporary hotel directly across from the Gendarmenmarkt with 92 small and simple rooms (white walls, chrome fixtures). 50-52 Charlottenstrasse; 800/763-4835

or 49-30/203-750; sofitel.com; doubles from $$.

MUNICH
Hotel Bayerischer Hof Family-owned hotel with a vaulted restaurant that serves Bavarian fare (sausage and strudel) and, on Sundays, a popular brunch. 2-6 Promenadeplatz; 800/223-6800 or 49-89/21200; bayerischerhof.de; doubles from $$$.

Hotel Cocoon Near the old city, small yet efficiently organized rooms with retro-futuristic touches, such as bubble chairs and hits of Day-Glo. 35 Lindwurmstrasse; 49-89/5999-3907; hotel-cocoon.de; doubles from $.

Hotel Vier Jahreszeiten Kempinski Built by a Bavarian king in 1858 and still full of royal furnishings, including the original Belle Époque spiral staircase. 17 Maximilianstrasse; 800/426-3135 or 49-89/212-500; kempinski-vierjahreszeiten.com; doubles from $$$.

OBERWESEL
Schönburg Castle Hotel One of the most hauntingly romantic places in Europe—a 13th-century fortress overlooking the Rhine Valley. 49-6744/93930; hotel-schoenburg.com; doubles from $.

GREECE
ATHENS
Astir Palace Complex of two properties on a private Mediterranean peninsula—the Westin Athens; Arion, a Luxury Collection

Resort & Spa; and, in 2011, a third, the W Athens. 40 Apollonos St., Vouliagmeni; 800/937-8461 or 30-210/890-2000; astir-palace.com; Arion doubles from $$$; Westin doubles from $$$.

Athenaeum InterContinental Grand white-stone building with the largest hotel rooms (averaging 810 square feet) in Athens. 89-93 Syngrou Ave.; 800/327-0200 or 30-210/920-6000; intercontinental.com; doubles from $$.

Classical 2, Fashion House Hotel Flamboyant and quirky rooms in the heart of town, with public spaces that include a soccer-themed restaurant. 2 Pireos St.; 30-210/523-5230; classicalhotels.com; doubles from $.

MANI PENINSULA
Kyrimai Hotel Stone-turreted family-run hotel on a private bay with a waterfront pool and an award-winning chef. 30-27330/54288; kyrimai.gr; doubles from $.

MYKONOS
Santa Marina, a Luxury Collection Resort Low-slung whitewashed bungalows built into the hills above a secluded beach. Ornos Bay; 800/325-3589 or 30-22890/23220; luxurycollection.com; doubles from $$$, including breakfast and port transfers. Open seasonally, May–September.

HUNGARY
BUDAPEST
Art'otel Budapest Within walking distance of the Hungarian National

Portego Hall at Ca' Sagredo Hotel, in Venice.

Gallery; more than 600 works by American artist Donald Sultan are on display, including carpets and dinnerware. 16-19 Bem Rakpart; 800/814-7000 or 36-1/487-9487; artotels.com; doubles from $.

Four Seasons Hotel Gresham Palace Art Nouveau masterpiece at the base of the Chain Bridge and a short walk from Vaci Street. 5-6 Roosevelt Tér; 800/332-3442 or 36-1/268-6000; fourseasons.com; doubles from $$$.

Lánchíd 19 Striking contemporary hotel on the bank of the Danube, with a luminous façade and glass bridges between guest rooms. 19 Lánchíd Utca; 800/337-4685 or 36-1/419-1900; lanchid19hotel.hu; doubles from $.

Marriott Hotel Affordable, unadorned guest rooms with Danube views. 4 Apáczai Csere János U.; 800/228-9290 or 36-1/486-5000; marriott.com; doubles from $$.

IRELAND
COUNTY KERRY
Aghadoe Heights Hotel & Spa Modern stone structure with a wellness focus (the hotel is home to an Aveda spa, and staffers encourage guests to explore the nearby national park). Killarney; 353-64/663-1766; aghadoeheights.com; doubles from $$.

COUNTY KILDARE
Kildare Hotel, Spa & Country Club Notable amenities at the 19th-century château known as the K Club include two championship golf courses and a 20,000-square-foot spa. Straffan; 353-1/601-7200; kclub.com; doubles from $$.

COUNTY KILKENNY
Mount Juliet Estate Georgian estate with a full roster of activities that include golf, fly-fishing, and horseback riding. Thomastown; 800/525-4800 or 353-56/777-3000; mountjuliet.ie; doubles from $$.

COUNTY LIMERICK
Adare Manor Hotel & Golf Resort 1832 Gothic Revival château on a sprawling parcel of parkland that includes a Robert Trent Jones Sr.–designed golf course. Adare; 800/462-3273 or 353-61/396-566; adaremanor.com; doubles from $$$.

DUBLIN
The Clarence A 49-room boutique property built in 1852 and updated in 1996 by U2's Bono and the Edge (the hotel's co-owners). 6-8 Wellington Quay; 877/227-2869 or 353-1/407-0800; theclarence.ie; doubles from $$$.

GALWAY
G Hotel Steel-and-glass low-rise, with bold, eye-popping interiors by the Irish milliner Philip Treacy. 353-91/ 865-200; theghotel.ie; doubles from $.

ITALY
BOLOGNA
Grand Hotel Baglioni Luxe rooms and standout service (Italian chocolate at turndown, wine-cellar tours) in an 18th-century palazzo and former seminary on the main square. 8 Via Indipendenza; 800/223-6800 or 39-051/225-445; baglionihotels.com; doubles from $$$.

CAPRI
Hotel La Scalinatella Intimate property—just 30 rooms—on one of the most peaceful stretches of the Italian island. 39-081/837-0633; scalinatella.com; doubles from $$$.

FLORENCE
Four Seasons Hotel Firenze Renaissance-era structure with 15th-century frescoes and the largest private garden in town. 99 Borgo Pinti; 800/332-3442 or 39-055/26261; fourseasons.com; doubles from $$.

Grand Hotel Villa Cora Once this was the residence of Napoleon III's widow, Empress Eugénie; now it's a boutique hotel that overlooks the city center. 18 Viale Machiavelli; 39-055/271-840; villacora.it; doubles from $$. The hotel is closed until June 2010 for renovations.

Hotel J. K. Place Stylish, small, and welcoming, with a clubby, masculine feel. 7 Piazza Santa Maria Novella, 800/525-4800 or 39-055/264-5181; jkplace.com; doubles from $$$.

Villa La Massa Sixteenth-century Medicean villa, the sister property to Lake Como's Villa d'Este. 24 Via della Massa Candeli; 800/223-6800 or 39-055/62611; villalamassa.it; doubles from $$$$.

GARGNANO

Grand Hotel a Villa Feltrinelli Restored 19th-century villa with four charming guesthouses—there are just 21 rooms in total—on the western shore of Lake Garda. 39-036/579-8000; villafeltrinelli. com; doubles from $$$$$. Open seasonally, April–October.

LADISPOLI

Hotel La Posta Vecchia Lavish 17th-century mansion (J. Paul Getty's former residence) built atop Roman ruins by the Tyrrhenian Sea. Palo Laziale; 800/735-2478 or 39-06/994-9501; lapostavecchia. com; doubles from $$$.

MILAN

Le Méridien Gallia Art Nouveau icon with Liberty-style interiors; downstairs there's a lobby bar, a Mediterranean restaurant, and an on-site florist. 9 Piazza Duca D'Aosta; 800/543-4300 or 39-02/67851; lemeridiengallia.com; doubles from $$.

Westin Palace Marble-clad hotel with Turkish baths in its fitness center. 20 Piazza della Repubblica; 800/228-3000 or 39-02/63361; westin.com; doubles from $$$.

MOMBARUZZO

La Villa Hotel Understated country retreat surrounded by vineyards in the hills of Piedmont. 39-0141/793-890; lavillahotel.net; doubles from $.

PADUA

Villa Pisani Built in the 1500's by the noble Pisani dynasty, this eight-room B&B is known for the original Veronese frescoes in its ballroom. Vescovana; 39-042/592-0016; villapisani.it; doubles from $$.

POSITANO

Il San Pietro Cliff-hanging architectural wonder above an Amalfi Coast cove overlooking the sea, with plenty to keep active types busy—from tennis courts to a mosaic-tiled pool. 2 Via Laurito; 800/735-2478 or 39-089/875-455; ilsanpietro.it; doubles from $$$$.

La Rosa dei Venti Seven-room hotel with simple accents, sweeping sea views, and a 400-step walkway to see-and-be-seen Fornillo Beach. 39-089/875-252; larosa deiventi.net; doubles from $.

RAVELLO

Hotel Caruso Belvedere 11th-century palace on a limestone bluff, once favored by celebrities (Jackie Kennedy, Greta Garbo, Humphrey Bogart); there's also a heated infinity pool, 15 private gardens, and two restaurants. 800/237-1236 or 39-089/858-801; hotel caruso.com; doubles from $$$$$.

Palazzo Sasso Pink-hued villa (built in the 12th century) high above the Mediterranean. Guests pick their linens from a Frette sheet menu and are granted access to a private seaside villa. 39-089/818-181; palazzosasso. com; doubles from $$$.

ROME

Grand Hotel Palace A 100-room structure with 1930's frescoes immortalizing Roman high society. 70 Via Veneto; 800/267-2656 or 39-06/478-719; boscolohotels.com; doubles from $$.

Hotel d'Inghilterra Fifteenth-century royal guesthouse, now a fashionable hideaway in the city's haute Via Condotti shopping district. 14 Via Bocca di Leone; 39-06/699-811; royaldemeure.com; doubles from $$$.

Portrait Suites Sexy urban retreat owned by the Ferragamo family; the Spanish Steps can be seen from the rooftop terrace. 23 Via Bocca di Leone; 39-06/6938-0742; lungarno hotels.com; doubles from $$$.

SORRENTO

Grand Hotel Excelsior Vittoria Family-run since 1834; the three adjoining brick buildings look out onto the Bay of Naples. 800/223-6800 or 39-081/807-1044; exvitt. it.com; doubles from $$$.

TAORMINA

Grand Hotel Timeo Former palazzo of Sicilian nobility, near Mount Etna and the Bay of Naxos. 39-0942/23801; grandhoteltimeo. com; doubles from $$$.

Hotel Villa Sant'Andrea Patrician villa that retains the charm of a private residence; divers will love the sea life in the marine preserve nearby. 39-094/223-125; villasantandreahotel.com; doubles from $$$.

VENICE

Bauer Il Palazzo Opulent details and heirloom furnishings in an 82-room hotel on the Grand Canal. San Marco 1413/D; 800/223-6800 or 39-041/520-7022; bauerhotels. com; doubles from $$$$$.

Ca' Sagredo Hotel Fifteenth-century palazzo with an elaborate marble staircase and frescoes. Campo Santa Sofia, Cannaregio 4198-99; 800/525-4800 or 39-041/241-3111; casagredohotel. com; doubles from $$.

Charming House IQs Four-room hidden gem furnished with contemporary pieces by Moroso and B&B Italia. Campiello Querini Stampalia, Castello 4425; 39-041/241-0062; thecharminghouse. com; doubles from $$.

Hotel Cipriani Giuseppe Cipriani's legendary 1950's getaway—silk curtains, gilded ceilings, and all-marble bathrooms—flanked by two 15th-century palazzos. Giudecca 10; 800/223-6800 or 39-041/520-7744; hotelcipriani.com; doubles from $$$$$. Open seasonally, April–October.

Hotel Excelsior Moorish architecture and old-guard–style rooms on the island of Lido. 41 Lungomare Marconi; 39-041/526-0201; ho10. net; doubles from $$$$.

KEY TO THE PRICE ICONS   **$** UNDER $250   **$$** $250–$499   **$$$** $500–$749   **$$$$** $750–$999   **$$$$$** $1,000 AND UP

Hotel Flora Behind St. Mark's Square, 43 rooms in a former art school with a serene courtyard garden. San Marco 2283/A; 39-041/520-5844; hotelflora.it; doubles from $$.

Luna Hotel Baglioni A 900-year-old palazzo, located steps from the Piazza San Marco. San Marco 1234; 800/223-6800 or 39-041/528-9840; baglionihotels.com; doubles from $$$$.

Novecento Boutique Hotel Nine-room boutique hotel run by a charming Italian couple and decorated with Oriental and Venetian tapestries and furniture. San Marco 2683; 39-041/241-3765; novecento.biz; doubles from $$.

LUXEMBOURG

Hôtel Le Royal Tucked into a leafy stretch of the city's main business thoroughfare, with two restaurants: one serving international cuisine, the second, French-inflected. 12 Blvd. Royal; 352/241-616-715; leroyalluxembourg.com; doubles from $$$.

MONACO
MONTE CARLO

Hôtel Hermitage Belle Époque structure facing Monte Carlo's Marina. Square Beaumarchais; 800/223-6800 or 377/98-06-40-00; hotelhermitagemontecarlo.com; doubles from $$$.

Hôtel Metropole Palatial hotel with a soaring glass atrium and Joël Robuchon's first Japanese restaurant, Yoshi. 4 Ave. de la Madone; 800/223-6800 or 377/93-15-15-15; metropole.com; doubles from $$$$.

THE NETHERLANDS
AMSTERDAM

Hotel Patou On a high-fashion corridor, 12 rooms and a brasserie that's a hit with café society. 63 P.C. Hooftstraat; 31-20/676-0232; hotelpatou.nl; doubles from $.

VLIELAND

Badhotel Bruin Affordable beach resort that's popular with young families from Amsterdam, on an island known for its bike paths and bird-watching. 31-562/452-828; badhotelbruin.com; doubles from $.

NORTHERN IRELAND
COUNTY FERMANAGH

The West Wing, Crom Castle For groups of up to 12 guests, six bedrooms in the historical seat of the Earls of Erne. 44-2867/738-004; cromcastle.com; weekend rates (three nights) from $$$$$ for up to 12 people.

POLAND
KRAKÓW

Hotel Pod Róza Centuries-old Renaissance palace made for modern travelers. 14 Florianska Ul.; 48-12/424-3300; hotel.com.pl; doubles from $$.

PORTUGAL
ÉVORA

Convento do Espinheiro, a Luxury Collection Hotel & Spa Former convent, now a 92-room hotel with candlelit arches and three pools on 23 acres in the Portuguese countryside. 800/325-3589 or 351-26/678-8200; luxurycollection.com; doubles from $.

LISBON

Fontana Park Hotel Former iron factory reimagined with glass-and-concrete staircases and a disciplined palette. 2 Rua Engenheiro Vieira da Silva; 800/337-4685 or 351-210/410-600; fontanapark hotel.com; doubles from $.

SAGRES

Memmo Baleeira Hotel At Europe's southwestern edge, a 144-room property with an in-house surf school. 351-282/624-212; memmo baleeira.com; doubles from $.

RUSSIA
ST. PETERSBURG

Hotel Astoria Elegant interiors opposite St. Isaac's Cathedral and within walking distance of the Russian Museum. 39 Bolshaya Morskaya Ul.; 888/667-9477 or 7-812/494-5757; thehotelastoria.com; doubles from $$$$$.

SCOTLAND
EDINBURGH

Caledonian Hilton 1903 hotel built on top of a 19th-century railway station, a 10-minute walk from Edinburgh Castle. Princes St.; 800/445-8667 or 44-131/222-8888; hilton.com; doubles from $.

Hotel Missoni Edinburgh On the city's Royal Mile, a statement hotel with colorful rooms and a fashionable bar and restaurant. 1 George IV Bridge; 44-131/220-6666; hotelmissoni.com; doubles from $$.

ISLE OF SKYE

Kinloch Lodge Food-focused retreat where cookbook author Lady Claire Macdonald runs on-site culinary demonstrations. Sleat; 44-1471/833-333; kinloch-lodge.co.uk; doubles from $$, including breakfast and five-course dinner.

SPAIN
BARCELONA

ME Barcelona Fifteen minutes from the city center by car, a glass-and-steel structure with 258 rooms and a much-hyped restaurant. 272 Carrer Pere IV; 877/954-8363; me-barcelona.com; doubles from $.

MADRID

Hotel Villa Magna (formerly Park Hyatt Villa Magna) Granite building with 150 rooms that sparkle after a renovation. 22 Paseo de la Castellana; 800/745-8883 or 34/91-587-1234; hotelvillamagna.com; doubles from $$$.

SAN SEBASTIÁN

Hotel Maria Cristina, a Luxury Collection Hotel Belle Époque property known for its old-world style on the Urumea River. 800/325-4545 or 34/94-343-7600; hotel-mariacristina.com; doubles from $$.

TUDELA

Hotel Aire de Bardenas Single-story cubical structures set against an austere landscape in northeastern Spain. 34/948-116-666; airede bardenas.com; doubles from $.

The indoor pool at Suvretta House, in St. Moritz, Switzerland.

SWITZERLAND
GSTAAD

Grand Hotel Park The first and still the finest luxury hotel in Gstaad. 800/745-8883 or 41-33/748-9800; grandhotelpark.ch; doubles from $$$$$. The hotel will be closed for renovations March–December 2010.

LAUSANNE

Lausanne Palace & Spa An institution for international high rollers since 1915, with a happening English colonial–style bar. 800/745-8883 or 41-21/331-3131; lausanne-palace.com; doubles from $$$.

ST. MORITZ

Suvretta House Castle-like property with a family-friendly vibe, just outside St. Moritz. 800/223-6800 or 41-81/836-3636; suvretta house.ch; doubles from $$$$.

ZERMATT

Seiler Hotel Monte Rosa Zermatt's oldest hotel, on a coveted corner near the Matterhorn. 41-27/966-0333; monterosazermatt.ch; doubles from $$$, seven-night minimum in winter.

ZURICH

Dolder Grand After a four-year makeover by Foster + Partners, an 1899 main building flanked by two futuristic glass-and-steel wings. 65 Kurhausstrasse; 41-44/456-6000; thedoldergrand.com; doubles from $$$$.

TURKEY
BODRUM

The Butterfly Six-room seaside villa where garden patios have panoramic views of the Aegean and the Greek island of Kos. 90-252/313-8358; thebutterfly bodrum.com; doubles from $$.

The Marmara These 95 rooms on a steep hill have views of the bay and either ground-floor terraces or sunny balconies. 90-252/313-8130; themarmarahotels.com; doubles from $$.

ISTANBUL

Ceylan InterContinental Near Taksim Square; the new spa has a relaxation room overlooking the Bosporus. 1 Asker Ocagi Cad.; 800/327-0200 or 90-212/368-4444; intercontinental. com; doubles from $$$.

Park Hyatt Maçka Palas 1920's town house in the fashionable Nişantaşi district; a favorite with media types. 4 Bronz Sk.; 800/233-1234 or 90-212/315-1234; park. hyatt.com; doubles from $$.

KEY TO THE PRICE ICONS $ UNDER $250 $$ $250–$499 $$$ $500–$749 $$$$ $750–$999 $$$$$ $1,000 AND UP

Fez
Marrakesh
Jerusalem
Alexandria
Amman
Cairo
Luxor
Zighy Bay
Dubai
Abu Dhabi

Samburu National Reserve
Nanyuki
Ol Pejeta Conservancy
Mount Kenya Park
LAIKIPIA
Serengeti National Park
Nairobi
Ngorongoro Crater
Masai Mara
Amboseli National Park
Karatu
Lake Manyara

HARTMANN VALLEY
Livingstone
Ongava Game Reserve
Linyanti Wildlife Reserve
Moremi Game Reserve
Chobe National Park
Okavango Delta Reserve
Makgadikgadi Pans
Kulala Wilderness Reserve
Mauritius
KRUGER NATIONAL PARK AREA
Madikwe Game Reserve
Johannesburg
KWAZULU-NATAL
Cedar Mountains Wilderness Area
EASTERN CAPE
Cape Town
Franschhoek

AFRICA
+ THE MIDDLE EAST

BOTSWANA

CHOBE NATIONAL PARK

Chobe Game Lodge Moorish-themed, eco-conscious property on a river frequented by elephants. 27-11/394-3873; desertdelta.com; doubles from $$$$$, all-inclusive.

Savute Elephant Camp Cluster of canvas tents in Chobe National Park; accessible only by chartered aircraft. 800/237-1236 or 2721/483-1600; orient-express.com; doubles from $$$$$, all-inclusive.

LINYANTI WILDLIFE RESERVE

DumaTau Camp Ten thatched-roof tents with en-suite bathrooms and outdoor showers, on the edge of a hippo-filled lagoon. 27-11/807-1800; wilderness-safaris.com; doubles from $$$$$, all-inclusive.

MAKGADIKGADI PANS

Jack's Camp A 1940's safari feel in the otherworldly salt pans, plus a shaded swimming pool. 27-11/447-1605; unchartedafrica.com; doubles from $$$$$, all-inclusive.

MOREMI GAME RESERVE

Camp Okavango Activities at this renovated tent encampment include canoeing in the river delta and guided tours on nearby islands. 27-11/394-3873; desertdelta.com; doubles from $$$$$, all-inclusive.

Eagle Island Camp Remote island tent retreat surrounded by water lilies and reeds. 800/237-1236 or 27-21/483-1600; orient-express.com; doubles from $$$$$, all-inclusive.

Khwai River Lodge Forty-year-old lodge and thatched-roof tents with muted interiors, set in a riverside forest. 800/237-1236 or 27-21/483-1600; orient-express.com; doubles from $$$$$, all-inclusive.

Mombo Camp and Little Mombo Camp Two groups of tents with plunge pools and decks for prime bird-watching. 27-11/807-1800; wilderness-safaris.com; doubles from $$$$$, all-inclusive.

Sanctuary Chief's Camp Traditional bush lodge on an island teeming with the Big Five. 27-11/438-4650; sanctuaryretreats.com; doubles from $$$$$, all-inclusive.

OKAVANGO DELTA RESERVE

Xudum Delta Lodge Contemporary safari camp offering a part-land, part-water wildlife experience on 62,000 acres. 888/882-3742; andbeyond.com; doubles from $$$$$ per person, all-inclusive.

EGYPT

ALEXANDRIA

Four Seasons Hotel at San Stefano In a crescent-shaped tower on the Corniche, 118 rooms designed by Pierre-Yves Rochon. 399 El Geish Rd.; 800/332-3442 or 20-3/581-8000; fourseasons.com; doubles from $$$.

CAIRO

Conrad Popular with corporate travelers; all 617 rooms have terraces overlooking the Nile. 1191 Corniche el Nil; 800/266-7237 or 20-2/2580-8000; conradhotels.com; doubles from $$.

Four Seasons Hotel Cairo at Nile Plaza Comfortable blend of business and luxury amenities; located on the riverbank. 1089 Corniche el Nil; 800/332-3442 or 20-2/2791-7000; fourseasons.com; doubles from $$.

Four Seasons Hotel Cairo at the First Residence High-rise on the Nile with interiors influenced by Egyptian and Neoclassical design. 35 Giza St., Giza; 800/332-3442 or 20-2/3573-1212; fourseasons.com; doubles from $$.

Mena House Oberoi Restored 19th-century hunting lodge on 40 acres abutting the Great Pyramid of Khufu. Pyramids' Rd., Giza; 800/562-3764 or 20-2/3377-3222; oberoihotels.com; doubles from $$.

LUXOR

Al Moudira Hotel Forty acres of gardens and a heady Arabian Nights ambience. Hager Al Dabbeya; 20-012/392-8332; moudira.com; doubles from $$.

ISRAEL

JERUSALEM

American Colony Hotel Just north of the Damascus Gate, a favored meeting place for diplomats, journalists, and UN officials. 23 Nablus Rd.; 800/745-8883 or 972-2/627-9777; americancolony.com; doubles from $$.

JORDAN

AMMAN

Four Seasons Hotel Stone-and-glass structure between the financial district and the quiet Al Sweifiyah residential area. Fifth Circle, Al-Kindi St.; 800/332-3442 or 962-6/550-5555; fourseasons.com; doubles from $$.

Grand Hyatt A 311-room hotel in the center of the business district. Hussein Bin Ali St.; 800/233-1234 or 962-6/465-1234; grand.hyatt.com; doubles from $$.

KENYA

AMBOSELI NATIONAL PARK

Amboseli Serena Safari Lodge Inspired by Masai architecture; the swimming pool is fed by melting ice from Mount Kilimanjaro. 254-20/284-2333; serenahotels.com; doubles from $$.

Tortilis Camp Eco-friendly tents facing Mount Kilimanjaro; the chef prepares Italian dishes with herbs grown in the property's garden. 254-20/603-090; chelipeacock.com; doubles from $$$$.

LAIKIPIA

Lemarti's Camp Five tastefully furnished tents of locally loomed cotton on raised wooden platforms above a river bend. 888/436-2040; lemartiscamp.com; doubles from $$$$$, all-inclusive, four-night minimum.

MASAI MARA

Fairmont Mara Safari Club Fifty tents on the Mara River, a prime hippo-viewing spot; traditional African dinners are served in a *boma*. 800/441-1414 or 254-20/221-6940; fairmont.com; doubles from $$$.

KEY TO THE PRICE ICONS   **$** UNDER $250   **$$** $250–$499   **$$$** $500–$749   **$$$$** $750–$999   **$$$$$** $1,000 AND UP

A deck at Little Kulala, in Namibia's Kulala Wilderness Reserve.

Governors' Camp Riverside tents and some of the area's best guides, on the former hunting grounds of colonial-era governors. 254-20/273-4000; governorscamp. com; doubles from $$$$.

Kichwa Tembo Two tented camps— one vintage-style, the other distinctly modern—in the heart of the Mara. 888/882-3742 or 27-11/809-4300; andbeyondafrica. com; doubles from $$$$$.

Little Governors' Camp Privacy is guaranteed at these 17 tents set around a watering hole: the property is accessed by a hand-pulled river ferry. 254-20/273-4000; governorscamp.com; doubles from $$$$$.

Mara Serena Safari Lodge Hillside domed huts are modeled after a Masai village and look onto a migratory path for elephants and giraffes. 254-20/284-2333; serenahotels.com; doubles from $$$.

MOUNT KENYA PARK
Serena Mountain Lodge Timber lodge 6,000 feet up in Mount Kenya's rain forest canopy. 254-20/284-2333; serenahotels.com; doubles from $$.

NAIROBI
Fairmont the Norfolk Tudor-style hotel in the city center that just underwent a $12 million overhaul. Harry Thuku Rd.; 800/441-1414 or 254-20/226-5000; fairmont.com; doubles from $$.

Giraffe Manor Ivy-covered 1932 lodge with grounds that are home to a herd of giraffes. Langata; 254-20/251-3166; giraffemanor.com; doubles from $$$$.

NANYUKI
Fairmont Mount Kenya Safari Club Recently renovated 1950's-era hunting lodge in the Mount Kenya foothills. 800/441-1414 or 254-723/786-992; fairmont.com; doubles from $$.

OL PEJETA CONSERVANCY
Sweetwaters Tented Camp Collection of 39 tents set on a 90,000-acre private reserve; the lodge has the largest rhino-breeding colony in East Africa. 254-62/32-430; serenahotels.com; doubles from $$$.

SAMBURU NATIONAL RESERVE
Samburu Serena Safari Lodge Rustic shingled cottages on the edge of the Northern Frontier District, home to the Grévy's zebra

KEY TO THE PRICE ICONS   **$** UNDER $250   **$$** $250–$499   **$$$** $500–$749   **$$$$** $750–$999   **$$$$$** $1,000 AND UP

and the Somali ostrich. 254-20/284-2333; serenahotels.com; doubles from $$.

MAURITIUS

Four Seasons Resort Mauritius at Anahita Far-flung getaway with 123 villas overlooking a lagoon or mountains. Beau Champ; 800/332-3443 or 230/402-3100; fourseasons.com; doubles from $$$$.

MOROCCO
FEZ

Sofitel Fés Palais Jamaï Formerly the residence of the grand vizier of Jamaï, overlooking the Fez medina. Bab Guissa; 800/763-4835 or 212-535/634-331; sofitel.com; doubles from $$.

MARRAKESH

La Mamounia Legendary hideaway revamped by designer Jacques Garcia, with an opulent new spa. Ave. Bab Jdid; 800/223-6800 or 212-5/2438-8600; mamounia.com; doubles from $$$$.

NAMIBIA
HARTMANN VALLEY

Serra Cafema Camp Main lodge on stilts overlooking the Kunene River; eight canvas-and-thatch-roof chalets. wilderness-safaris.com; doubles from $$$$, all-inclusive.

KULALA WILDERNESS RESERVE

Little Kulala Adjacent to stunning thousand-foot sand dunes, 11 villas with bleached plank floors and rooftop terraces with "sky beds" for stargazing. wilderness-safaris.com; doubles from $$$$, all-inclusive.

ONGAVA GAME RESERVE

Little Ongava One of the country's most luxurious compounds: private infinity pools and African objets d'art in three cottage suites. wilderness-safaris.com; doubles from $$$$$, all-inclusive.

OMAN
ZIGHY BAY

Six Senses Hideaway Between jagged mountains and a wide beach, Omani-style stone villas and a spa with two hammams. Musandam Peninsula; 800/591-7480; sixsenses.com; doubles from $$$$$.

SOUTH AFRICA
CAPE TOWN

Cape Grace Mansard-roof hotel with 121 elegant rooms on its own private quay. W. Quay Rd.; 800/223-6800 or 27-21/410-7100; capegrace.com; doubles from $$$.

Grand Daddy Hotel Boutique property with a rooftop "trailer park"—seven custom-designed Airstreams. 38 Long St.; 27-21/424-7247; granddaddy.co.za; doubles from $.

Mount Nelson Hotel Pink stucco property on nine leafy acres. 76 Orange St.; 800/237-1236 or 27-21/483-1000; mountnelson.co.za; doubles from $$$.

Table Bay Hotel Waterfront gabled building adjoining an upscale shopping mall. Quay 6, Victoria & Alfred Waterfront; 27-21/406-5000; suninternational.com; doubles from $$$.

Twelve Apostles Hotel & Spa Cape Dutch–style hotel tucked between the mountains and sea, a 15-minute drive from downtown. Victoria Rd., Camps Bay; 800/223-6800 or 27-21/437-9000; 12apostleshotel.com; doubles from $$.

Westin Grand Arabella Quays Sleek tower with a spa on the V&A Waterfront. Lower Long St.; 800/228-3000 or 27-21/412-9999; westin.com; doubles from $$$.

CEDAR MOUNTAINS WILDERNESS AREA

Bushmans Kloof Number one in T+L's 2009 World's Best Awards, with access to over 130 Bushmen rock art sites. 27-21/481-1860; bushmanskloof.co.za; doubles from $$, all-inclusive.

EASTERN CAPE

Shamwari Game Reserve Seven lodges on a conservation-conscious Big Five preserve that's home to dozens of big cats. 877/354-2213 or 27-41/407-1000; shamwari.com; doubles from $$$$$, all-inclusive.

FRANSCHHOEK

Le Quartier Français Charming inn with one of South Africa's top restaurants; located in a historic Winelands village. 800/735-2478 or 27-21/876-2151; lequartier. co.za; doubles from $$$.

JOHANNESBURG

Michelangelo Hotel Italian Renaissance–style hotel with grand public spaces on Sandown's

Nelson Mandela Square. 135 West St.; 800/223-6800 or 27-11/282-7000; michelangelo.co.za; doubles from $$$.

Saxon Boutique Hotel & Spa Gated estate best known for its indoor-outdoor spa, in tony Sandhurst. 36 Saxon Rd.; 800/223-6800 or 27-11/292-6000; thesaxon.com; doubles from $$$$.

The Westcliff Palatial guest rooms in nine villas on a ridge overlooking the city. 67 Jan Smuts Ave.; 800/237-1236 or 27-11/481-6000; westcliff.co.za; doubles from $$$.

KRUGER NATIONAL PARK AREA

Bush Lodge at Sabi Sabi Private Game Reserve Thatched-roof suites around a busy watering hole; courtyards have carvings by South African sculptors. 27-11/447-7172; sabisabi.com; doubles from $$$$$, all-inclusive.

Earth Lodge at Sabi Sabi Private Game Reserve Thirteen butler-serviced suites built into the hillside; an uprooted tree serves as the property's bar. 27-11/447-7172; sabisabi.com; doubles from $$$$$, all-inclusive.

Lion Sands Private Game Reserve All 30 rooms have fireplaces and plunge pools that overlook the Sabie River. 27-11/484-9911; lionsands.com; doubles from $$$$$, all-inclusive.

Londolozi Private Game Reserve Five family-run lodges on 42,000 wilderness acres known for leopard sightings. 800/735-2478 or 27-13/735-5653; londolozi.com; doubles from $$$$$, all-inclusive.

MalaMala Game Reserve Three lodges on South Africa's largest private Big Five preserve. 27-11/442-2267; malamala.com; doubles from $$$$$, all-inclusive.

Ngala Private Game Reserve Colonial-style lodge and six raised tents on an eco-friendly reserve. 888/882-3742 or 27-11/809-4300; andbeyondafrica.com; doubles from $$$$$, all-inclusive.

Royal Malewane Refined 20-room bush camp on the western edge of Kruger. 27-15/793-0150; royalmalewane.com; doubles from $$$$$, all-inclusive.

Singita Kruger National Park Two raised lodges with interiors by up-and-coming African designers. 800/735-2478 or 27-21/683-3424; singita.com; doubles from $$$$$, all-inclusive.

Singita Sabi Sand Pair of stunning lodges—Boulders is rustic; Ebony, distinctly African colonial–style—along the Sand River. 800/735-2478 or 27-21/683-3424; singita.com; doubles from $$$$$, all-inclusive.

KWAZULU-NATAL
Phinda Private Game Reserve Six conservation-minded lodges in a 56,800-acre reserve; initiatives include lion reintroduction. 888/882-3742 or 27-11/809-4300; andbeyondafrica.com; doubles from $$$$$, all-inclusive.

MADIKWE GAME RESERVE
Molori Safari Lodge Five distinctive suites; activities range from bush walking and game drives to cooking classes and golf. 27-82/613-5723; molori.com; doubles from $$$$$ per person, all-inclusive.

TANZANIA
KARATU
Gibb's Farm Located on a coffee plantation in the Ngorongoro Forest foothills. 255-27/253-4397; gibbsfarm.net; doubles from $$$, including meals.

LAKE MANYARA
Lake Manyara Serena Safari Lodge Series of circular, brightly decorated buildings on a cliff overlooking a lake frequented by migrating birds. 254-20/284-2333; serenahotels.com; doubles from $$$, including meals.

Lake Manyara Tree Lodge Shingled tree houses in the bush; the only lodge that lies within Lake Manyara National Park. 888/882-3742 or 27-11/809-4300; andbeyondafrica.com; doubles from $$$$$, all-inclusive.

NGORONGORO CRATER
Ngorongoro Crater Lodge Masai-inspired huts with romantic Victorian touches (gilt mirrors, velvet bedspreads) along the rim of a volcano. 888/882-3742; andbeyondafrica.com; doubles from $$$$$.

Ngorongoro Serena Safari Lodge Rooms have prehistoric wall paintings in this eco-lodge, which is built of river rock and covered in vines. 254-20/284-2333; serena hotels.com; doubles from $$$, including meals.

Ngorongoro Sopa Lodge Thatched-roof rondavels have floor-to-ceiling windows that look down into the crater. 800/806-9565 or 255-27/250-0630; sopalodges.com; doubles from $$, including meals.

SERENGETI NATIONAL PARK
Kirawira Luxury Tented Camp Edwardian-style camps on a ridge in the western Serengeti. 800/525-4800 or 254-20/284-2333; serenahotels.com; doubles from $$$$$, all-inclusive.

Serengeti Migration Camp Twenty tents with wraparound porches and attentive service along the Grumeti River, a drinking spot for hippos. 800/806-9565 or 255-27/250-0630; elewana.com; doubles from $$$$$, all-inclusive.

Serengeti Sopa Lodge Secluded hotel with traditional African interiors in an acacia grove that overlooks the Serengeti Plains. 800/806-9565 or 255-27/250-0630; sopalodges.com; doubles from $$$, including meals.

Singita Grumeti Reserves Two opulent lodges and a 1920's-inspired nine-tent camp, located on a 347,000-acre wilderness preserve. 800/735-2478 or 27-21/683-3424; singita.com; doubles from $$$$$, all-inclusive.

UNITED ARAB EMIRATES
ABU DHABI
Emirates Palace Dome-bedecked hotel with a staff of nearly 2,000. W. Corniche Rd.; 800/426-3135 or 971-2/690-9000; emiratespalace. com; doubles from $$.

DUBAI
Atlantis, The Palm Sprawling, maximalist fantasy compound on 114 acres, with a mile of man-made beachfront. 971-4/426-1000; atlantisthepalm.com; doubles from $$$.

Burj Al Arab Iconic sail-shaped hotel on its own island off Jumeirah Beach. 877/854-8051 or 971-4/301-7777; jumeirah.com; doubles from $$$$$.

ZAMBIA
LIVINGSTONE
Livingstone River Club Cluster of chalets surrounded by manicured lawns on the banks of the Zambezi River. 27-11/807-1800; wilderness-safaris.com; doubles from $$$$$, all-inclusive.

Royal Livingstone Colonial-style rooms feature wildlife sketches and views of Victoria Falls. 27-11/780-7878; suninternational. com; doubles from $$$$.

Tongabezi Lodge Houses and rondavels at a bend in the Zambezi, where guests can opt to dine on a raft serviced by waiters who row out on canoes. 260-21/332-7468; tongabezi.com; doubles from $$$$$, all-inclusive.

KEY TO THE PRICE ICONS   **$** UNDER $250   **$$** $250-$499   **$$$** $500-$749   **$$$$** $750-$999   **$$$$$** $1,000 AND UP

A vaulted wing at Emirates Palace, in Abu Dhabi, United Arab Emirates.

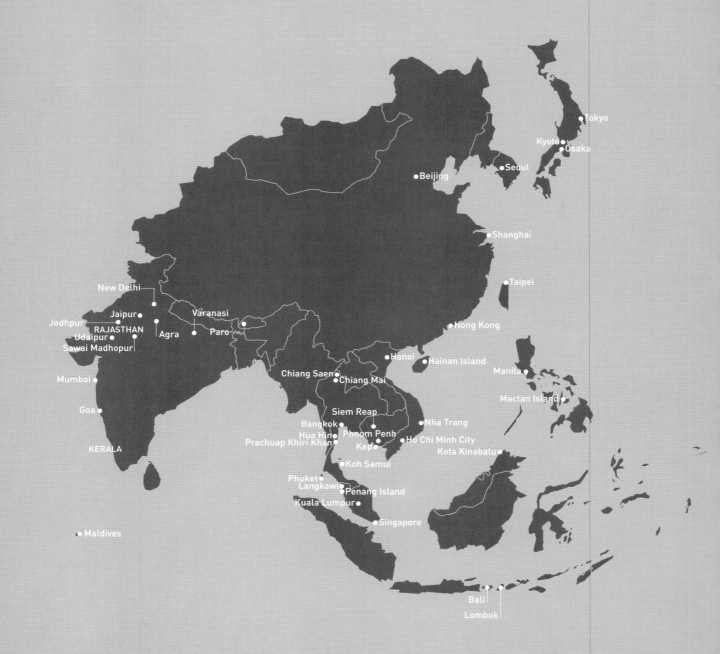

New Delhi
Jaipur
Jodhpur
RAJASTHAN
Udaipur
Sawai Madhopur
Mumbai
Goa
KERALA

Varanasi
Agra
Paro

Beijing

Shanghai

Taipei

Hong Kong

Tokyo
Kyoto
Osaka
Seoul

Hanoi
Hainan Island
Chiang Saen
Chiang Mai
Siem Reap
Bangkok
Hua Hin
Phnom Penh
Prachuap Khiri Khan
Kep
Koh Samui
Phuket
Langkawi
Penang Island
Kuala Lumpur
Singapore

Nha Trang
Ho Chi Minh City

Manila
Mactan Island

Kota Kinabalu

Maldives

Bali
Lombok

ASIA

BHUTAN
PARO
Amankora Five stylish eco-lodges in western and central Bhutan; guests are provided with a guide and driver. 800/477-9180 or 975/233-1333; amanresorts.com; doubles from $$$$$, all-inclusive.

CAMBODIA
KEP
Knai Bang Chatt Eleven rooms in Modernist villas along a stretch of coast poised to recapture its former glory. 855-12/349-742; knaibangchatt.com; doubles from $.

PHNOM PENH
Raffles Hotel Le Royal A 170-room French-colonial icon; don't miss the Jackie Kennedy–inspired Femme Fatale cocktail in the Elephant Bar. 92 Rukhak Vithei Daun Penh; 800/768-9009 or 855-23/981-888; raffles.com; doubles from $.

SIEM REAP
Hôtel de la Paix Art Deco and traditional Khmer design elements in 107 rooms encircling an inner courtyard, plus a fabulous (and affordable) spa. 855-63/966-000; hoteldelapaixangkor.com; doubles from $$.

Raffles Grand Hotel d'Angkor Carefully restored French-colonial retreat featuring a lap pool inspired by Angkor's royal baths. 800/768-9009 or 855-63/963-888; raffles.com; doubles from $.

Sofitel Angkor Phokeethra Golf & Spa Resort Stately property with 238 guest rooms, five restaurants, and its own off-site golf course. 800/763-4835 or 855-63/964-600; sofitel.com; doubles from $.

CHINA
BEIJING
Aman at Summer Palace Evocative 51-room hotel in a painstakingly restored Qing dynasty complex next to the former residence of the dowager empress Cixi. 1 Gonqmenqian St.; 800/477-9180 or 86-10/5987-9999; amanresorts.com; doubles from $$$.

China World Hotel Inspired by China's imperial palaces, with escalator access to one of the city's most upscale shopping malls. 1 Jianguomenwai Rd.; 866/565-5050 or 86-10/6505-2266; shangri-la.com; doubles from $$.

Park Hyatt Muted spa-like rooms atop a 66-story skyscraper—the tallest on Chang'an Avenue. 2 Jianguomenwai Rd.; 800/233-1234 or 86-10/8567-1234; park.hyatt.com; doubles from $$.

Peninsula Beijing Classic Chinese-inflected design meets of-the-moment amenities, such as 42-inch plasma TV's. 8 Goldfish Lane; 866/382-8388 or 86-10/8516-2888; peninsula.com; doubles from $$.

The Regent A mile from Tiananmen Square, with 500 streamlined rooms, top service (waiters remember how you take your coffee), and an indoor pool. 99 Jinbao St.; 800/967-9044 or 86-10/8522-1888; regenthotels.com; doubles from $$.

Ritz-Carlton Financial Street Glass-and-chrome tower in the Financial District, a quick cab ride from the now-hip alleys of Nanluoguxiang. 1 Jin Cheng Fang St. E.; 800/241-3333 or 86-10/6601-6666; ritzcarlton.com; doubles from $$.

Shangri-La Hotel A 24-story building on well-manicured grounds; the Chi spa offers treatments from Thailand, Tibet, and China. 29 Zizhuyuan Rd.; 866/565-5050 or 86-10/6841-2211; shangri-la.com; doubles from $$.

St. Regis Ritzy high-rise with a service focus (all rooms have 24-hour butlers) and Alexandra Champalimaud–designed interiors. 21 Jianguomenwai Rd.; 877/787-3447 or 86-10/6460-6688; stregis.com; doubles from $$.

HAINAN ISLAND
Ritz-Carlton Sanya Tropical-island getaway with lush gardens, lagoons, and a private white-sand beach. 800/241-3333 or 86-898/8858-8888; ritzcarlton.com; doubles from $.

HONG KONG
Conrad Set on 21 floors of the Pacific Place Towers skyscraper, with larger-than-average guest rooms; downstairs is the upscale Pacific Place Mall. Pacific Place, 88 Queensway; 800/266-7237 or 852/2521-3838; conradhotels.com; doubles from $$.

Four Seasons Hotel In the International Finance Center, 399 rooms with either Western or Chinese design elements. 8 Finance St.; 800/332-3442 or 852/3196-8888; fourseasons.com; doubles from $$.

Grand Hyatt Stunning views and sleek design; a favorite of business travelers to Hong Kong, as it's connected to the convention center. 1 Harbour Rd.; 800/233-1234 or 852/2588-1234; grand.hyatt.com; doubles from $.

InterContinental Seventeen floors cantilevered on stilts above Victoria Harbour, with an Alain Ducasse outpost and a Nobu Matsuhisa restaurant. 18 Salisbury Rd.; 800/327-0200 or 852/2721-1211; intercontinental.com; doubles from $$.

Island Shangri-La The city's tallest hotel attracts business travelers and shoppers, thanks to its proximity to banks and the Pacific Place Mall. Pacific Place, Supreme Court Rd.; 866/565-5050 or 852/2877-3838; shangri-la.com; doubles from $$$.

Kowloon Shangri-La Seven hundred rooms on the Tsim Sha Tsui East waterfront, with floor-to-ceiling bay windows throughout. 64 Mody Rd.; 866/565-5050 or 852/2721-2111; shangri-la.com; doubles from $$.

Mandarin Oriental There's a 1-to-1 staff-to-guest ratio at this art-filled icon; many of the 501

The Chairman Suite's indoor garden at the Park Hyatt Shanghai.

rooms have balconies overlooking Victoria Harbour. 5 Connaught Rd.; 800/526-6566 or 852/2522-0111; mandarinoriental.com; doubles from $$$.

Peninsula Hong Kong Neoclassical landmark with a dazzling Philippe Starck–designed rooftop restaurant. Salisbury Rd.; 866/382-8388 or 852/2920-2888; peninsula.com; doubles from $$.

W Hong Kong Nightclub-worthy vibe and cutting-edge amenities tailored to the tastes of its urban clientele. 1 Austin Rd. W., Kowloon Station, Kowloon; 877/946-8357 or 85-2/3717-2222; whotels.com; doubles from $$.

SHANGHAI

Four Seasons Hotel Business-oriented hotel with a gleaming spa, a block from the shopping on Nanjing Road. 500 Weihai Rd.; 800/332-3442 or 86-21/6256-8888; fourseasons.com; doubles from $$$.

Grand Hyatt One of the world's tallest hotels, with a rooftop bar and an Art Deco–meets–Chinese aesthetic. 88 Century Ave.; 800/233-1234 or 86-21/5049-1234; grand.hyatt.com; doubles from $$.

Hyatt on the Bund Two-tower skyscraper; most of the 631 rooms have views of the nearby Huangpu River. 199 Huangpu Rd.; 800/233-1234 or 86-21/6393-1234; hyatt.com; doubles from $$.

JW Marriott Hotel at Tomorrow Square Twisting steel-and-glass structure facing People's Park. 399 Nanjing W. Rd.; 800/228-9290 or 86-21/5359-4969; marriott.com; doubles from $$.

Park Hyatt On 16 floors of the Shanghai World Financial Center. 100 Century Ave.; 800/233-1234 or 86-21/6888-1234; park.hyatt.com; doubles from $$$$.

Peninsula Shanghai Opulent property with a 1934 Rolls-Royce Phantom for tours of the city. 32 Zhongshan Dong Yi Rd.; 866/288-8889 or 86-21/2327-2888; peninsula.com; doubles from $$.

Portman Ritz-Carlton Fresh from a $40 million renovation, with

Asian elements such as cabinets inspired by Chinese medicine chests. 1376 Nanjing Rd. W.; 800/241-3333 or 86-21/6279-8888; ritzcarlton.com; doubles from $$.

Pudong Shangri-La Two connected buildings with a 10,764-square-foot spa offering treatments inspired by ancient Asian remedies. 33 Fu Cheng Rd.; 866/565-5050 or 86-21/6882-8888; shangri-la.com; doubles from $$.

Sofitel Shanghai Jin Jiang Oriental Pudong Business amenities and 445 simple rooms, next to the New International Expo Centre. 889 Yang Gao Nan Rd.; 800/763-4835 or 86-21/5050-4888; sofitel.com; doubles from $.

St. Regis Some of the largest rooms in the city; hotel butlers are trained as both city guides and translators. 889 Dongfang Rd.; 877/787-3447 or 86-21/5050-4567; stregis.com; doubles from $$.

Westin Bund Center Two towers—one earthy, one sleek—that look out on every major Shanghai landmark. 88 Henan Central Rd.; 800/228-3000 or 86-21/6335-1888; westin.com; doubles from $.

INDIA
AGRA

Oberoi Amarvilas Mughal palace that mirrors the Taj Mahal just a few blocks away: Moorish archways, patterned domes, and intricate pavilions. Taj East Gate; 800/562-3764 or 91-562/223-1515; oberoihotels.com; doubles from $$$.

KEY TO THE PRICE ICONS $ UNDER $250 $$ $250–$499 $$$ $500–$749 $$$$ $750–$999 $$$$$ $1,000 AND UP

GOA

Casa Britona Riverside warehouse revamped into a 10-room property with frescoed walls and colonial antiques. Bardez; 91-832/241-6737; casaboutiquehotels.com; doubles from $.

Casa Palacio Siolim House 17th-century former Goan governor's mansion with formal sitting rooms and an enormous pool. Siolim; 91-832/227-2138; siolimhouse.com; doubles from $.

Panchavatti Four-suite hotel on 24 acres overlooking a river and paddy fields; owner Loulou Van Damme fosters a slumber-party atmosphere. Island of Corjuem, Aldona; 91-082/258-0632; islaingoa.com; doubles from $.

Taj Exotica On a swath of Benaulim Beach, 140 rooms—each with a private veranda—in a Mediterranean-style complex. 866/969-1825 or 91-832/668-3333; tajhotels.com; doubles from $$.

JAIPUR

Oberoi Rajvilas Modern Rajasthani retreat made up of well-appointed tents and villas and an Oberoi spa. Goner Rd.; 800/562-3764 or 91-141/268-0101; oberoihotels.com; doubles from $$$.

Rambagh Palace Once home to the maharajahs of Jaipur, a 19th-century Mughal palace with 79 high-ceilinged rooms and suites. Bhawani Singh Rd.; 866/969-1825 or 91-141/2211-919; tajhotels.com; doubles from $$$$.

JODHPUR

Umaid Bhawan Palace Formerly one of the largest private

residences in the world; Art Deco interiors now fuse Indian and European design. 866/969-1825 or 91-291/251-0101; tajhotels.com; doubles from $$.

KERALA
Kumarakom Lake Resort

Lakefront cottages on 25 acres filled with rice paddies, mangrove forests, and tropical birds, in southwestern India. Kottayam; 91-481/252-4900; thepaul.in; doubles from $$.

MUMBAI

The Oberoi Reopening this year with restored interiors and upgraded security (luggage scanners, metal detectors, more security cameras) after the November 2008 attack. Nariman Point; 800/562-3764 or 91-22/5632-5757; oberoihotels.com; price not available at press time.

Taj Mahal Palace & Tower

A 1903 grande dame with dramatic interiors overlooking the 85-foot-high Gateway of India; the Heritage Wing is reopening in March after the attack. Apollo Bunder; 866/969-1825 or 91-22/6665-3366; tajhotels.com; doubles from $$.

Taj President In the heart of the city, yet set back from the chaotic neighborhood of Colaba; the posh hideaway of choice among Mumbai's glitterati. 90 Cuffe Parade; 866/969-1825 or 91-22/6665-0808; tajhotels.com; doubles from $$.

NEW DELHI

Aman New Delhi Manicured lawns and vast expanses of stone add up to a restful cocoon. Lodhi Rd.; 800/477-9180 or 91-11/4363-3333;

amanresorts.com; doubles from $$$$.

The Oberoi Business-friendly, with a romantic bar, a dim sum restaurant, and a new gourmet-food store (the first in India). Dr. Zakir Hussain Marg; 800/562-3764 or 91-11/2436-3030; oberoihotels.com; doubles from $$.

Taj Palace Hotel Behemoth that's big enough to host conventions yet still provides personal service

(a 24-hour concierge and a doctor are on call). Sardar Patel Marg Diplomatic Enclave; 866/969-1825 or 91-11/2611-0202; tajhotels.com; doubles from $$.

SAWAI MADHOPUR

Oberoi Vanyavilas Luxe jungle tents outfitted with four-poster beds, freestanding bathtubs, and teak floors, next to Ranthambhore National Park and Tiger Reserve. 800/562-3764 or 91-7462/223-999; oberoihotels.com; doubles from $$$.

The Writer's Room at Panchavatti, in Goa, India.

The courtyard at the Oberoi
Udaivilas, in Udaipur, India.

UDAIPUR

Oberoi Udaivilas Mewari-style
rooms along Lake Pichola; guests
can take a cruise in a Kashmiri
wooden boat. 800/562-3764 or 91-
294/243-3300; oberoihotels.com;
doubles from $$$.

Taj Lake Palace A 263-year-old
white marble palace that rises
from a rock foundation on its
own island in Lake Pichola.
866/969-1825 or 91-294/252-8800;
tajhotels.com; doubles from $$$.

VARANASI

Taj Nadesar Palace Once a
maharajah's residence, now a
hotel and a spa incorporating
ancient Indian healing therapies.
Nadesar Palace Grounds; 866/969-
1825 or 91-542/250-300-119;
tajhotels.com; doubles from $$.

INDONESIA
BALI

**Ayana Resort & Spa (formerly
Ritz-Carlton, Bali Resort & Spa)**
High on a precipice above the
Indian Ocean, with the world's
largest seawater pool. Jimbaran;
62-361/702-222; ayanaresort.com;
doubles from $.

Nusa Dua Beach Hotel & Spa
Balinese-wood rooms on 23
beachfront acres dotted with
sculpted gardens in an exclusive
enclave. Denpasar; 62-361/771-
210; nusaduahotel.com; doubles
from $.

The Shaba Three-suite colonial
mansion in a coconut grove;
rooms have antique teak floors
and claw-foot tubs. Jimbaran;
62-361/701-695; shaba-bali.com;
doubles from $$.

LOMBOK

Hotel Tugu Lombok On the
unspoiled northwestern coast,
garden villas and oceanfront
suites inspired by the island's
blend of cultures. 62-370/620-111;
tuguhotels.com; doubles from $.

JAPAN
KYOTO

Hyatt Regency Contemporary
interiors with traditional touches
(silk kimono textiles, cedar tubs).
644-2 Sanjusangendo-mawari;
800/233-1234 or 81-75/541-1234;
hyatt.com; doubles from $$$.

OSAKA

Imperial Hotel Classic hotel with
a five-story atrium, state-of-
the-art business center, and 380
rooms along the Okawa River.
8-50 Temmabashi 1-chome;

KEY TO THE PRICE ICONS   **$** UNDER $250   **$$** $250–$499   **$$$** $500–$749   **$$$$** $750–$999   **$$$$$** $1,000 AND UP

81-6/6881-1111; imperialhotel.co.jp; doubles from $$.

TOKYO

Four Seasons Hotel Tokyo at Chinzan-so On 17 acres of Japanese gardens downtown, with some of the largest guest rooms in the city. 10-8 Sekiguchi 2-chome; 800/332-3442 or 81-3/3943-2222; fourseasons.com; doubles from $$$.

Grand Hyatt Modern city-view rooms and limestone *ofuro*s (Japanese soaking tubs). 6-10-3 Roppongi; 800/233-1234 or 81-3/4333-1234; grand.hyatt.com; doubles from $$$.

Hotel Okura Understated Japanese style, with expert service and an art museum spotlighting more than 2,000 Buddhist works. 2-10-4 Toranomon; 81-3/3582-0111; okura.com; doubles from $$$.

MALAYSIA

KOTA KINABALU

Shangri-La's Tanjung Aru Resort & Spa Just 10 minutes away from downtown Kota Kinabalu, a 492-room resort with views of nearby islands. 866/565-5050 or 60-88/327-888; shangri-la.com; doubles from $.

KUALA LUMPUR

Mandarin Oriental Soaring 88-story building defined by its panoramic views of the Petronas Twin Towers and the KL City Centre Park gardens. Kuala Lumpur City Centre;

800/526-6566 or 60-3/2380-8833; mandarinoriental.com; doubles from $$.

Shangri-La Hotel Recently renovated high-rise with a marble lobby and four restaurants. 11 Jalan Sultan Ismail; 866/565-5050 or 60-3/2032-2388; shangri-la.com; doubles from $.

LANGKAWI

Bon Ton Restaurant + Resort Eight antique Malay wooden stilt houses around a lotus lagoon; the restaurant specializes in Malay-influenced curries. 60-4/955-1688; bontonresort.com.my; doubles from $.

PENANG

Shangri-La's Rasa Sayang Resort & Spa Oceanside resort features two tree-shrouded pools; near Taman Rimba National Forest Reserve. 866/565-5050 or 60-4/888-8888; shangri-la.com; doubles from $$.

MALDIVES

DHIGU ISLAND

Anantara Dhigu Resort & Spa String of 110 overwater suites and beach villas on a 10-acre private island that's part of the South Male Atoll. 011-960/664-4100; anantara.com; doubles from $$$$.

PHILIPPINES

MACTAN ISLAND

Shangri-La's Mactan Resort & Spa, Cebu Set on its own beachfront cove, with palm-filled grounds, two pools, a child-friendly indoor playroom, and a Chi spa.

866/565-5050 or 63-32/231-0288; shangri-la.com; doubles from $$.

MANILA

Makati Shangri-La Curvilinear wood-paneled rooms in the upscale business district of Makati. Ayala Ave. and Makati Ave.; 866/565-5050 or 63-2/813-8888; shangri-la.com; doubles from $$.

SINGAPORE

Conrad Centennial Business hotel near the Fountain of Wealth (the world's largest fountain). 2 Temasek Blvd.; 800/266-7237 or 65/6334-8888; conradhotels.com; doubles from $$.

Four Seasons Hotel Steps from Orchard Road boutiques, with high-tech amenities and 1,500 local works of art. 190 Orchard Blvd.; 800/332-3442 or 65/6734-1110; fourseasons.com; doubles from $$.

Mandarin Oriental Fan-shaped façade near Marina Square; all 527 rooms have floor-to-ceiling harbor views. 5 Raffles Ave., Marina Square; 800/526-6566 or 65/6338-0066; mandarinoriental.com; doubles from $$.

Pan Pacific Black-and-taupe rooms and a John Portman–designed atrium, on Marina Bay Harbor. 7 Raffles Blvd., Marina Square; 877/324-4856 or 65/6336-8111; panpacific.com; doubles from $$.

Raffles Hotel Low-rise colonial buildings with rooms named for illustrious former guests, including Noël Coward and Ava Gardner. 1 Beach Rd.; 800/768-

9009 or 65/6337-1886; raffleshotel.com; doubles from $$$$.

Ritz-Carlton Millenia This 32-story high-rise on Marina Bay has works by Frank Stella and Andy Warhol on display. 7 Raffles Ave.; 800/241-3333 or 65/6337-8888; ritzcarlton.com; doubles from $$$.

Shangri-La Hotel Unusually shaped rooms (imagine odd angles and curves) on 15 landscaped acres a few blocks from pedestrian-friendly Orchard Road. 22 Orange Grove Rd.; 866/565-5050 or 65/6737-3644; shangri-la.com; doubles from $$.

SOUTH KOREA

SEOUL

Westin Chosun Business-district hotel overlooking Seoul Plaza, with all of the expected amenities (in-room espresso makers, flat-screen TV's). 87 Sogong-dong, Jung-gu; 800/228-3000 or 82-2/771-0500; westin.com; doubles from $$.

TAIWAN

TAIPEI

Shangri-La's Far Eastern Plaza Hotel Frequent host to visiting dignitaries, with sweeping city and mountain views from most of the 420 rooms as well as the 43rd-floor rooftop pool. 201 Tun Hwa S. Rd., Section 2; 866/565-5050 or 886-2/2378-8888; shangri-la.com; doubles from $$.

THAILAND

BANGKOK

Banyan Tree All-suite skyscraper that's also home to the popular 61st-floor Vertigo Grill & Moon

---

KEY TO THE PRICE ICONS $ UNDER $250 $$ $250–$499 $$$ $500–$749 $$$$ $750–$999 $$$$$ $1,000 AND UP

Overlooking the Rauk River at the Four Seasons Tented Camp Golden Triangle, in Thailand.

Bar and a signature spa. 21/100 S. Sathon Rd., Sathon; 800/591-0439 or 66-2/679-1200; banyantree.com; doubles from $$.

Conrad A 391-room hotel located in the central business district, near major embassies and the Bangkok Transit System. 87 Wireless Rd., Pathumwan; 800/266-7237 or 66-2/690-9999; conrad hotels.com; doubles from $.

Dusit Thani The 517 rooms are small, but make up for it with private balconies and views of nearby Lumpini Park. 946 Rama IV Rd.; 66-2/200-9000; dusit.com; doubles from $.

Four Seasons Hotel French-colonial hotel with hand-painted silk ceilings and the city's largest lap pool. 155 Rajadamri Rd.; 800/332-3442 or 66-2/126-8866; fourseasons.com; doubles from $.

JW Marriott Hotel Black marble high-rise with a roster of business amenities and a prime location on Bangkok's main shopping drag. 4 Sukhumvit Rd., Soi 2; 800/228-9290 or 66-2/656-7700; marriott. com; doubles from $.

Le Méridien A 24-story hotel with plush interiors off ritzy Silom Road. 40/5 Surawong Rd.; 800/543-4300 or 66-2/232-8888; lemeridien.com; doubles from $.

Mandarin Oriental Bangkok's prime hotel since 1876; rooms in the River Wing now have balconies after a recent renovation. 48 Oriental Ave.; 800/526-6566 or

66-2/659-9000; mandarinoriental. com; doubles from $$.

Peninsula Bangkok Within a tower that overlooks the Chao Phraya River, 370 rooms with teak floors, silk-covered furniture, and high-tech control panels. 333 Charoennakorn Rd., Klongsan; 866/382-8388 or 66-2/861-2888; peninsula.com; doubles from $$.

Shangri-La Hotel Riverside hotel with Bangkok's largest treatment rooms at the property's Chi spa. 89 Soi Wat Suan Plu, New Rd.; 866/565-5050 or 66-2/236-7777; shangri-la.com; doubles from $.

CHIANG MAI
dusitD2 Next to the night bazaar, a 131-room hotel with tongue-in-cheek touches (the staff performs a chorus line during the afternoon shift switch). 66-5/399-9999; d2hotels.com; doubles from $.

Four Seasons Resort Just outside Chiang Mai proper, with 12 newly opened poolside villas and pavilions that look onto rice paddies. 800/332-3442 or 66-53/298-181; four seasons.com; doubles from $$.

Mandarin Oriental Dhara Dhevi Complex of 54 suites and 64 free-standing Thai pavilions on intricately landscaped grounds. 800/526-6566 or 66-53/888-888; mandarin oriental.com; doubles from $$$.

CHIANG SAEN
Anantara Golden Triangle Resort & Spa On a ridge in Thailand's hill country, with its own elephant

conservation center. 66-53/784-084; anantara.com; doubles from $$.

Four Seasons Tented Camp Golden Triangle Luxury tents outfitted with hand-hammered copper bathtubs; activities include elephant trekking and rafting down the Mekong River. 800/332-3442 or 66-53/910-200; four seasons.com; doubles from $$$$, all-inclusive, two-night minimum.

HUA HIN
Anantara Hua Hin Resort & Spa A series of teak pavilions with ocean views and terraces on 16 acres of gardens. 66-32/520-250; anantara. com; doubles from $$.

KOH SAMUI
Anantara Koh Samui Resort & Spa A 106-room waterfront property with varied activities on Phuket's longest beach. 66-77/428-300; anantara. com; doubles from $$.

PHUKET
Anantara Phuket Resort & Spa Villas outfitted in teak and raw silk, and a spa with ayurvedic treatments. 800/223-6800 or 66-76/336-100; anantara.com; villas from $$$$$.

Amanpuri Amanresorts' flagship set the bar for intimate private escapes; a cluster of pavilions and villas are serviced by an inconspicuous staff. 800/477-9180 or 66-76/324-333; amanresorts. com; doubles from $$$$.

JW Marriott Resort & Spa Elegant property that welcomes children, on secluded Mai Khao Beach; the

three restaurants were renovated in 2009. 800/228-9290 or 66-76/338-000; marriott.com; doubles from $$.

Le Méridien Beach Resort Beachside resort with lagoon-style pools and a shuttle to Patong Beach. 800/543-4300 or 66-76/370-100; lemeridien.com; doubles from $$.

PRACHUAP KHIRI KHAN
X2 Kui Buri On an underdeveloped stretch of coast, 23 modern stone villas with private plunge pools. 66-32/601-412; x2resorts.com; doubles from $.

VIETNAM
HANOI
Sofitel Legend Metropole The city's French Quarter is the setting for this 1901 colonial hotel, recently updated with a new three-level spa. 15 Ngo Quyen St.; 800/763-4835 or 84-4/3826-6919; sofitel.com; doubles from $$.

HO CHI MINH CITY
Park Hyatt Saigon Colonial splendor—four-poster beds, ironwork, and shutters—on Saigon's central square. 2 Lam Son Square, District 1; 800/233-1234 or 84-8/3824-1234; park. hyatt.com; doubles from $$.

NHA TRANG
Evason Ana Mandara & Six Senses Spa The only beachfront resort in Nha Trang, with an aesthetic and design reminiscent of a traditional Vietnamese village. 800/591-7480 or 84-58/352-2222; sixsenses.com; doubles from $$.

KEY TO THE PRICE ICONS   **$** UNDER $250   **$$** $250–$499   **$$$** $500–$749   **$$$$** $750–$999   **$$$$$** $1,000 AND UP

FRENCH POLYNESIA

Marquesas Islands •

• Bora-Bora

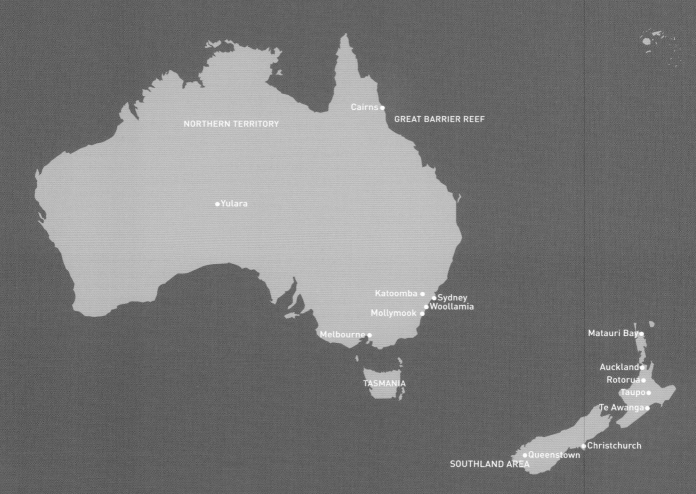

NORTHERN TERRITORY

Cairns •

GREAT BARRIER REEF

• Yulara

Katoomba •   • Sydney
                • Woollamia
Mollymook •

Melbourne •

TASMANIA

Matauri Bay •

Auckland •
Rotorua •
Taupo •
Te Awanga •

• Christchurch
• Queenstown
SOUTHLAND AREA

AUSTRALIA
+ NEW ZEALAND
+ THE SOUTH PACIFIC

AUSTRALIA

CAIRNS

Kewarra Beach Resort Cluster of bungalows and suites between lush rain forest and a stretch of private beach. 61-7/4058-4000; kewarra.com; doubles from $$, two-night minimum.

GREAT BARRIER REEF

Hayman Private island resort with a PADI dive center, a 1-to-1 staff-to-guest ratio, and tours galore. 800/223-6800 or 61-7/4940-1234; hayman.com.au; doubles from $$$.

Lizard Island Resort Beachfront accommodations on an island 50 minutes by motor-powered dive boat from the Great Barrier Reef. 800/225-9849 or 61-7/4043-1999; lizard-island.com.au; doubles from $$$$$, all-inclusive, two-night minimum.

KATOOMBA

Lilianfels Blue Mountains Resort & Spa Storybook country-house hideaway that's best known for its roster of outdoor activities, including walking tours through the rain forest. 800/237-1236 or 61-2/4780-1200; lilianfels.com.au; doubles from $$.

MELBOURNE

Crown Towers High-rise casino complex that's secluded enough to attract non-gamers. 8 Whitemen St.; 61-3/9292-6868; crowntowers.com.au; doubles from $$.

The Langham On the Southbank Promenade, with traditional British touches such as afternoon tea and Waterford Wedgwood chandeliers. 1 Southgate Ave.; 800/588-9141 or 61-3/8696-8888; langhamhotels.com; doubles from $$.

Park Hyatt Well-rounded 20-story hotel with Art Deco interiors and a top-notch spa, next to the Fitzroy Gardens downtown. 1 Parliament Square; 800/233-1234 or 61-3/9224-1234; park.hyatt.com; doubles from $$.

Sofitel Melbourne On Collins Comfortable, contemporary rooms in the city's shopping and theater district. 25 Collins St.; 800/763-4835 or 61-3/9653-0000; sofitel.com; doubles from $$.

MOLLYMOOK

Bannisters Point Lodge Revamped seaside motel with 33 rooms and a restaurant by chef Rick Stein. 61-2/4455-3044; bannisterspointlodge.com.au; doubles from $$.

NORTHERN TERRITORY

Bamurru Plains Remote bush camp just west of Kakadu National Park, home to a spectacular array of wildlife. Swim Creek Station; 61-2/9571-6399; bamurruplains.com; doubles from $$$$$, all-inclusive, two-night minimum.

SYDNEY

Four Seasons Hotel Polished, updated rooms and public spaces on 34 floors, plus the largest outdoor pool in the city. 199 George St.; 800/332-3442 or 61-2/9250-3100; fourseasons.com; doubles from $$.

InterContinental Centrally located tower atop the 1851 Treasury Building. 117 Macquarie St.; 800/327-0200 or 61-2/9253-9000; intercontinental.com; doubles from $$.

Observatory Hotel One hundred rooms at a property reminiscent of a manor house (mahogany furniture and brocade tapestries). 89-113 Kent St.; 800/237-1236 or 61-2/9256-2222; observatoryhotel.com.au; doubles from $$.

Park Hyatt A prime location, directly across the harbor from the Opera House and a walkway's width from the water. 7 Hickson Rd.; 800/233-1234 or 61-2/9241-1234; park.hyatt.com; doubles from $$$.

Shangri-La Hotel The city's largest rooms and a new Chi spa that opened in December. 176 Cumberland St.; 866/565-5050 or 61-2/9250-6000; shangri-la.com; doubles from $$.

Sydney Harbour Marriott Hotel at Circular Quay Along the harbor, a glass-and-concrete skyscraper featuring a grand three-floor lobby. 30 Pitt St.; 800/228-9290 or 61-2/9259-7000; marriott.com; doubles from $$$.

Westin Sydney The city's best hotel for business travelers, with a central downtown location and plenty of executive-level amenities. 1 Martin Place; 800/937-8461 or 61-2/8223-1111; westin.com.au; doubles from $$.

TASMANIA

Priory Country Lodge Four-bedroom Tudor Gothic-style house and three pavilions; a good base for game hunting. 61-3/6259-4012; thepr{i}orycountrylodge.com.au; doubles from $$, including breakfast, afternoon tea, and dinner.

WOOLLAMIA

Paperbark Camp An Aussie eco-safari: tents imported from Africa, and a treehouse restaurant. 571 Woollamia Rd.; 800/227-9246 or 61-2/4441-6060; paperbarkcamp.com.au; doubles from $$.

YULARA

Voyages Longitude 131° Futuristic tented camp with adventurous daily itineraries and dramatic views of Uluru. 800/225-9849 or 61-8/8957-7131; longitude131.com.au; doubles from $$$$$, all-inclusive, two-night minimum.

FRENCH POLYNESIA

BORA-BORA

InterContinental Resort & Thalasso Spa Eighty overwater bungalows around an islet off Bora-Bora. 800/327-0200 or 689/607-600; intercontinental.com; doubles from $$$$$.

Four Seasons Resort Bora Bora On a private isle, 100 overwater bungalows with thatched roofs and seven beachfront villas. 800/332-3442 or 689/603-130; fourseasons.com; doubles from $$$$$.

MARQUESAS ISLANDS

Hiva Oa Hanakee Pearl Lodge Fourteen bamboo-lattice

KEY TO THE PRICE ICONS   **$** UNDER $250   **$$** $250–$499   **$$$** $500–$749   **$$$$** $750–$999   **$$$$$** $1,000 AND UP

A cottage suite at Huka Lodge, in Taupo, New Zealand.

Otahuna Lodge Homestead with Arts and Crafts interiors and 30 acres of landscaped grounds on what was once New Zealand's largest private residence. Tai Tapu; 64-3/329-6333; otahuna.co.nz; doubles from $$$$$, including breakfast and dinner.

MATAURI BAY

Lodge at Kauri Cliffs Cliffside lodge and golf course on 6,500 acres with panoramic views of the South Pacific. 800/735-2478 or 64-9/407-0010; kauricliffs.com; doubles from $$$$$, including breakfast and dinner.

ROTORUA

Treetops Lodge & Wilderness Experience Timber-and-stone lodge and villas surrounded by a 2,500-acre nature reserve on a volcanic plateau. 64-7/333-2066; treetops.co.nz; doubles from $$$$$, including breakfast, dinner, and some activities.

QUEENSTOWN

Eichardt's Private Hotel Five-suite main building and a four-suite cottage in the heart of Queenstown, overlooking Lake Wakatipu and Walter Peak. Marine Parade; 64-3/441-0450; eichardtshotel.co.nz; doubles from $$$$.

Sofitel Queenstown Hotel & Spa Centrally located, with refined rooms and a spa that incorporates Maori rituals into its treatments. 8 Duke St.; 800/763-4835 or 64-3/450-0045; sofitel.com; doubles from $.

SOUTHLAND AREA

Fiordland Lodge Ten lakeshore rooms and two log cabins in the midst of spectacular scenery; run by a veteran park ranger and his wife, with a wealth of guided activities. Te Anau; 64-3/249-7832; fiordlandlodge.co.nz; doubles from $$$, including breakfast and dinner.

Lodge at Tikana Ultra-private and refined eco-conscious retreat on a working farm, for single-party bookings of up to four people. Winton; 64-3/236-4117; tikana.co.nz; from $$$$$, including breakfast and dinner.

Mandeno House Elegant bed-and-breakfast with welcoming rooms and a formal rose garden in a quaint university town. 667 George St., Dunedin, Otago; 64-3/471-9595; mandenohouse.com; doubles from $.

TAUPO

Huka Lodge Exclusive 25-room lodge beloved by celebrities for its well-appointed rooms and premier fishing, hiking, and golf along the banks of the Waikato River. 800/223-6800 or 64-7/378-5791; hukaretreats.com; doubles from $$$$$, including breakfast and dinner.

TE AWANGA

Farm at Cape Kidnappers A 26-room inn on a working sheep and cattle ranch, 800 feet above the sea. 800/735-2478 or 64-6/875-1900; capekidnappers.com; doubles from $$$$$, including breakfast and dinner.

bungalows on a hill overlooking Mount Temetiu and the bay of Tahauku. 800/657-3275 or 689/927-587; spmhotels.com; doubles from $$.

NEW ZEALAND
AUCKLAND

The Hilton Modern hotel on Waitemata Harbor, a five-minute stroll from the business center. Princes Wharf, 147 Quay St.; 800/445-8667 or 64-9/978-2000; hilton.com; doubles from $.

Hotel DeBrett Eclectic 25-room property in an Art Deco building given a top-to-bottom redo. 2 High St.; 64-9/925-9000; hoteldebrett.com; doubles from $.

Westin Auckland Lighter Quay A 172-room hotel on Viaduct Harbour, within walking distance of lively Queen Street. 21 Viaduct Harbour Ave.; 800/228-3000 or 64-9/909-9000; westin.com; doubles from $.

CHRISTCHURCH

The George Boutique hotel overlooking Hagley Park with minimalist lithographs and 53 light-filled rooms. 50 Park Terrace; 800/525-4800 or 64-3/379-4560; thegeorge.com; doubles from $$.

Guest tents at
Voyages Longitude 131°,
in Yulara, Australia.

A view of Île aux Chats, a private island at the Four Seasons Resort Mauritius at Anahita

TRIPS
DIRECTORY

VENTURE ARTS AND CULTURE BEACH CITY DESIGN ECO
NSCIOUS FAMILY FOOD AND WINE GREAT VALUE HISTORIC ISLAN
UNTAIN REMOTE ESCAPE ROMANTIC SPA ADVENTURE ART
D CULTURE BEACH CITY DESIGN ECO-CONSCIOUS FAMILY FOO
D WINE GREAT VALUE HISTORIC ISLAND MOUNTAIN REMOT
CAPE ROMANTIC SPA ADVENTURE ARTS AND CULTURE BEAC
Y DESIGN ECO-CONSCIOUS FAMILY FOOD AND WINE GREAT VALU
TORIC ISLAND MOUNTAIN REMOTE ESCAPE ROMANTIC SP
VENTURE ARTS AND CULTURE BEACH CITY DESIGN ECO

The Oak Bar at the Plaza Hotel, in New York City.

INDEX

A terrace at the Peninsula House, in the Dominican Republic.

CONTRIBUTORS

Christine Ajudua
Dara Albanese
Gini Alhadeff
Richard Alleman
Kurt Andersen
Katie Arnold
Tom Austin
Luke Barr
Lily Becker
Laura Begley
Thomas Beller
Mary Bianco
Rocky Casale
Paul Chai
Jennifer Chen
Tanvi Chheda
Jennifer V. Cole
Yolanda Crous

Anthony Dennis
Robyn Eckhardt
Pamela Edwards
Matthew Evans
Amy Farley
Andrew Ferren
Jennifer Flowers
Eleni Gage
Charles Gandee
Ozgur Gezer
Alice Gordon
Jaime Gross
Michael Gross
James Patrick Herman
Latilla Isaac
Karrie Jacobs
Sarah Kantrowitz
David Kaufman

Stirling Kelso
Sharon Leece
Peter Jon Lindberg
Bruno Maddox
Alexandra Marshall
Ralph Martin
Connie McCabe
Alex Frew McMillan
Alison Miller
Shane Mitchell
Robert Morris
Ian Mount
Monalika Namchoom
John Newton
Kathryn O'Shea-Evans
Lauren Quaintance
Bruce Schoenfeld
Clara O. Sedlak

Swapan Seth
Dani Shapiro
Maria Shollenbarger
Scott Spencer
Jeff Spurrier
Rima Suqi
Mary Justice Thomasson-Croll
Guy Trebay
Meeghan Truelove
Bonnie Tsui
Alison Tyler
Anya von Bremzen
Valerie Waterhouse
Jennifer Welbel
Jeff Wise
Michael Z. Wise
Elizabeth Woodson

Inside a tent at Lemarti's Camp, in Laikipia, Kenya.

PHOTOGRAPHERS

A magazine of modern global culture, *Travel + Leisure* examines the places, ideas, and trends that define the way we travel now. T+L inspires readers to explore the world, equipping them with expert advice and a better understanding of the endless possibilities of travel. Delivering clear, comprehensive service journalism, intelligent writing, and evocative photography, T+L is the authority for today's traveler. Visit us at **TravelandLeisure.com.**